Cadres for Conservatism

Cadres for Conservatism

*Young Americans for Freedom
and the Rise of the Contemporary Right*

Gregory L. Schneider

NEW YORK UNIVERSITY PRESS
New York and London

NEW YORK UNIVERSITY PRESS
New York and London

Library of Congress Cataloging-in-Publication Data
Schneider, Gregory L., 1965–
Cadres for conservatism : young Americans for freedom and the
rise of the contemporary right / Gregory L. Schneider.
p.   cm.
Includes bibliographical references and index.
ISBN 0-8147-8108-X (cloth : alk. paper)
1. Young Americans for Freedom.   2. Conservatism—United States.
3. United States—Politics and government—1945-1989.   I. Title.
JC573.2.U6 S35 1999
320.52'0973—ddc21   98-25355
                          CIP

Manufactured in the United States of America

10 9 8 7 6 5 4 3 2 1

For Reg, Nancy, Hail, and Grace

Contents

Acknowledgments

This work has benefited from the close support of many colleagues and institutions. Foremost among those who gave their wisdom and insight on recent American politics was my dissertation advisor, Richard Fried. His editorial skills, helpfulness, and involvement with the project have been invaluable to me. His sense of humor, good cheer, and friendship have been most appreciated throughout the completion of this work. He epitomizes the attributes of scholarship and mentoring that are most sought after by any graduate student.

Other scholars who contributed in various ways to strengthening the manuscript, although they are in no way responsible for the final content, include Alonzo Hamby, James Sack, Richard Jensen, Melvin Holli, Richard Braungart, James Andrew, Rick Perlstein, Kenneth Heineman, and George Nash. The staffs at the Hoover Institution at Stanford University, the Sterling Library at Yale, the Chicago Historical Society, and the Herbert Hoover and John F. Kennedy Presidential Libraries were most helpful and courteous in their handling of requests for material. Niko Pfund and the editorial staff of New York University Press greatly facilitated the improvement of the manuscript. I am grateful for their professionalism.

I owe special thanks to those members of YAF who agreed to interviews and took time away from their busy schedules to tell me something about their history. Among those who deserve special recognition are William F. Buckley and William Rusher for allowing me to examine and cite from their personal papers and for their good-natured comments on the manuscript; Douglas Caddy, for sending me documents relating to YAF's early history; James Lacy, for providing me material regarding his tenure as national chairman; and most importantly, Jameson Campaigne, who graciously allowed me to use and photocopy his personal collection of YAF papers and provided encouragement, professional and personal, for the duration of this project.

This manuscript would never have been completed without the love I receive every day from my wife, Petra. Her constant support for research trips, high phone bills resulting from "another interview" and her encouragement for my scholarly endeavors have gone beyond what the requisite words of gratitude and love can encompass. Our dog Sydney kept reminding me (and Petra) that books and jobs should take second place to interminable games of Frisbee and Kong. I am thankful for the dog's obsessiveness, however, since it dragged me outside and away from the flickering blue of the computer screen.

The dedication pays tribute to two sets of parents to whom I am increasingly grateful for pointing the way, steady and true.

List of Abbreviations

ACU   American Conservative Union
ASG   Association of Student Governments
CYR   College Young Republicans
JBS   John Birch Society
FCM   Fund for a Conservative Majority
HUAC   House Un-American Activities Committee
ISI   Intercollegiate Society of Individualists
NSA   National Student Association
PL   Progressive Labor
SDS   Students for a Democratic Society
SCFC   Student Committee for a Free China
SFC   Students for a Free Campus
SIL   Society for Individual Liberty
WYCF   World Youth Crusade for Freedom
YAF   Young Americans for Freedom
YR   Young Republicans
YRNF   Young Republican National Federation

Introduction

In attempting to explain the rise and consequent success of conservatism in recent American politics, historians have tended to describe the situation in two ways: as a phenomenon reactive to the excesses of liberalism and radicalism during the 1960s, or as a product of status-anxious ethnic groups upset over their station in American life. Although these are certainly defensible positions, they explain little of the appeal and character of the modern American conservative movement. The fact that many Americans felt that Ronald Reagan—and Barry Goldwater before him—addressed what was flawed with American politics and foreign policy cannot be owed solely to Archie Bunker archetypes in working-class enclaves or to oil men in the Southwest. What historians have long ignored, but are beginning to recover, is the tradition of conservative politics in America—the development and shaping of a key set of principles and affectations that eventually led to political activism and the capture of a major political party.

One key element in this tradition was a group of young people who formed an organization in 1960 called Young Americans for Freedom. While radical students in the 1960s reshaped American society by addressing persistent issues of inequality, racism, poverty, and war, young conservatives refashioned American politics by building cadres of conservative activists intent on challenging liberalism both as an ideology and as a mode of governance. In the end the radicals, upset at how unbending some institutions were to change, disappeared into the smoky pall of exploded buildings or into the purple haze of personal politics. The conservatives remained, worked at the grass roots to construct an alternative political culture based on their ideas, captured the Republican Party, and wound up profoundly reshaping American politics in the process.

At this time only one scholarly study of YAF exists, John Andrew's *The Other Side of the Sixties*.[1] Andrew tells YAF's story through the Goldwater presidential campaign in 1964, neglecting the rich history of YAF after that year. Because Andrew believed that YAF was fully integrated into main-stream Republican and conservative politics after 1964, his book is limited to YAF's early history but is not a complete history of the organization and its effect on conservative politics. It is important to remember that YAF continued as a major student organization well into the 1980s, collapsing only because the conservative movement YAF helped create became so successful. It played a crucial role in opposing the student Left during the late 1960s and in mobilizing young conservative activists during (and after) those years.

Unlike Andrew's otherwise fine study of YAF, the current volume shines light on YAF's whole history, a story of an independent grassroots organization that helped young people mobilize for political action and provided the conservative movement with activist cadres for their causes. As Morton Blackwell, one of the youngest delegates to the 1964 Republican convention, stated years later, the Goldwater defeat did not represent the end of conservative hopes for victory, but rather their beginning. "Sometimes in politics, you win by losing," Blackwell intoned.[2] The historical investigation contained in the following narrative tends to support his point. The cadres of activists built up through participation in groups like YAF helped foment the conservative counterrevolution against liberalism. This is their story.

This book is a narrative history of the Young Americans for Freedom from the 1950s through its collapse in the mid-1980s. YAF was a large organization with several hundred individual chapters throughout the country. Because the archival collections containing YAF materials are scattered and of varied worth, the only feasible approach to this topic was to study YAF from a national perspective, concentrating only peripherally on specific campus chapters where they were relevant to the story. YAF, unlike Students for a Democratic Society, its radical counterpart during the 1960s, left no central archive for scholarly use. Most members I have contacted long ago disposed of their documents from that era, although several individual collections proved of crucial importance for the narrative.

With archival material available but rather thin, I decided to contact key national leaders and sponsors of the organization and encourage them to participate in recalling their own history. The oral histories contained herein, selected from the twenty-six interviews conducted, add a dimension to the history of YAF that is lacking from other histories of the conservative movement. Through the interviews I have gained insights into the motivations and views of individuals within YAF and the conservative movement that are not readily apparent from the documented sources.

Accordingly, this book offers a challenge to historians to broaden their studies of recent American politics to include the Right. Conservatives, however many historians may think otherwise, were not only, or even mainly, a concoction of pro-McCarthy zealots, antifluoridationists, anti-Semitic crackpots and racist kooks. The majority of the conservatives were well-intentioned, concerned citizens, mostly college-educated, motivated to take action by what they believed were the excesses of American liberalism. A historiography of modern American politics should take this into account, while fully documenting and criticizing the excesses of more extreme members of the conservative coalition. If historians are ever to understand fully the seismic shift in American politics away from a progressive-liberal state during the past quarter-century, they are going to have to deal with the legacy and ideas of conservatives on their own terms. To do any less is to ignore the importance of a social, intellectual, and political movement that has helped reshape America in our time.

Part 1 of the book examines YAF during the early years. Chapter 1 emphasizes the intellectual foundations that emerged after World War II and played a role in shaping a conservatism around which young people mobilized. Chapter 2 discusses YAF's founding conference and a disruptive internal schism that nearly paralyzed the organization during its first year. Attention then shifts (chapter 3) toward an examination of YAF's position on liberalism and anticommunist issues during the early 1960s, finally turning, in chapter 4, to a study of YAF's role during the Goldwater campaign.

Part 2 documents the revolt on the campus, beginning with the YAF fight for a provictory strategy in Vietnam (chapter 5); that struggle included both supporting American policy and resisting the New Left and the antiwar movement (chapter 6). Chapter 7 then focuses on an ideological schism that plagued the organization during 1969, partly because of the development of radical libertarianism during the late 1960s and its popularity on campus.

Part 3 examines YAF as an integral part of the conservative movement: chapter 8 documents its experience in the Nixon administration, and chapter 9 highlights the organization's revival in the buildup for Reagan during the late 1970s and then its collapse during the Reagan administration.

Forging a New Politics

1

Stirrings on the Right

Bliss was it in that dawn to be alive, But to be young was very
heaven!   —William Wordsworth

We fight for lost causes because we know that our defeat and dismay
may be the preface to our successors' victory, though that victory
itself will be temporary; we fight rather to keep something alive than
in the expectation it will triumph.   —T. S. Eliot

Nineteen forty-five was to be a year of victorious relief. After
six years of war, German arms were stilled behind the might of the most
powerful military union ever assembled. Japan lay prostrate before the
unforgettable fire. Around the world liberated nations and peoples celebrated the end of bondage from cruel tyranny. American power, technological and military, had vanquished its foes; American ideals seemed
equally invulnerable to challenge. Nineteen forty-five was to offer the
world a new breath of freedom, a respite from bloodshed and a release
from the geopolitical conflicts induced by the war that was expected to end
all wars.

Yet, as the dawn rose on the American age, Communist military power
presented a formidable challenge. The Soviet Union, not the democratic
West, occupied the Eurasian heartland. Despair and devastation in postwar
Europe proved alluring, it was thought, to the Communists' empty prom-
ises of bread and peace. As Americans yearned to bring the boys back home
quickly, new geopolitical realities induced an expanded internationalist role
for American power and influence in the affairs of Europe. The new world
would immerse itself in solving the problems of the old.

Little noticed in the year of victory, when a new role in European
power politics threatened America's traditional sense of its own exception-
alism, the old individualist Albert Jay Nock died. Nock was, in words that

would influence a later generation of conservatives, a "superfluous man." Critical of mass democracy, Nock conceived of the ideal of the remnant— a select few who would save Western civilization. Strongly aristocratic and pessimistic, Nock was, according to historian George Nash, representative of a "philosophical individualism" that in its singularity made its practitioner certainly superfluous by the standards of 1945.[1]

But Nock was more than eccentric. His superfluity made him attractive to the happy few who read *Our Enemy, the State* and *Memoirs of a Superfluous Man*, or who had the good fortune to read the early *Freeman,* the fine, but shortlived, individualist journal founded in the 1920s and reflective of Nock's own Jeffersonian leanings.[2] Nock's influence appealed both to traditionalists, who found in his rejection of democracy and his veneration for permanent things a perspective that matched their own, and to libertarians, who believed his defense of individualism was a tradition that needed resurrection in the twentieth century.[3] Albert Jay Nock represented both currents in postwar American conservative thought. His death in 1945 would bring the remnant to life.

For both traditionalists and libertarians, 1945 and the years that followed represented the antithesis of freedom. Austrian economist Friedrich August von Hayek, who had labored in England since before the war, gave voice to this in *The Road to Serfdom,* a well-received polemic that warned of the fate that would befall those democracies intent on following the socialist model of state centralized planning. "It is necessary to now state the unpalatable truth that it is Germany whose fate we are in some danger of repeating," Hayek wrote in 1944.[4] If present trends in the democracies continued, Hayek believed, America and the West would find themselves in the totalitarian trap that ensnared the German and Russian people, choosing security over liberty and state planning over a competitive economic order.

The shrill alarums of both Nock and Hayek suggested to individualists that the year of victory represented little more than a continuing battle against the forces of growing state power and collectivism. Little had changed as Soviet power replaced fascism and growing state economic power in America imperiled individual freedoms. If Hayek's program of maximizing the freedom of the individual over government were ever to succeed, it would represent only the "beginning of a new, long, and arduous process" in which a new world, built upon the abandoned road of nineteenth-century liberalism, was created.[5] Even as individualists like Nock and Hayek longed for the restoration of lost orders, they realized that the battle ahead would be difficult.

For traditionalists, Nockian skepticism concerning democracy matched certain affinities presented in the critique of modernism undertaken by scholars such as Richard Weaver, Leo Strauss, Eric Voegelin, and Russell Kirk. Weaver, a southerner trained in the Vanderbilt agrarianism of his mentors John Crowe Ransom and Cleanth Brooks, found himself teaching in the Department of English at the University of Chicago, the epitome of the modern university (with its Gothic edifice designed by the antimodernist architect Ralph Adams Cram). Weaver believed the root of modern man's troubles had begun in the rejection of universals, which occurred as early as the thirteenth century when William of Occam suggested the doctrine of nominalism. For Weaver, "the defeat of logical realism in the great medieval debate was the crucial event of Western culture."[6] The consequence of this defeat at the hands of William's doctrine of nominalism was the rejection of universal truth and the heresy that "man is the measure of all things."[7] This medieval debate greatly affected the modern world for it allowed man to be judged without the leveling power of original sin; it allowed for the belief that man is capable of endless good; and it disallowed transcendence by cutting man off from God, which offered man salvation only out of this world and not in it and caused the totalitarian temptation brought on by positivism and put into practice by the Bolsheviks.[8] The replacement of faith by ideology was known all too clearly in the twin nightmares of fascism and Communism in the twentieth century.

Other antimodernists, such as Leo Strauss and Eric Voegelin, offered their critique of modernity, but the depth of their philosophical inquiries into the nature of truth made their works less accessible to a general audience.[9] Unlike Strauss and Voegelin, Weaver offered a relatively discernible historical-literary approach to the issue of modernism, an approach made even more palatable by the publication of Russell Kirk's *The Conservative Mind: From Burke to Santayana* in 1953.

Kirk had been influenced by Nock when he was a soldier stationed in the vast deserts of Utah during World War II. There he read *Our Enemy, the State,* eagerly corresponded with its author, and digested its individualist ethos. After the war Kirk held an assistant professorship at Michigan State University before matriculating at Saint Andrew's University in Scotland. There he chose the topic of men who stood against their age—and in 1953 that learned dissertation was published by the Henry Regnery Company in Chicago as *The Conservative Mind.*[10]

Kirk's exegesis was monumental. He delineated in the book six canons of conservatism, which included the belief that a divine intent ruled society, a respect for the mystery of life, the conviction that society requires orders and classes, the view that property and freedom are interconnected, a faith in prescriptive tradition, and the belief that innovation and change are not to be held as ends in themselves but rather as means to maintain as much as possible the continuity of social order.[11] Kirk offered a traditionalist conservatism that placed emphasis on the decline of the West but offered, unlike the gloomier Weaver's analysis, hope for renewal. As Kirk later wrote in an injunction to young conservatives, change comes when one "begin[s] by brightening the corner where you are; by improving one human unit, yourself, and by helping your neighbor."[12] A man of letters in the truest sense, writing from his familial home in rural Mecosta, Michigan, Kirk lived the life of a conservative sage from a preliberal past. Though he was pessimistic about the state of American culture in the twentieth century, Kirk's cheerfulness negated his pessimism and provided wellsprings for action, for those so inclined.

Other areas for active engagement appeared at the beginning of the Cold War. For if conservatism was advanced by the writings of Hayek, Weaver, and Kirk, it was made politically palatable by the anticommunist issue, which dominated American politics in the late 1940s and early 1950s. The Soviet Union, viewed by many conservatives as a monolith centered in Moscow, was intent on conquest. The Truman administration's efforts to contain Communism where it was in Eastern Europe, while redressing the lure of Communism elsewhere through rehabilitative measures such as the Marshall Plan, did little to ease the fears of the red menace at home. Even though liberals dominated anticommunist activity during the late 1940s, through the formation of groups like the Americans for Democratic Action (ADA), which helped create a "vital center" of liberalism that was strongly anticommunist (or at least anti-Stalinist), conservative anticommunists, many of them former radicals and Communists themselves, reawakened to fight the subversive menace they saw at home.[13]

Conservative anticommunists responded to the Cold War by reinvigorating the dormant view, held by Eugene Lyons among others, that the "red decade" of the 1930s was the explanation for Soviet advances and the impotence of American diplomacy in the face of Soviet violations of the Yalta treaty.[14] In the 1930s a Communist underground apparatus used the tumult of depression and the statism of New Deal liberalism to advance its agenda. The revelations in 1948 before the House Committee on Un-American Activities by former communists Elizabeth Bentley and Whittaker Chambers of an underground spying apparatus that had infiltrated New

Deal agencies confirmed to many conservative anticommunists that Soviet influence reached deep within the American government. The disclosures by Bentley that Harry Dexter White, a high official at the Treasury Department had given her information for Soviet intelligence, and by Whittaker Chambers that Alger Hiss, a lawyer in the Agricultural Adjustment Administration (where a Communist cell was active) and later in the State Department, had been active in espionage confirmed the earlier views of many on the Right that a Communist presence remained active in America and was encouraged, if not aided, by liberal reformers in FDR's New Deal.[15]

Chambers, especially, had a tremendous influence on conservative anticommunism. Although a rumpled, melancholy figure who believed the West had already lost the battle against Communism and who despaired of any active effort against the Soviets, Chambers would be one of the key influences, through his magisterial chronicle *Witness,* for many conservative anticommunists in the postwar period. Pilloried by the media and well-connected Democratic politicians for his role in the Hiss case, a vilification from which his reputation has never fully recovered, even though evidence regarding his charges against Hiss have been verified, Chambers withdrew to his Westminster, Maryland, farm to continue in solitude his jihad against the unholy menace of Communism.[16]

If Chambers's work stressed the religious impulse of the Cold War anticommunist crusade, it was up to former Trotskyite James Burnham to articulate a geopolitical case for conservative anticommunism. Both strains of anticommunist thought and activity, geopolitical and internal subversion, dominated conservative views of Communism for the remainder of the Cold War.[17]

Burnham was the preeminent intellectual of the Trotskyite Left during the 1930s but had moved away from his allies on the Left during the 1940s; by the mid-1950s he was fully ensconced in conservative intellectual life after accepting an editorship at *National Review.*[18] Burnham was not alone in making the pilgrimage from Left to Right after World War II, but it was surprising that he did so in light of his intellectual work on behalf of Trotskyism. A brilliant social theorist, Burnham had articulated a conception of social organization that would emerge in the wake of World War II—a new "ruling class" of managers would defy both the capitalist and the socialist systems and reign supreme in the postwar era. A full decade before C. Wright Mills's famous theories on the power elite and managerialism had emerged in the 1950s, Burnham had suggested just such a possibility.[19] After publishing *The Machiavellians,* a book further developing his conception of a ruling class, Burnham turned his attention to foreign affairs and the Communist threat.

Burnham embraced, in *The Struggle for the World,* a view of geopolitics similar to that of American policymakers after the war. Influenced by British geopolitician Halford Mackinder, Burnham argued that the Cold War represented "the third world war" and that America must take the offensive against Communist expansionism.[20] Containment, Burnham believed, would ultimately fail because of its defensive posture. Conjoining realism with anticommunist moralism, Burnham argued that the United States should exploit Soviet weaknesses in Eastern Europe through an aggressive strategy of propaganda and "offensive-subversive war." Even after the American atomic monopoly was broken by the Soviet bomb explosion in 1949, Burnham argued, much like containment architect George F. Kennan, that the Soviet state suffered from internal weaknesses that could be exploited. Burnham and Kennan differed over the means, not the ends, necessary to contain the Soviet Union.[21] Burnham's means included an anticommunist moralism leading to the strategy of liberation, which, even after the Soviet invasion of Hungary in 1956, would remain a preferred means for conservatives for dealing, at least rhetorically, with the Communists.[22]

An articulation of conservative principles was well under way in the early years of the Cold War. The strands of Hayekian individualism and antistatism were opposed by Weaver's and Kirk's "new conservatism"—a label applied to the traditionalist reawakening in the early 1950s.[23] Straddling those two positions stood the anticommunist Right, a diverse and amorphous grouping of ex-communists and radicals that included Catholics, Jews, Protestants, extremists, libertarians, and traditionalists.[24] The "fusion" of those three entities into one unified conservative movement was a process begun in the 1950s, in the wake of McCarthyism, which was responsible for the development of a unified "vital center" conservatism centered around the magazine *National Review* and the political leadership of Barry Goldwater.[25] With conservative principles articulated, it was up to a new generation of conservative young people to bring about the quest for philosophical order.

One of those young people was a graduate of Yale University named William F. Buckley, Jr. Buckley had been raised in privilege. His father was a successful oil and real estate entrepreneur in Mexico during the early twentieth century and the tumultuous years of the Mexican Revolution. A self-professed counterrevolutionary and supporter of Victoriano Huerta, William Buckley grew alarmed when rebel generals attacked property and the ruling elite in Mexico. After his real estate and oil holdings were lost in the wake of Huerta's removal from power, Buckley returned to the United States in 1921 eager to regain his fortune, to marry, and to raise a family, all the while instilling in his progeny a respect for order, veneration for the Catholic faith, and hatred of revolution.[26]

William F. Buckley, Jr., was born into the wellspring of his father's beliefs. One of ten children, William junior developed an interest in learning and music from his mother, a South Carolinian of refined tastes and morals. William senior designed an elaborate home educational system in which the children were taught foreign languages, the classics, and music. He would question the children around the dinner table about contemporary events and their education. Wealth allowed the Buckley children the privilege of the finest tutors, lengthy stays abroad, and the development of cultural affectations certainly at odds with their homespun Yankee Protestant neighbors in Sharon, Connecticut.[27]

The Buckley children were loyal to their father's political faith, combining strong anticommunism, conservative Catholicism, hostility to intervention in European affairs, and hatred of revolutionary change. The Buckley children published an anti-interventionist newsletter, *The Spectator,* in 1939, which showcased these views. The patriarch of the Buckley family would join the America First Committee and young William would be drawn to an isolationist position before Pearl Harbor. William junior often participated in discussions with his father's intellectual friends, including Albert Jay Nock, and attended Millbrook School after a year in public school in England. In 1943, after graduating from Millbrook, Buckley was drafted into the army and completed Officer Candidate School while serving uneventfully stateside. In 1946 he matriculated at Yale.[28]

At Yale Buckley thrived. He delighted in antagonizing the faculty, primarily drawn to New Deal liberalism, by offering a clear alternative to the collectivism being taught in New Haven. A disciple of political scientist Willmoore Kendall, Buckley was active in the political union, the debating team (where his future brother-in-law, L. Brent Bozell, and he defeated Oxford University's touring team in 1949), and the student newspaper the *Yale Daily News,* of which he became chairman in the 1949–50 school year.[29]

After leaving Yale in 1950, Buckley worked for the Central Intelligence Agency in Mexico, where his fluent Spanish and family connections came into play. Bored with intelligence work (Mexico was not exactly a hot spot in the Cold War), Buckley decided to take time to write an exposé of his college, a book he entitled *God and Man at Yale*. To young conservatives during the 1950s, Buckley's book was a manifesto akin to what C. Wright Mills's *The Power Elite* or Paul Goodman's *Growing Up Absurd* were for left-wing students. Buckley attacked the Yale administration for allowing the teaching of atheism and collectivism in religion and economics courses. Religion was taught at Yale devoid of any serious appreciation for its moral canon; economic instruction emphasized collectivist approaches, such as the New Deal, to economic problems rather than solutions that advocated free market principles. Forgotten by the Yale faculty, in Buckley's view, were the individualist and moral traditions that remained the backbone of freedom in the West. To Buckley, an emphasis on individualism (free market economics) was the *sine qua non* of freedom. By not stressing the role of free markets and religion, Yale instructors ignored the traditional strengths of Western civilization.[30]

The book was harshly received by the Yale administration and by several reviewers in the mainstream press. McGeorge Bundy wrote the "unofficial" Yale reply in the *Atlantic Monthly*. Bundy pointed to the irony of having the Catholic Buckley defending Yale's Protestant religious tradition. "In view of the pronounced and well recognized difference between Protestant and Catholic views on education in America," he argued with more than a hint of anti-Catholicism, "it seems strange for any Roman Catholic to undertake to speak for the Yale religious tradition."[31] But he missed Buckley's point. Buckley argued that no one was speaking for *any* religious tradition at Yale. If the Yale administration had eschewed its Protestant heritage, should not it be up to some defender of tradition to take a stand, no matter his religious background?

For conservatives Buckley's book was a godsend, despite negative reviews in the mainstream press. Here was an articulate, handsome, debonair, and cocky Yale graduate telling the world that his university made a sham of academic integrity. After the book's publication and the reception it received, there was little doubt that its author was a dynamic new spokesman for conservatism in America.

Other young people took different routes to their conservatism in the postwar period. Marvin Liebman, who would become one of the conservative movement's premier public relations professionals and organizers, was a Communist and a Zionist before converting to anticommunism in the 1950s. With the help of his mentors, former New Jersey governor

Charles Edison (the youngest son of the inventor) and Walter Judd, a former missionary to China and a congressman from Minnesota, Liebman organized groups like the Aid Refugee Chinese Intellectuals committee and, most importantly, the Committee of One Million (Against the Admission of China into the United Nations).[32] Liebman had perfected the establishment of conservative "letterhead" organizations, many of them bipartisan, designed to sustain anticommunist intellectuals and politicians in their work against Communism. In this manner, Liebman would be instrumental in bringing together diverse and often conflicting intellectuals for anticommunist political purposes.

William Rusher, a lawyer who worked in the Young Republicans during the 1950s to move that organization in a conservative direction, and who would later, in 1957, become publisher of *National Review,* also entered conservatism from a different direction than Buckley. Born in Chicago in 1923, Rusher grew up in New York, graduated from Princeton University in 1943, and served a three-year stint as an officer in the Army Air Corps. In 1946 he attended Harvard Law School, graduated in 1948, and took a job at a Wall Street law firm. While at Harvard he was involved in Young Republican activities, becoming the first president of Harvard's YR club.[33] Rusher claimed that it was the atmosphere of the Cold War and particularly the Korean War that brought about his transformation to staunch anticommunism (he worked as a counsel for the Senate Internal Security Subcommittee).[34] His reading in conservative intellectual thought, everything from Hayek to Kirk to Chambers, was what turned him into a conservative. For Buckley, Liebman, and Rusher, a group who would represent the first wave of youth revolt in favor of conservative principles, anticommunism and growing state power in America were common themes bringing them to the Right during the 1950s.

Organizationally, however, even with the intensification of conservative activity in the YR during the mid-1950s, there were very few organizations for conservative activists to join at this time. The Young Republicans remained, much like the wider party, controlled by a liberal country-club establishment who looked with disdain on conservative influence. Although John Ashbrook, with the help of Rusher and F. Clifton White, a YR activist from Cornell University in New York, won the chairmanship of the YR National Federation in 1957, the eastern wing quickly reasserted its influence in YR affairs and won out again the next year.[35] The national party was equally indifferent to youth activists. Tom Charles Huston, who would later become national chairman of YAF, recalled that he worked for

Democrats in the 1950s because the party members in his small Indiana town wanted little to do with young people. When he enrolled at Indiana University in 1959, he thought it important to establish a conservative club on campus in order to compete with the YR, who were liberal Republicans no different in principle from Eisenhower.[36]

What helped young conservatives shake Republican Party disinterest and emerge into the forefront of campus politics by the late 1950s was the Intercollegiate Society of Individualists (ISI), an organization created to distribute conservative publications to students. Founded in 1953 by Frank Chodorov, a former editor of the journal *analysis* and the newsletter *Human Events,* ISI was meant to be a clearinghouse for the publication and distribution of conservative literature on college campuses. Self-consciously emulating the Intercollegiate Socialist Society established in 1905 by novelist Jack London, among others, ISI was created "to uproot the collectivist seed which had been implanted in people's minds over the past generation" and "to create a conservative leadership for America."[37] Through education and ideas, conservatives would build on the individualist principles that Hayek and others helped resurrect after the war.

ISI, although relatively unknown outside conservative circles, was immensely successful in laying the groundwork for a conservative intellectual movement on campus.[38] Among the books ISI distributed to students, free of charge or for a minimal fee, were Hayek's *Road to Serfdom,* Felix Morley's *Freedom and Federalism,* Richard Weaver's *Ideas Have Consequences,* and Buckley's and Brent Bozell's *McCarthy and His Enemies.* ISI also published its own newsletter, *The Individualist,* as well as distributing numerous monographs and pamphlets of its own by leading conservative scholars.[39] Chodorov and his principal associate, Vic Milione, the son of Italian immigrants and graduate of tiny Saint Joseph College, were intent on keeping ISI an organization that helped students learn the individualist-conservative intellectual tradition. It was not an activist organization, but its success on campuses encouraged the formation of conservative clubs, where the issues and ideas in ISI-sponsored publications would be discussed and debated.[40] Young conservatives from many of these clubs would later play instrumental roles in the formation of YAF and the development of an activist conservative movement in the 1960s.

M. Stanton Evans was one such person in the 1950s who helped transform ideas into action, and much like Buckley, Rusher and Liebman, he represents a transition between the older intellectual Right and the younger, more activist-oriented conservatism. Between 1951 and 1955

Evans attended Yale; there he helped form a conservative club, the Calliopean Society, and edited its publication, *The Independent.* In 1956 he joined
the staff of *Human Events,* where, for three years, he gained acclaim as an
editor. He left *Human Events* in 1959 and, at the age of twenty-six, became
the youngest editor of a major American daily newspaper, the *Indianapolis
News.*[41] Within a year he published his first book, *Revolt on the Campus,*
which explored the rise of conservative thought among young people. In
this book Evans documented the importance of ISI to him as a Yale
freshman. He recalled, "Through ISI, I received books by Frederic Bastiat,
Frank Chodorov, and F.A. Harper as well as the newsletter *Human Events,*
and I became aware of the existence of conservative publishers—Henry
Regnery and Devin Adair. . . . It was a discovery beyond price for it meant
that I was no longer alone."[42]

At Williams College Jameson Campaigne, Jr., the son of a columnist for
the *Indianapolis Star,* founded a conservative club and made active inroads
into what he considered to be the one-sided and biased view of his instructors. Campaigne and cohorts put out book lists of "recommended read-
ings" for courses, challenging the reading lists put together by faculty.
Hugely popular, the reading lists caused faculty much consternation as
interested students began to challenge and question the views of their
professors with growing confidence. The Williams Conservative Club also
established a taped radio program called "Radio Free Williams" and
brought to campus speakers such as Buckley and radio commentator Fulton
Lewis, Jr.[43] Some thirty people joined in the activities at Williams.

The diversity of conservative student activity during the late 1950s could
be laid at the doorstep of ISI and its efforts to reawaken a conservative
presence at the nation's colleges. But though ISI was a necessary organization, it was not sufficient in and of itself to explain the conservative student
renascence. The founding of *National Review* in 1955 was of even greater
importance. For some time the only conservative publication in existence
was the biweekly newsletter *Human Events.* Published in Washington,
D.C., *Human Events* kept an eye on national politics from a conservative
perspective, but it was altogether inadequate as a source for conservative
intellectuals. *The Freeman,* an intellectual organ, was founded in the 1920s
by the libertarian Albert Jay Nock and resurrected in 1950 through a
merger with Isaac Don Levine's anticommunist journal *Plain Talk.* However, *The Freeman* was a money-losing proposition during the height of its
influence between 1950 and 1954. Reduced to a monthly published under
the auspices of the Foundation for Economic Education, *The Freeman* was

a fine intellectual journal but never reached a large audience.[44] By mid-1955, therefore, not a single weekly periodical with a conservative viewpoint was printed in the United States; there were eight such liberal outlets. As Buckley claimed in the inaugural issue of *National Review,* that imbalance represented a loss in the war of ideas.

Buckley was intent on reaching intellectuals with *National Review* and eschewing the more conventional populist label that haunted once-prominent right-wing magazines like *The American Mercury.*[45] The masthead of the magazine was symbolic of Buckley's efforts. Each school of conservative thought was represented. Russell Kirk headed up the traditionalist position (along with contributors such as Donald Davidson, Richard Weaver, and Austrian monarchist Erik von Kuehnelt-Leddihn). Libertarians on the masthead included journalists such as John Chamberlain and Frank Chodorov. Many ex-radicals and ex-Communists also contributed, including James Burnham, Frank Meyer, Max Eastman, Chambers, Chamberlain, and Buckley's mentor Willmoore Kendall. The ex-radicals gave the magazine an obvious anticommunist flavor through its early years of publication, but Communism was not the only enemy. Liberalism, which Buckley and the other editors assaulted with great vigor, was also a target. To the writers and readers of *National Review,* growing state power in America was tantamount to a loss of individual freedom. Although Soviet totalitarianism represented the extreme threat to freedom, the editors believed that liberalism was headed down the same road.

Buckley's magazine, much like *The Freeman,* was a money-losing venture, yet it had a profound impact on the conservative movement. (Frank Meyer, one of the editors, called it the conservative movement's *Iskra,* referring to the Bolshevik publication that was instrumental in the Russian Revolution).[46] Buckley himself edited it, giving him and his causes a national audience and media exposure. The successful effort to gather the support of conservative intellectuals encouraged the further development and elaboration of their ideas in a public forum. The attractiveness of the magazine itself, which was crisply edited and witty, helped conservatives gain support from all sectors of society, and especially from the young people who now held *National Review* and its young editor in esteem.

Nevertheless, even with a growing cadre of conservatives throughout the country, the emerging conservative movement remained solely an intellectual movement. One of the problems conservatives had in the 1950s involved side-stepping Wisconsin senator Joseph McCarthy and his anticommunist activities. Many on the nascent political Right supported the senator's ends, but anticommunist activity as a whole was hurt by McCarthy's actions. The polarization of American politics during the 1950s over the Communist issue meant that those who practiced any form of anticommunism were suspect McCarthyites. Painting with a broad brush (and ironically, mimicking McCarthy in the process), the anti-anticommunists were quite successful in marginalizing the impact of anticommunist attacks during the 1950s and 1960s.[47]

This is not to say that those who played a crucial role in the formation of the conservative movement during the 1950s wished to distance themselves too much from McCarthyism. Many, such as Buckley, Burnham, and Bozell, wrote in favor of McCarthy's anticommunism, while others on *National Review*'s masthead, such as Max Eastman and Whittaker Chambers, were never comfortable with the senator's activities.[48] Yet, even without McCarthy, the Right would still have reflected an intense disregard for Communism and its progenitors, and overall the junior senator from Wisconsin, who was more a demagogue with a few followers than an ideologue with many, had very little effect on the galvanization of the postwar conservative movement. He may have been seen by many younger conservatives as one who articulated what was necessary—a strong anticommunism that pointed out the dangers in American policy both abroad and at home—but for the most part, McCarthyism diminished the political impact anticommunism possessed forever after. Only the Left, which may have otherwise truly died a quiet death in the 1950s, given postwar America's economic abundance and complacent ease, seemed to benefit from the senator's activities.[49]

That does not mean that the young people who would come to form YAF were not supporters of McCarthy. Lee Edwards, the son of Willard Edwards of the *Chicago Tribune,* echoed his father's staunch support for McCarthy and later worked for Senator John Marshall Butler from Maryland, who supported McCarthy and voted against his censure from the Senate in 1956.[50] Douglas Caddy manned a table in the French Quarter in New Orleans, getting signatures in favor of McCarthy during the Army-McCarthy hearings. He then forwarded the signatures to Maj. Gen. Albert Wedemeyer and Gen. Bonner Fellers, who were leaders of a drive to support the embattled senator.[51] Other future YAF members, if not supporting McCarthy outright, did at least support his anticommunist goals and held to the view that an internal threat was a serious matter. Yet, overall, though McCarthy had his defenders among young people, his dogmatism was not instrumental in formulating a conservative youth movement during the late 1950s.[52]

Events that had a greater effect on the creation of a conservative political movement during the 1950s focused mainly on the perception of Eisenhower's weakness vis-à-vis the Communist bloc. One of those events occurred in November 1956 when the Hungarian government of Imre Nagy withdrew from the Warsaw Pact. In response, after three days of delay and rising tension, Soviet tanks already stationed in Hungary crushed the Hungarian government and installed a puppet regime loyal to Moscow. The Eisenhower administration did little, even though its own rhetoric of liberation, itself a ploy to gain anticommunist support, may have encouraged the Hungarian government to take action against Soviet control. As Eisenhower's biographer Stephen Ambrose claimed, "liberation was a sham. Eisenhower had always known it. The Hungarians had yet to learn it."[53]

Sham or not, for conservatives the failure of the United States to stop the rape of Hungary was abhorrent. The editors of National Review published editorials condemning the Soviet action and Eisenhower's tepid response. They also wrote and signed a pledge to have nothing to do with the Soviet Union until their troops withdrew from Hungary.[54] Marvin Liebman organized a picket line outside the Soviet Union's United Nations headquarters in New York. Hungarian movie stars such as Eva and Zsa Zsa Gabor and Illona Massey were recruited to join the picket line, luring media attention in the process. The most recognizable of all Hungarian actors, Bela Lugosi, was unavailable but sent his best wishes. Liebman also organized an "Army of Liberation" made up of volunteers from Ivy League universities that was going to march into Hungary, declare solidarity with Hungarian students, and tell the Russians to get out. Transport was arranged, funded by former New Jersey governor Charles Edison, and students from several Ivy League schools were all ready to go to Hungary, with Liebman leading them. Then midterms intervened and the "army" collapsed.[55]

Another motivating factor for action developed a year later. In October 1957 the Soviets launched the space satellite Sputnik, which for two days circled the Earth depicting American weakness in the new missile age. Eisenhower's reaction was again laconic, suggesting that there was little to fear from the tiny satellite. The Democratic Congress, in reaction to Sputnik and with the encouragement of Eisenhower's scientific advisory panel, passed the National Defense Education Act in 1958, which increased spending on scientific and technical training in American schools and universities. The act contained a loyalty oath provision stipulating that students who received loan moneys from the government must swear loyalty to the Constitution as well as sign a disclaimer affidavit certifying that they were not members of any subversive organization.[56]

The presidents of Yale and Harvard reacted by stating that they would not accept the provisions of the act if the loyalty oath was included, since they believed it to be a denial of academic freedom.[57] Democratic senator John F. Kennedy offered a Senate bill to rescind the clause.[58] Educators and the media indicated their support for repeal of the oath and the affidavit, and it appeared that with the opening of the spring session of Congress in 1960, they would get it.[59] Then something strange happened. Two students, one from Georgetown University and the other from George Washington University, both dismayed at the controversy, decided to fight for the oath's preservation and formed the Student Committee for the Loyalty Oath.[60]

It was not unusual, for those who knew them, that Douglas Caddy and David Franke would take such action in support of the loyalty oath. Caddy, at Georgetown, was chairman of the District of Columbia College Young Republicans. Franke was editor of ISI's publication, *The Individualist,* as well as *The Campus Republican,* the organ of the national College YR. Both had been fellows, along with William Schulz—who worked with conservative radio commentator Fulton Lewis III—in the first college journalism class sponsored by *Human Events.* Franke had been an activist since junior high school, when he became a dedicated anticommunist after reading his aunt's copy of John T. Flynn's *The Road Ahead,* an excoriation of creeping socialism. In college, one of his mentors was a conservative history professor at Delmar Community College in Corpus Christi, Texas, who "turned him on" to constitutionalism and conservative thought.[61] Caddy, the son of an executive for an oil company, grew up in Louisiana and Texas. He attended Georgetown University School of Foreign Service, where he became active in forming YR chapters in the Washington area. He had volunteered to pass out pro-McCarthy leaflets during the Army-McCarthy hearings and had worked for Kent and Phoebe Courtney's newspaper *The Independent American.*[62]

With connections made nationwide in their work for ISI and the YR, Caddy and Franke established a network of loyalty oath chapters on thirty college campuses, including Harvard and Yale.[63] Several colleges arranged votes supporting the loyalty oath provisions in their student senates. One occurred at a small women's college in Washington, D.C., Dunbarton College of Holy Cross, attended by Carol Dawson, a conservative activist friendly with both Caddy and Franke.

Dawson had been raised in a Republican home but in 1958 had been a conservative for only a short time. Born in Indianapolis, where her father was a newspaperman, Dawson's conservatism sprouted from her involvement with friends like Caddy and Franke. Her future husband, and Franke's roommate, Robert Bauman, also played a role in her movement right. A member of the College YR and student government as well as a writer for the student newspaper, Dawson was active in making the loyalty oath movement a success.[64]

By early 1960, strong support for keeping the loyalty oath provision in the National Defense Education Act had been achieved. Individual letters from young people throughout the country poured into Washington, and congressmen were pressured into taking a public stand on the issue. Caddy and Franke, working at the YRNF and ISI respectively, where they had connections to the adult conservative world, haggled with congressmen to keep the oath in the legislation. Most of these legislators, many of them conservatives themselves, gave speeches in support of the loyalty oath for submission in the *Congressional Record*.[65] Caddy and Franke also worked over college administrations, attacking A. Whitney Griswold at Harvard for denying students "freedom of choice" in deciding whether or not to sign the oath and receive funds. As Caddy stated in a New York address, "not a single student in the United States is being compelled to participate in the defense education program. The student's right to choose freely whether he will take the oath and participate in the program or not is his sacred American birthright. If his conscience or convictions forbid, he can choose not to."[66]

In an article in ISI's *Individualist,* Franke argued that those who, like Griswold, counted themselves as defenders of academic freedom at colleges and universities were not speaking for the majority of American universities. Within a week of Harvard's and Yale's withdrawal from the provisions of the NDEA in November 1959, more than 1,365 other colleges were fully participating in the program.[67] Also, if the act was passed for "defense" purposes, what logic would it be to have a disloyal person working on behalf of American defense?[68]

The pressure was unrelenting. Through letter-writing campaigns to congressmen, press releases, and public exposure of the arguments of those against the oath, the students began to see results. Kennedy's bill for repeal of the act was passed in the Senate, with no record of who voted for it, but it died in committee in the House. The loyalty oath was saved.

Young people working on the Student Committee for the Loyalty Oath gained something aside from preservation of the oath itself. They acquired experience in working the corridors of power in Congress and in using the press to their advantage. Conservative connections also benefited their movement. Lee Edwards, the son of *Chicago Tribune* Washington correspondent Willard Edwards, was employed as a press secretary to Senator John Marshall Butler (R–Md.). Edwards, who had attended Duke University and later did graduate work at the Sorbonne in Paris, met Franke, Caddy, and Robert Bauman through activities in the Washington, D.C., YR and mobilized his influence as press secretary for a U.S. senator who was behind the Student Committee for the Loyalty Oath.[69]

Building on their success with the loyalty oath, young conservatives began to seek out an avenue for political advancement as the 1960 election neared. The Republican Party was mired, they lamented, in the liberal "modern Republicanism" of Dwight Eisenhower and New York governor Nelson Rockefeller, who was the current East coast liberal kingmaker in the Republican Party. Although they had moved much more to the right in the late 1950s, primarily because of the influence of William Rusher and numerous others, the YR were still not an organization hospitable to conservative activism. ISI was growing in the late 1950s, but as a political vehicle its influence was negligible, primarily because it saw its mission as encouraging young conservatives through ideas. *National Review* served as an important resource in the conservative movement, but it was only a forum for ideas, not a place from which to capture a political party. Where would young conservatives turn as the 1960 election approached?

The answer came like a sirocco out of the Arizona desert. Barry Goldwater, a Republican senator from Arizona since 1953, was the epitome of the American success story. His grandfather, Mike Goldwasser, a Jewish immigrant from Russia, had established himself in the dry goods business in the Arizona Territory in the early 1870s. Mike's son, Baron Goldwater, inherited the business and turned the dry goods store into the largest modern department store in Arizona. Barry Goldwater, as the grandson of one of Arizona's first families, inherited the prestige of the family name and learned the department store trade after spending several uneventful years at the University of Arizona. Like many men of his generation, Goldwater served in World War II as an Army Air Corps major (he would later rise to the rank of brigadier general in the reserves), returned to the family business, and, out of boredom as well as civic duty, became active in Phoenix politics. Because of his wide name recognition, rugged good looks, and ideological beliefs, Goldwater was selected to run for a U.S. Senate seat in 1952. He easily defeated his Democratic opponent, Ernest McFarland. McFarland was the Senate majority leader during the Eighty-Second Congress and one of the most popular politicians in Arizona history to that time, but in 1952 he was an old New Dealer in a conservative age.[70]

In the Senate Goldwater became an outspoken conservative. He voted against McCarthy's censure in 1954 and, from his perch on the Senate Labor and Public Welfare Committee, fought against the expansion of labor union influence in politics. Goldwater was also a virulent anticommunist. He believed Communism represented a threat to Western freedom and individualism and recommended increased defense expenditures to fight it, but, unlike most conservative politicians during the 1950s, he did not think there was much to fear from internal security threats—the foreign threat that the Soviet Union represented was enough for him.

As a first-term senator, Goldwater fought the growing graft and corruption in labor unions. Opposed to most of Eisenhower's foreign policy, he believed the president could have reacted in stronger fashion to the Hungarian situation and ought to have built up America's defenses in the wake of *Sputnik*. In 1958, after his reelection, Goldwater was anointed as chairman of the prestigious Republican Senatorial Campaign Committee, an organization designed to raise money and guide strategy for electing Republicans to the Senate. Goldwater later claimed that he relished this role, because it gave him the chance to study the Republican Party nationwide.[71] It also allowed him to make public appearances before local Republican audiences. One such audience would change people's perceptions of the Republican from Arizona practically overnight and make him one of the best-known and most admired of Republican officials.

The appearance was at the Western Republican Conference in November 1959 in Los Angeles. Nelson Rockefeller, who had announced for the 1960 Republican presidential nomination, spoke before Goldwater did and echoed liberal views concerning how government could spend its way out of social problems. To the fiscally prudent Goldwater, Rockefeller's speech represented the major problem of the Republican Party in the eyes of the public—"me-tooism." Goldwater followed Rockefeller by staking his claim for the Republican Party: he would commit that party to freedom, limited central power, a reduction in bureaucracy, and a balanced budget.[72]

The reaction was thunderous. Goldwater was heralded by the *Los Angeles Times* as "the leading conservative thinker in American life" and asked to write a newspaper column articulating his views on prominent issues. Within a year, 140 newspapers were running Goldwater's column.[73]

Goldwater's public enunciation of conservative principles was a blessing to the emerging movement. Buckley and others at *National Review* had long hailed the senator's stance on political issues, especially his handling of the Ervin-Kennedy Bill of 1958, a law designed to reform labor unions that Goldwater voted against. A strengthened bill, the Landrum-Griffith Act, passed because of Goldwater's stand.[74] William Rusher, *National Review*'s publisher, had "discovered" Goldwater in 1955 when the senator addressed the Young Republican National Federation Executive Committee in Colorado Springs; Rusher returned to New York a Goldwater enthusiast.[75] After joining *National Review* as publisher in 1957, Rusher kept up the Goldwater enthusiasm, seeing in the young senator presidential possibilities.

It did not take long for conservatives and Goldwater to form a relationship. Although Goldwater was a charter subscriber to *National Review* and a hero to the developing conservative movement in the late 1950s, he was true to his political party and not interested in running for any office without its endorsement. With the Republicans controlled by the Eastern establishment, it was necessary for conservatives to take over the party if they ever hoped to put a conservative into the highest office in the land. Goldwater became the tool, most of the time an unwilling tool, around whom conservatives built their political base and captured the GOP.[76]

The use of Goldwater by conservatives happened in two ways. First, a group of prominent conservatives and anticommunists pressured Goldwater to express his views in a book. The publication of Goldwater's *Conscience of a Conservative* in March 1960 was the culmination of an effort led by retired Notre Dame University Law School dean Clarence "Pat" Manion, the host of a weekly syndicated radio show from South Bend, Indiana, called the Manion Forum. Manion was deeply interested in constitutional questions regarding the distribution of powers between the federal government and the states. He was also a virulent anticommunist who joined the John Birch Society and its board of directors after its founding in 1958. Although not one to fall prey to the more ridiculous views of Birch Society founder Robert Welch (who suggested in a privately distributed book, *The Politician,* that Eisenhower was "A conscious articulate instrument of the Soviet conspiracy"),[77] Manion stayed on the Birch board, seeing the organization as a vital force in the struggle against Communism.

As early as 1957, Manion and other Republicans had sought a political candidate to challenge the eastern domination of the Republican Party. For Manion, this was personal. Dismissed from the President's Commission on Inter-Governmental Relations in 1954 because of his "orthodox" right-wing views (he supported passage of the controversial Bricker Amendment), Manion and other right-wing figures, such as T. Coleman Andrews, a former commissioner of the Internal Revenue Service, sought to change the Republican Party to one more representative of their views on constitutional and anticommunist matters.[78] In a letter to his friend Senator William Jenner of Indiana Manion argued that the right wing of the Republican Party should bolt the party and establish itself as an independent American Party:

> If you, Goldwater, McCarthy and perhaps a few others, could come out now and announce your intention to run for the Constitution and the United States the whole country would be electrified. Suppose you by-passed the Republican Convention and let them nominate a "modern Republican" to divide the Internationalist- Socialist vote with the Democrats. Do you mean to tell me that you wouldn't get more than a third of the votes in November, which would be all that you would need to win?[79]

Whether Jenner seriously considered a run as an independent candidate or not, the right wing of the Republican Party was searching for a candidate to support in the 1960 election.

Goldwater was the perfect fit. All that was needed was a vehicle in which the senator could articulate his views. Goldwater later claimed that Manion "was responsible for the writing of the book *The Conscience of a Conservative*."[80] This was only partially true. Manion secured the funds and the publisher, but he was not the book's author. The author was recruited from the ranks of *National Review*. L. Brent Bozell, Buckley's brother-in-law and an editor at the magazine, agreed to help Goldwater polish some of his speeches in order to turn them into book material. The objective, as Manion wrote Buckley in September 1959, was threefold: "to give Goldwater an authentic platform"; "to wean him off Nixon (if it had not been for this movement, I am sure that Barry would have been plumping for Nixon all over the place by this time)"; and to preserve the "hope" that they could make a "fight in the convention."[81] Manion was realistic, however. He understood that Goldwater had "a Chinaman's chance," as he put it, to win the nomination for the presidency, particularly with Rockefeller's millions behind either Nixon or his own candidacy, but he found throughout his canvass of Republicans "universal admiration for Goldwater and an almost unanimous wish to see him bear the Republican standard."[82]

Goldwater's book was a triumph. It sold over ten thousand copies in March, mainly to business and corporate interests solicited by Manion, and had over fifty thousand in print by May. It would sell 3.5 million copies by the time of Goldwater's nomination in 1964. This success made for an interesting dilemma. Could Goldwater now be considered a national figure strong enough to challenge Nixon for the Republican presidential nomination at the convention, or should he pursue the vice-presidential nomination?

For Manion and other right-wing elements in the Republican Party, part of the success of Goldwater's book lay clearly in the fact that his conservative principles resonated with thousands of people throughout the nation. As an example, in March 1960 Goldwater won the presidential straw poll vote of the South Carolina Republican State Convention. A month later, he was pledged the fourteen delegates of the Arizona delegation as a favorite-son candidate, even though Goldwater had promised Congressman John Rhodes and Arizona state Republican chairman Richard Kleindienst that the votes would be freed up for Nixon at the convention.[83]

Goldwater and his ideas also excited young people. At an April 1960 meeting of the Midwest Federation of College Young Republican Clubs held in Des Moines, Iowa, conservative students pushed through a surprising endorsement of Goldwater for vice president. Although most of the college students were too young to vote, Goldwater had excited them enough to work for his nomination during the spring and summer of 1960. A month after the Des Moines meeting, a new organizational committee, Youth for Goldwater for Vice-President, was formed.[84] Headed by Northwestern University graduate student Robert Croll, the group included prominent young conservatives such as David Franke and Doug Caddy of the loyalty oath committee, as well as Robert Harley and Richard Noble, who had cut their organizational teeth in the College YR.[85]

The press paid little attention to the Youth for Goldwater drive before the convention. On May 12, 1960, Croll announced that the Youth for Goldwater drive had two distinct purposes: to get Goldwater nominated as the vice-presidential candidate and "to work within the YR National Federation for the political and economic philosophies represented in Goldwater's book, *Conscience of a Conservative*."[86] Croll also announced the formation of forty-five chapters at various colleges throughout the country dedicated to this cause.[87]

Youth for Goldwater represented an intersection of various streams of the conservative movement. First, the young people in the organization were working for principles that they believed differentiated them from other Republicans. Goldwater's book was a warning shot fired across the bow of the liberal Republicanism represented by Eisenhower, Nelson Rockefeller, and the majority of the party. The book stressed conservative principles such as individualism, anticommunism (emphasizing victory over rather then coexistence with the Soviet Union), and states' rights. It showed how conservatives were intent on maximizing individual freedom by turning back the growth of federal power. Goldwater stated, "The conservative looks upon politics as the art of achieving the maximum amount of freedom for individuals that is consistent with the maintenance of social order."[88]

Young conservatives received key operational support from their elders. *National Review* ran advertisements soliciting financial support for Youth for Goldwater. Frank Meyer argued that "the emergence of Barry Goldwater as a principled conservative gives us a public political symbol through which our position is expressed in the political arena."[89] As a result, at the end of the school year David Franke was hired as an intern at the *National Review,* where he would be able to continue his work for Goldwater. Marvin Liebman also volunteered his talents on behalf of the young conservatives, hiring Doug Caddy to work for him at his New York offices when he graduated from Georgetown in the spring. Older conservatives such as former New Jersey governor Charles Edison encouraged the youngsters with advice and financial support.

Young people who were separated by distance or membership in other conservative organizations came together in their campaign for Goldwater's nomination. Young Republicans, College YR, members of independent college conservative clubs, and ISI played active roles in the committee, gaining not only vital tactical political experience, but also networking with like-minded young people. Part of this networking involved the merger of eastern groups like the loyalty oath committee with Young Republican groups from the Midwest, represented by Bob Croll and others.[90] Conservatism, by 1960, was not the lonely life it had been a short ten years earlier.

The efforts on behalf of Goldwater by older and younger conservatives were indeed electrifying. By the time of the Republican convention in July, Goldwater was a firm possibility for vice president in the minds of

Republican delegates. A week before the convention, however, Nixon had flown to New York to meet with Governor Rockefeller. In return for Rockefeller's withdrawal of his name as a candidate, Nixon agreed to certain terms which were perceived by right-wing Republicans to include nominating an East Coast Republican as his running mate. (Nixon subsequently chose Massachusetts Republican Henry Cabot Lodge as his running mate). The Fifth Avenue Treaty (Goldwater less generously referred to it as a "domestic Munich") was the nail in the coffin for the Goldwater drive, yet young people still persevered despite the odds.[91]

When Goldwater arrived in Chicago, he was greeted by a large conservative presence at the convention. Walter Judd, a Minnesota congressman and cofounder, with Marvin Liebman, of the Committee of One Million, was to give the keynote address to the convention. Liebman, working with Charles Edison, began a Judd for Vice President committee, which succeeded in getting the congressman a meeting with Nixon, but little else.[92] The Youth for Goldwater forces also fought for their man, but to no avail.[93] Even after Goldwater allowed his name to be placed in nomination, he went along with the prearranged scenario and asked that his name be withdrawn.

During Goldwater's speech to the convention, a demonstration organized by the Youth for Goldwater forces took place. When Goldwater was introduced to the crowd, as M. Stanton Evans recalled, "the words were suddenly lost in bedlam. A great wave of sound exploded into the vaulted regions of the [hall] . . . the ovation for the outspoken senator was real and deep and it was overwhelming."[94] The young conservatives, many of whom could not vote and were not delegates to the convention, conspired with friendly state delegations, such as Arizona's, to be sneaked onto the convention floor for demonstrations in support of Goldwater. Given false credentials, they battled with security forces to stay on the floor, supporting Goldwater when his turn came to speak.[95]

There was also a public presence at the convention. Doug Caddy recalled that young people were out on the street marching with pictures of Goldwater mounted on poles sixteen feet high. "When Nixon came in on the motorcade, I remembered the look on his face when he passed. He was about ten feet from me as his car passed, and he had the most shocked look on his face. . . . He could sense that here was a real factor which he had never considered, that there was an emerging voice of conservatism."[96]

However, the efforts went for naught. Putting the party first and his conservatism second, Goldwater announced what conservatives like Manion and others had dreaded—the Republican Party was the historic house of conservatives, and Goldwater would do what he could to work for the election of the top ticket of Nixon and Lodge. If conservatives wanted to elect one of their own, they would need to "grow up" and take control of the Republican Party.[97] Although it did not appear that this was possible in the wake of the 1960 convention, within four years Goldwater would be sitting atop the national Republican ticket, and it would be young people who were instrumental in getting him there.[98]

The day after the convention, with Nixon and Lodge holding the banner of the Republican Party, the Youth for Goldwater executive committee, as well as six or seven other young people,[99] met at a luncheon organized by Liebman and Charles Edison in the Columbia Room of the Pick-Congress Hotel. Unnoticed and uncovered by the press, Edison enjoined the young people to keep in contact, to keep fighting for conservative principles and conservative candidates, and to organize conservative clubs on campus.[100] Determined not to let their past success slip away, Doug Caddy, with Liebman's support, put together an interim committee for a national student conservative organization. By the end of the summer of 1960, with the aid of mailing lists and contacts made in the Youth for Goldwater drive, as well as networks in the YR and College YR, the seeds of a conservative youth organization were sown. In the early fall they would germinate in the upper reaches of Connecticut in the ancestral manse of William F. Buckley, Jr., the young conservative more responsible than any other for bringing together and making possible the movement toward political action.

2

Join Together and Fall Apart, 1960–1962

We knew we had made an impact with the Goldwater for Vice-President operation and we had some success with the loyalty oath . . . and there was a need for an organization on the outside that could exert influence on American politics.　　　—Lee Edwards

[The Sharon Statement] wasn't the Declaration of Independence, it wasn't the Gettysburg Address—it was a very common sense statement, I think, of what American conservatives believed then and believe now.　　　—M. Stanton Evans

Sharon, Connecticut, was a sleepy little backwater town tucked in the northwest corner of the state, far away from urban Hartford and New Haven, and even farther away in time from the New York suburbs that had developed along Connecticut's southwestern shore. Sharon was founded before the American Revolution, and many of the town's residents could still claim descent from Yankees who settled the interior of that colony in the late 1600s and fought against the British. More recent immigrants to Sharon had little in common with the natives, however. The most famous family of Sharon, the Buckleys, were Irish Catholics who sensed that they did not fit in with their Protestant neighbors.[1]

William F. Buckley, Sr., had moved the Buckley family to Sharon in the early 1920s after returning to New York to raise investment capital for an oil venture in Venezuela. Wanting his children to grow up in the countryside, Buckley purchased the forty-seven-acre estate of Great Elm, so called because the state's largest elm tree stood in its front yard. Built in 1763, the house had once claimed the governor of Connecticut as its tenant, but it was the Buckleys who would bring the house, and the town, fame.[2]

After laying the groundwork for a national student conservative organization at the Chicago convention, Doug Caddy and Marvin Liebman sought a place to hold a founding meeting. For Liebman, "the Buckley name was a substantial lure," and it was decided that he would approach Buckley about a meeting at his ancestral home in Sharon.[3] After arrangements were made with the Buckley family, Caddy and Liebman called for a meeting the weekend of September 10–11, 1960.

The Sharon conference can be viewed, like the radical congress held at Port Huron in 1962, as one of the most significant student meetings of the 1960s. Long ignored by historians, the Sharon conference represented the beginnings of a movement that would help catapult conservatives into political power within two decades. Like their counterparts in the New Left, young conservatives were tired of the complacency of American politics. Specifically, they were weary of liberal dominance within the Republican Party and demanded change.[4] Buckley later wrote in the warm afterglow of the conference, "What is so striking in the students who met at Sharon is their appetite for power. Ten years ago, the struggle seemed so long, so endless, even, that we did not dream of victory. . . . The difference in psychological attitude is tremendous."[5]

Even though Sharon signified the start of something big for young conservatives, no written transcripts were kept of the meeting itself. Nonetheless, more than ninety young activists, including many from the Young Republicans and other organizations such as the national Youth for Goldwater for Vice-President, gathered at Sharon and founded Young Americans for Freedom.[6] Doug Caddy assumed the role of national director of the organization and, as one person in attendance related, masterminded the choice of the organization's first national board of directors.[7] The Sharon conference typified the efforts made by young conservatives over the previous several years in that it was inclusive. Though the organization drew support from various conservative groups and the YR, YAF was to be an independent and non-partisan group and would seek sponsorship and advisory support from prominent conservative Democrats, such as Strom Thurmond, as well as Republicans.

Of those in attendance at Sharon, close to two-thirds were from the East, with the Midwest representing about two-thirds of the remainder. The other ten people were split somewhat evenly between the West Coast and the South, with one making the trip from Canada.[8] The ethnic makeup of YAF's founding generation represented groups whom sociologists David

Westby and Richard Braungart called old Americans, people of English, Scotch-Irish, French, Dutch, or German ethnicities; indeed, some 78 percent of all YAF members were representative of this ethnic category.[9] The majority of YAF members came from lower-middle- and working-class families; the fathers of some 64 percent of the YAF members surveyed never went to college.[10] What is surprising in such research is the fact that the majority of conservative students came from less privileged backgrounds than comparable radical student groups and were seemingly old-stock Americans, not the status-anxious ethnic groups often depicted as being members of right-wing movements.[11] Many early YAF members came to their conservatism from issues like McCarthyism and the 1956 invasion of Hungary or because of shared religious and political family backgrounds. Their political views did not represent a sharp generational break with their elders, as happened on the Left during the 1960s.[12]

In regard to religious belief, Catholicism was the dominant faith. This should not be surprising given the anticommunist emphasis that YAF imbibed. Yet, as Douglas Caddy related, religion was not a big issue in the formation of YAF. There were several Jews present at the Sharon conference, including Howard Phillips and Robert Schuchman, two of YAF's major leaders in the early years, and many more Protestants, including Carl McIntire, Jr., the son of the prominent conservative anticommunist evangelist.[13] Catholicism remained more of a concern in the early history of YAF primarily because of the influence of Buckley and *National Review,* which took a strongly traditionalist pro-Catholic line during the early 1960s.[14] But YAF overall was not an organization concerned with religious issues and remained primarily a secular-oriented organization throughout its history.

To be invited to the Sharon conference or to participate there, one did not need to be a college student. Of the roughly ninety-six people attending, seventy-five listed a college affiliation, with the majority attending five schools: Harvard, Yale, Northwestern University, the University of Chicago, and the University of Minnesota. The latter three midwestern schools were represented by activists from the Collegiate YR Midwest Federation, including Robert Croll from Northwestern University and John Weicher, who would later edit the *New Individualist Review,* the journal of the University of Chicago's chapter of the Intercollegiate Society of Individualists. Ten of the collegians reported graduate school and law school affiliations. The other twenty-odd attendees included conservative elders, for example, William Rusher, Frank Meyer, Marvin Liebman, novelist John Dos Passos, Charles Edison, Buckley, and interested staff members from various conservative organizations.

The program at Sharon was informal, with meetings held throughout the first day.[15] There were plenty of chances to hobnob with prominent conservatives such as Buckley, Meyer, Edison, and Dos Passos. Loosely organized committees were established to discuss the organization's program and its focus.

One such committee, made up of David Franke, Carol Dawson, and M. Stanton Evans, was to review the statement of principles, which had been drafted en route by Evans, and to offer it to the conference for a final vote.[16] The statement emphasized several prominent themes of contemporary conservative thought. First, it had a traditionalist supposition that God-given free will was fundamental to mankind, especially in man's desire to be free from arbitrary force. Second, it offered a classical liberal analysis of the functioning of the free market and the desirability of limiting government's interference in it. Finally, it took the view that international Communism was the single greatest threat to America's liberties and that American foreign policy should stress victory over rather than coexistence with Communist governments.[17] There was no worry that the anticommunist position adopted in the statement might contradict the idea that government's role should be limited. For the young conservatives at Sharon, Communism was a force opposed to human freedom, one that should be resisted with force. There was a role for the government in defeating the Communist world's threat to America's liberties.

Many conservatives, at the meeting itself and in its aftermath, found the Sharon Statement's delineation of common conservative principles fallacious. The juxtaposition of classical liberalism with traditional beliefs that a divine intent ruled society angered some of the more skeptical or agnostic libertarians. Lee Edwards recalled that one clause concerning the use of the word *God* in the statement caused some of the most vociferous debate. The motion to include God in the statement passed only by a 44–40 vote.[18] Jameson Campaigne recalled that a heated argument between Stan Evans and one young conservative took place at the meeting but added that "this happens whenever you get conservatives of different persuasions in the same room."[19]

Some of the more critical comments on the statement came after the conference. John Weicher and Ed Facey, two YAF members from the University of Chicago who were present at Sharon, criticized the statement in the first issue of the *New Individualist Review*. Both considered themselves individualists and were upset that YAF would take positions that would diminish the power of the individual vis-à-vis the state. When the author of the Sharon Statement announced the view that victory over Communism and the concomitant rise in defense spending that would be needed to achieve this were vital to maintaining individual liberties, and when YAF supported governmental agencies like HUAC in its battle with "un-Americans," did these actions not diminish individual freedom?[20]

To Evans, however, the statement was an articulation of what most American conservatives supported anyway—they believed in God and in freedom. According to Evans, "The idea that there is some kind of huge conflict between religious values and liberty is a misstatement of the whole problem. The two are inseparable."[21] Therefore, to label the document a "fusionist" statement, as did its critics, put the cart before the horse. It allowed for a quite natural pairing to become falsely split. As Evans related, "if there are no moral axioms, why should there be any freedom?"[22]

On the other hand, one prominent traditionalist conservative was quite critical of Evans's reading of conservative thought and was certain that the libertarianism put forth in the Sharon Statement was unequivocally wrong. Gerhart Niemeyer, a professor of political science at the University of Notre Dame, argued that the Sharon Statement's position on conservatism stressed classical liberalism at the expense of tradition. For Niemeyer, classical liberalism was the enemy.

> It was classical liberalism which, by insisting on the primacy of private will, destroyed the basis for genuine political community, which in turn led to the modern totalitarian perversions. It was classical liberalism which divorced the public order from the historical world of Western culture, positive law from natural law, political theory from religion. By all means, let us do some hard thinking before we trust our fate to the guidance of classical liberalism!

Niemeyer believed that the particulars recommended in the Sharon Statement left "the individual standing alone before the state, powerless before the sole possessor of power, normless before the sole creator of norms, a self-centered pigmy before the leviathan of government bureaucracy." For him, "conservatism was an awareness of pre-existent values." Twentieth-century man had been raised on liberal pieties, Niemeyer believed, and until he could break himself of those prejudices manifestos would have to wait. Although he understood that a statement of principles was a logical step for young conservatives who were so certain of their ideological beliefs, it represented an illusion. Like so much else in the search for truth, what was required was patience and confidence, not manifestos.[23]

Conservatives surrounding *National Review* found Niemeyer's criticism, however inspired, to be groundless. Although his traditionalist view had many adherents, for the majority of conservatives the Sharon Statement restated the belief that classical liberalism and traditionalism were not two halves of the proverbial walnut, but rather a unified whole. As Evans wrote years later, "the point is not that liberty and religious values can be 'fused' by some ingenious method, but rather that they are a necessary unity. . . . Western freedom is the product of our faith, and the precepts of that faith are essential to its survival."[24] To William Rusher, the statement came as close as "there will ever be to a statement of the original principles of the modern American conservative movement."[25] From the lack of debate over key portions of the manifesto (barring the close vote over the insertion of *God* in the statement), it was clear that the young people gathered at Sharon agreed. Evans's draft was adopted with little debate and modification.[26]

With the statement of principles out of the way, the question of what to call the organization took center stage. There was a deliberate effort to avoid using the word *conservative* because of negative connotations acquired by that term in the late 1950s.[27] Lee Edwards argued that the organization should include the word *American* because "we wanted to be open to young people of all parties and persuasions who could accept the principles enunciated in the Sharon Statement."[28] In order to prevent any hint of partisanship, the organization avoided the use of the word *Republican* in the name. Therefore, again with little debate, Young Americans for Freedom was chosen as the group's nom de guerre.

The other decision made at Sharon was to elect the first national chairman. Caddy had already appointed himself national director because of his work in establishing the organization, and, with his uncanny behind-the-scenes organizing ability, had come up with a proposed first chairman before the conference opened. David Franke would have been the logical choice, but he was uninterested, informing Caddy that he would rather return to New York to work at the grass roots.[29] That left the selection pretty much up to the whims of Caddy, and his choice was somewhat of a surprise to Franke and, indeed, the entire gathering at Sharon.

Robert Schuchman of Yale University became YAF's first national chairman. The selection was odd in one sense because few people had heard of Schuchman before Sharon, but in two other ways it made perfect sense. First, Schuchman was at Yale Law School, and the prestige of having someone from the Ivy League as national chairman was too tempting to pass up; second, Schuchman was Jewish, and although there is no direct evidence to support this supposition, the conservative movement needed to get beyond the public perception that it was mostly Catholic and anti-Semitic. A Jewish, Yale-educated conservative went a long way to defuse possible smears.[30]

A native of New York City, Schuchman was a graduate of the prestigious Bronx High School of Science.[31] There, with future YAF member William Schulz, he helped found a conservative club in the mid-1950s. He attended Queens College, where he graduated summa cum laude, and Yale Law School, where he was active in the Calliopean Society while writing for conservative publications on campus and off.[32] In his acceptance speech at Sharon, Schuchman echoed the feelings of the conference participants: "We believe an organized and dedicated conservative youth can materially affect the course of political events and help America attain the free society envisioned by its founders."[33]

A magazine was also planned at Sharon, and, with the logistical support of Marvin Liebman and organizational funds, *The New Guard* was established, with its premier issue appearing in March 1961 to coincide with a YAF rally in New York City. The editor of the magazine was Lee Edwards. A monthly, the publication focused on promoting YAF but also on furthering the "eternal truths" of the Sharon Statement. According to Carol Dawson, who would later serve as editor herself, the *New Guard* was "a forum for philosophical debate." Edwards was more elaborate about the magazine's purposes: it offered YAF's opponents "the pincers of liberty, individualism and initiative to free themselves of chains as rusty as the shibboleths which [they] will attempt to wrap around us."[34] No matter how the publication was seen by its editors, the *New Guard* served an important purpose in giving YAF and its members a public forum from which to debate conservative positions. Later-developing student organizations on the Left, such as Students for a Democratic Society, never possessed a comparable publication.

If the organization that emerged from the Sharon conference had a major weakness, it was its structure. What was the role of campus chapters in relation to the national office? Who determined policy and action? What was the role of the national chairman? Of the national director?

These questions, although addressed in YAF's bylaws, would quickly become, and remain, contentious issues in the organization's history. YAF's national board determined rules and policies but did little to provide a guiding hand over direct action on a local level. David Franke, who would head up the Greater New York Area Council of YAF until 1963, believed that work on the grass roots was fundamental to the organization's success. The New York Council, which represented all of the metropolitan New York area, including the New Jersey suburbs, claimed sixty active chapters, which organized anticommunist demonstrations in Washington, marched in support of HUAC hearings, picketed embassies and consular offices, held meetings to discuss important issues, and helped in local political campaigns. The council included groups made up of European expatriates on the Upper East Side of Manhattan, as well as "hipster-individualists" from Greenwich Village. The chapters took very little direction from the national office. Franke recalled, "We were pretty antagonistic toward things the national group were doing because we were in the trenches doing stuff and they were issuing press releases."[35] This eventually led to conflict concerning the purpose of YAF's national board—was it to be used to control the organization's activities, or was it to be used as an aid to local organizations that emphasized direct action? The YAF board and its leadership could never effectively address this question.

Other conservatives, such as William Rusher, noticed the weakness in YAF's organization from the start. The national board "chose all the full-time staff members of the organization and actively dominated its policies. The temptation to form factions and acquire majority control of the board was overpowering from the start to a number of healthy young conservative politicos."[36] Making things worse, in Rusher's view, was the fact that several of YAF's leaders fell under the sway of Marvin Liebman's financial influence. Liebman "became a rich and adoring uncle" to many of the YAF kids, "spoiling a number of them badly" in the process.[37] Housing YAF in his New York office, Liebman allowed the staff members expensive charge accounts, airline tickets, and other baubles.[38] Although Liebman did nothing wrong, his instincts to help out the young people in YAF encouraged excess on the part of the national leadership. As the young are wont to do, Rusher believed, they took advantage of Liebman's generosity.[39]

After the Sharon conference, YAF members dispersed to their respective campuses to fight for Nixon in the 1960 campaign. YAF activity during the fall of 1960 was primarily confined to getting the organization off the ground. Liebman had graciously donated office space to the new organization, and Caddy, who continued to work for Liebman with the McGraw-Edison Educational Fund, one of Liebman's fund-raising organizations, returned to New York to run YAF's affairs. YAF paid Liebman's firm a rate of $850 per month for its services, beginning in October 1960. Liebman then paid the office staff needed for YAF's activities. But as YAF grew in size, the staff also expanded to include six staff workers, who were bulging out of Liebman's tiny Lexington Avenue offices. By the spring of 1961 something had to give. Liebman proposed that the organization either move or pay Liebman $2,000 per month in fees and share in some of the miscellaneous office expenses with Liebman's other organizations such as the Committee of One Million. YAF decided to remain in Liebman's office but now paid him as a professional consultant.[40]

YAF's relations with *National Review* were also relatively cozy during the organization's infancy. In October 1960 YAF participated in a *National Review* Forum held at Hunter College in New York, discussing YAF's purpose as well as the renaissance of student conservatism on campus. Although *National Review* was criticized on several occasions for being too close to YAF, the elder conservatives were careful not to intervene in the organization's affairs. Buckley explained to one discontented correspondent, "It is true . . . that I encouraged its [YAF's] formation. That I should encourage the formation of a conservative youth movement should be about as surprising a datum as that Herbert Aptheker should encourage foundation of a Marxist or Communist youth group."[41]

The two members of *National Review*'s editorial board closest to YAF were Frank Meyer and William Rusher. Meyer served as an éminence grise to the young conservatives, delighting in talking to YAF's leaders well into the night over philosophical questions. Rusher, who had been active in YR politics for well over a decade, took a much more energetic role in tactical political maneuvering behind the scenes. At several times during the decade, Rusher's prodding and political savvy were crucial in keeping YAF on the conservative path the editors of *National Review* believed it should follow.

This relationship between the elder conservatives surrounding *National Review* and the national office of YAF was mostly constructive throughout YAF's history. Buckley was always available to give a speech at YAF conventions, Rusher and Meyer were active as advisors to the organization, and the editors of *National Review* publicized the major activities of YAF chapters as much as they could. When one compares the relationship of YAF and *National Review* with that of Students for a Democratic Society and its parent organization, the League for Industrial Democracy, the healthy interchange between younger and older conservatives explains much about the influence of YAF in conservative politics long after the tumults of the 1960s had passed.

YAF's activities that first year consisted of support for conservative candidates for office, such as John Tower of Texas, who won a special election for the vacant Senate seat of Lyndon Johnson. Tower was also the first Texas Republican senator since Reconstruction.[42] YAF chapters also spearheaded such anticommunist efforts as picketing in favor of the House Un-American Activities Committee when it held hearings in Washington in the fall and protesting in front of the White House over Kennedy's failure to adequately support Cuban rebels in the botched Bay of Pigs invasion the following spring. YAF members served as shock troops for the conservative movement, seizing on tactics such as picket lines and marches that had been employed by leftist and Communist groups in the past.[43]

YAF's main event of its first year was a conservative rally held in New York City. Liebman and Caddy felt it was important to have a rally that would show support for conservative principles and politics. On March 3, 1961, over three thousand people, with more than that number turned away, gathered at the Manhattan Center to recognize prominent conservative supporters of the organization and celebrate the arrival of conservatism among the youth of the country. Goldwater spoke at the rally on the topic "The Conservative Sweep on the American Campus." He echoed the sentiment of many on hand when he argued that the young people "are the national leaders of tomorrow concerned with their future and they don't want it mortgaged by political persuasions with which they are not in sympathy."[44] Awards were then passed out to Buckley, novelist Taylor Caldwell, Russell Kirk, industrialist Herbert Kohler, publisher Eugene Pulliam, columnist George Sokolsky, former Atomic Energy Commission chairman Lewis Strauss, and James Abstine of the Indiana YR and YAF.

The rally was important because of its drawing power, which showed growing conservative strength. For Liebman, this type of event yielded publicity for the organization and also served as a forum for advancing the purposes of conservative young people. Rallies, to the consummate impresario Liebman, were "like putting on a show and having the opening night work out beautifully."[45]

Because of activities like the rally, YAF grew in its first year. The national office was claiming over twenty-five thousand members (in reality YAF probably had closer to five thousand). For Liebman, however, "it was important that the membership be perceived at 25,000" in order to draw publicity.[46] Although the national office encouraged the probable fiction, the exaggerated number of members may not have been too far from the truth.[47] To become a member of YAF, one had to pay a negligible fee to the national office—one dollar. After March 1961, two additional dollars would get a subscription to the *New Guard*. Most students and younger people in communities would forgo paying the fee and would become "unofficial" members. There was little benefit to be an official member unless you wanted to make a name for yourself within the organization.[48] Much like comparable leftist student organizations during the 1960s, YAF's actual membership numbers may have been inflated, but by counting "fellow-traveling" conservative students as members, the organization may not have been stretching the truth too far.[49] Official membership was not necessarily an accurate indicator of an organization's potential influence. As Caddy related, neither YAF nor its left-wing counterpart, SDS, was ever a large organization, but the influence of both during the 1960s was significant.[50]

Although membership statistics appeared solid, and members were engaged in various activities, a focus on YAF's national office leaves one with an impression of inactivity during the organization's first year in operation. The rally and national office press releases, though important in gaining publicity, did little to further the organization's goal of building conservative cadres on campus. Internal conflicts were partly to blame for the inaction. The main issue was who would control the national office and direct national policy. But added into the dispute, which paralyzed the organization during its first year, was conflict between the young directors of YAF and their elder guides Bill Rusher and Marvin Liebman.

Caddy reportedly always loved the machinations of behind-the-scenes politics.[51] What he began to implement in the spring of 1961, according to his critics, was an effort to control the organization in a centralized manner, concentrating all power in a national office controlled by him and his supporters. The key question is, Why? Was there anything to the charge that Caddy was obsessed with controlling power over YAF?

The problem started in May 1961 with a conflict between Caddy and Franke concerning chapter applications from the New York Council. Franke decided to withhold the applications ostensibly because Caddy had engineered a change in YAF's Policy Committee that gave himself more power over local chapters.[52] Caddy argued that he only wanted to add one more member to the committee in order to make it function more efficiently. Franke protested because he saw the additional member as someone whom Caddy could control in policy debates. The elders at *National Review,* particularly Meyer and Rusher, actively intervened to avoid a public split, but it was clear to them by the end of May that Caddy had sought to control the organization and "alter the Policy Committee" to do so.[53] Rusher wished to prevent the emergence of power blocs and factional infighting that might seriously damage the organization.

Liebman, as an ex-Communist with some familiarity with factional infighting, offered a proposal that would change the Policy Committee. He recommended the appointment of one additional member (Caddy's goal), but he also recommended that local chapters be granted greater autonomy in pursuing their own programs. Buckley and Liebman met with Caddy and Franke, and all agreed on the Liebman memorandum.[54] The matter was apparently resolved to the satisfaction of everybody, yet Caddy, who was leaving for six months of military service in June, was accused of continuing his control of the organization by appointing William Cotter as acting national director while he was away. To achieve this, Caddy had gained the support of Howard Phillips and Robert Schuchman, along with Scott Stanley, a YAF board member from the University of Kansas Law School with alleged ties to the right-wing John Birch Society. Caddy, according to his critics, had agreed pro forma to the settlement while persisting in the de facto centralization of power in the national office he directed.[55]

Throughout the summer the situation stood at an impasse, with Cotter assuming the reins upon Caddy's departure. Caddy claimed that he appointed Cotter to take over when he left because Cotter, a student at Fordham University who lived in New York, was well qualified to do the work necessary to further the organization's goals. "Someone had to do the work," Caddy claimed.[56] Cotter had been present at Sharon and had formed a conservative club at Fordham. At the Sharon conference he was made organizational director and felt loyal to Caddy's leadership, believing YAF, as a student organization, should be led by young people and not guided by the likes of William Rusher and Marvin Liebman.[57] Caddy and Cotter were very critical of the continued dependence on Liebman in particular; Cotter charged years later that since YAF was one of the only conservative organizations in operation at the time, Liebman helped sustain his public relations business on YAF's back.[58] Liebman was distressed at the challenge he saw emanating from Caddy and Cotter, who had convinced Howard Phillips and Robert Schuchman of their views and seemed to be forming a faction intent on controlling YAF. Liebman called Rusher in midsummer, alarmed about the situation.[59] To Rusher, Caddy's faction appeared to be moving to centralize power in the national office, throw out Liebman, and control the organization for their own purposes. It was a dangerous situation, which could lead to the organization's quick demise.

Rusher decided to intervene (reluctantly, according to his account); with a faction including Liebman, Carol Bauman,[60] Edwards, Franke, Bob Croll, Bill Madden, William Schulz, and James Kolbe, he brought in Richard Viguerie to assume the new organizational position of executive secretary. It was a brilliant move. First, Franke knew Viguerie, having worked with him one summer to establish a conservative grassroots organization in Houston, Texas.[61] His duties were to be administrative, not policymaking. Second, Viguerie was to work as the organization's executive secretary in conjunction with Marvin Liebman's firm. This connection was indispensable to fund-raising and the promotion of the organization. Finally, having a professional executive secretary would free up the organizational director, William Cotter, for field work building chapters. Cotter could be kept out of the national office; Viguerie, "loyal to the faction who got him to New York," would take his place; and Caddy's power drive could be thwarted.[62] In advance of a September 2, 1961, board meeting,

> it was pointed out that even after nearly a year's work and considerable expense, YAF has not yet begun to realize its potential in total national membership and individual affiliated chapters. Since administrative duties to be taken over by Richard Viguerie will no longer hinder his travel, we feel that the Organizational Director should now spend at least [two-thirds] of his time "in the field."[63]

Not only would this benefit YAF, but it would keep Cotter away from YAF's offices while Viguerie established himself as executive secretary.[64]

William Cotter and Doug Caddy recalled a different scenario concerning the drive for power and influence among Rusher and ambitious young people. According to both men's recollections, Viguerie was a pawn of Rusher. The fact that he would vote for Rusher's faction against Caddy was owed to the simple fact that Rusher brought him to work for Liebman in New York, which Viguerie freely admitted.[65] Rusher allegedly offered the same temptations of power and influence within YAF (and presumably the conservative movement) to both Cotter and Howard Phillips. Phillips recalled an effort on the part of Rusher to get him to vote against Caddy by withholding funds from Phillips that were raised (by Phillips) to pay expenses for a YAF group attending a National Student Association meeting in Madison, Wisconsin. When Phillips told Rusher in no uncertain terms of his intention to stand by Caddy, Rusher withheld the funds until Phillips threatened to go public with the movement's dirty laundry.[66] The funds were subsequently released, which made Phillips more determined to support Caddy. Cotter recalled a time when "he was brought to the mountain top by Rusher" and shown all the things he could have if he supported him at the upcoming board meeting. Cotter rejected the offer.[67] Caddy's faction felt that the leadership of YAF should remain under the control of "authentic student leaders" such as Caddy, Cotter, Phillips, Stanley, and Schuchman. But it was also a question of friendship and loyalty. Caddy had been the main builder of YAF. Without him, according to Phillips, Stanley, and Schuchman, there would have been no organization.[68] The effort on the part of Rusher and Liebman represented the furthering of their own ambitions (to help with Liebman's fund-raising business and to create a loyal pro-Goldwater, pro–*National Review* conservative movement). As such, the hiring of Viguerie represented a "boarding party" by Rusher and others to move YAF their way and to gain personally from such an intervention.[69]

Nevertheless, Caddy's faction could not stand in the way of Viguerie's hiring, which, in the end, helped transform the organization. Viguerie had long been active in YR politics in Texas. A marginal student, Viguerie loved the organizational work of politics and worked on John Tower's first Senate campaign in Texas as well as in Harris County Republican politics. "Looking for any way he could to get to Washington," Viguerie responded to a *National Review* ad for an executive secretary, received high praise from Franke, and was brought to New York to interview with Rusher and Liebman.[70] Viguerie was a hardworking and ambitious young professional; finding YAF some twenty thousand dollars in debt, he began the task of restoring financial credibility to the young organization with Liebman's help. The addition of Viguerie as executive secretary introduced yet another potential power bloc into the YAF mixture, a bloc that, given the importance of handling the administrative duties of a membership organization, could (and would) challenge the power base of the elected national chairman. Viguerie never used the position for that purpose, content to learn and develop the skills that would turn him into one of the more influential fund-raisers (through direct mail operations) in the entire country by the 1970s, but the potential for abuse of power by a paid professional running the organization's affairs remained.

At the penultimate board meeting, held in Liebman's office over a hot

Labor Day weekend, Rusher and Liebman both threatened to withdraw their support from the organization—and the support of just about everyone else connected with them in the conservative movement—if Caddy's faction continued to cause trouble. The Caddy faction relented, but, as Rusher recalled, "Caddy [himself] had the unfortunate presence not to resign."[71] Partly this was because Caddy was not present at the meeting. He was still in the army in September and claims that Rusher called the meeting to control the organization for his purposes. "What was this old man doing fooling around with this youth organization?"[72] Howard Phillips, one of Caddy's supporters, concurred with Caddy's recollection, claiming that Rusher "killed the organization at this point." "I saw Rusher's operation as a boarding party and a lot of people rolled over for Rusher because of their ambitions in the Goldwater movement."[73]

Rusher was equally candid in admitting that when YAF was founded, the elder conservatives "overlooked the important fact that we were bringing into existence a social organization . . . composed of real people, who have to be dealt with in the old fashioned political mode."[74] He had previously told Liebman and Buckley, "We have scotched the snakes, not killed them. We must find friendly forces in YAF as strong and determined as Caddy and Cotter and Phillips. [U]pon whom can we build our church?"[75]

It would be a year before Rusher's Saint Peter came into the picture. In the meantime, factionalism continued to disrupt YAF, leading to a major schism in the organization and an unstable, barely functioning national office. Two more charges had been unleashed by Rusher's faction against Caddy. One was that Caddy was leading the organization toward New York governor Nelson Rockefeller; a second charge had to do with the closeness of one YAF board member, Scott Stanley, to the John Birch Society. Both charges, according to the accused, were absurd on the face of it. How could the same faction be pulling YAF toward the liberal Republican Nelson Rockefeller and toward the radical anticommunist Robert Welch?[76] To the accusers, most prominently Rusher and those on the board who supported his views, the least hint of Rockefeller or Birch influence on YAF's board was enough to prompt action against Caddy's faction.[77] In the end it became clear that both charges rested on flimsy evidence and represented means by which the faction could be eliminated rather than real dangers to the organization's vitality.

The first charge, concerning Caddy's flirtation with New York governor Nelson Rockefeller, emerged out of two events in 1961. The first involved a meeting with Rockefeller organized by Martin McKneally, Rockefeller's conservative conscience; the second event grew out of the candidacy of YAF member Ed Nash for the New York City Council. In August 1961, McKneally, the former national director of the American Legion and a stalwart conservative anticommunist, invited several members of YAF to meet with Governor Rockefeller in his New York office. William Cotter was acting national director at the time, while Caddy was in the army. Cotter, who had met McKneally earlier in the year and knew that he represented Rockefeller's window into the conservative movement, accepted the invitation, and on August 1, 1961, he and six others from YAF's national board, including Carol and Robert Bauman, met for a little over an hour with the governor, listening as he attempted to convince them he was really a conservative. No one, as Cotter recalled, was convinced of the governor's conversion and instead viewed Rockefeller as an "arrogant man," an unprincipled politician hoping to gain conservative support for future presidential ambitions. "You have to remember," Cotter recalled, "we hated Rockefeller the way we hated any Communist."[78]

Rusher saw the meeting quite differently, relating in a letter to Brent Bozell the danger that many conservatives would be "ready to believe that . . . [Rockefeller's] 'hard-line' . . . speeches and private assurances . . . are reliable guides to his real opinions."[79] He also connected the meeting organized by McKneally with the Caddy faction's effort to take control of the organization from Liebman and himself:

> By midsummer of this year [predating the meeting with Rockefeller], when I finally focused my attention on the problem [in YAF], all four of the strongest personalities in YAF (three of whom are also . . . its three highest officers) . . . had formed themselves into a well-disciplined clique, harassed their rivals nearly out of the organization, gone into barely concealed opposition to Marvin Liebman, and even formed a stealthy liaison with the aforementioned Martin McKneally.[80]

The reason to squelch the Caddy faction was to keep it out of Rockefeller's possession and to keep the organization in a pro-Goldwater mode. As an old YR activist who was experienced in factional infighting, Rusher seemed to be justifying his actions by using the rationale of Rockefeller taking over YAF for squeezing the "strongest personalities in YAF" right out of the organization.

For the Caddy faction, the episode reiterated the fact that young people— not Rusher and Liebman—should control the organization. Both were not needed. Liebman, according to charges made by Caddy, was squeezing the organization out of $3,580 per month, which was his charge for office space and his work on behalf of YAF.[81] Both Caddy and Cotter believed the organization could do its own fund-raising and did not need Liebman's help any longer.[82] Although both remained grateful for Liebman's help in getting the organization off the ground, his company was beginning to be a detriment to the financial health of the organization. If Viguerie was correct that YAF was twenty thousand dollars in debt when he became executive secretary in September 1961, where did that money go? According to Caddy and Cotter, it went to pay for Liebman's other fund-raising enterprises, which did not receive as many contributions in the early 1960s as YAF did.[83] More likely, it went to pay the growing expenses of an organization that had New York offices, a magazine, paid staff members, and several employees.[84]

A second issue related to the charges of Rockefeller influence in YAF stemmed from the New York City Council candidacy of YAF member Ed Nash in the fall of 1961.[85] Nash ran in the Republican primaries that fall and garnered 42 percent of the vote in his district, a sizable percentage for an acknowledged conservative candidate. David Franke, as Greater New York council chairman, received little financial support for Nash's campaign from the national office, partly, as Nash himself later charged, because "Caddy was echoing the Rockefeller line" and telling potential campaign workers that "they were wasting their time in taking part in" the campaign.[86] The charges by Nash, made some six months later in *Human Events*, may also represent little more than a rationalization designed to remove Caddy from his position as national director. During the Nash candidacy Caddy was not in charge of the organization. He claimed to have supported Nash during the early summer when Nash began preparing his candidacy.[87] The charges were also publicized at a time when a final push was being made to remove Caddy from his position in YAF in May 1962. This in and of itself does not discredit Nash's charges (David Franke reiterated that Caddy did not fully support the candidacy),[88] but their publication at that time makes them suspect. Whatever the charges, there is no evidence to sustain the charge that Caddy was "pushing a Rockefeller line." Caddy wondered why Rockefeller would be interested in a race for the New York City Council anyway, particularly one involving an upstart young conservative. "I doubt Rockefeller ever heard the name Ed Nash."[89]

There seems to be little evidence to substantiate the charges that the Caddy faction was deliberately moving the organization toward the Rockefeller camp. A meeting with the governor did take place, but all participants in the Caddy faction reiterated their contempt for Rockefeller as a politician then and now and believed the charges made against them had more to do with a power struggle in YAF that was designed to keep YAF loyal to Rusher and Liebman.[90] Caddy, Cotter and Phillips continue to see Rusher as the main manipulator, a veteran of YR infighting interested in making sure YAF stayed loyal to his views. They thought he should not have been interfering so much in a youth organization.

But Rusher had his reasons. From his perspective it was imperative that YAF remain wedded to the fusionist conservatism represented by *National Review* and Barry Goldwater. The fact that he was a YR veteran and understood the infighting that took place in politics (and the fact that this involved conflict between different viewpoints) made him more convinced that what the Caddy faction was up to involved trouble for the young organization. YAF was the only successful mainstream conservative organization existing in 1961. For it to wind up in the Rockefeller camp (even though the evidence that that might have happened is thin) after only a year would have been disastrous for the conservative movement. In this regard, Rusher was correct to insist that, for a while, the young people in YAF maintain ideological cohesiveness even if that meant sacrificing autonomy within their own organization.[91]

A second justification for action by Rusher was based on the equally overblown charge that the John Birch Society was interested and had the means to take over the organization. The John Birch Society, named for an American soldier who had been killed by the Chinese communists in 1945 (ostensibly the first American casualty in the Cold War), had been founded in 1958 by a Boston area candy manufacturer and vehement anticommunist named Robert Welch. Throughout the early 1960s the press showered attention on Welch's pronouncements and the activities of the organization, which claimed sixty thousand members nationwide. Welch believed any accommodation with Communism was an evil that must be eradicated, and when the Eisenhower administration began to implement a détente policy with the Soviet Union, Welch even labeled the sitting president "a conscious agent of the Communist conspiracy."[92]

For conservatives like those around *National Review* or organizations like YAF, anticommunism was a praiseworthy stand, but Welch's paranoia was another matter entirely. In early 1961 Buckley began an effort to expunge the conspiracy theory–prone Welch from the conservative movement. This road had to be navigated very carefully. Many conservatives supported the goals of the Birch Society, and many prominent activists, such as Clarence Manion, were members of the society. How could he act without offending a sizable element of *National Review*'s readership?

Buckley decided that Welch, not the society itself, should be the target of an attack, and in a *National Review* question–and–answer column, Buckley sought to diminish Welch's influence. For example, Buckley stated that the JBS "was an organization of men and women devoted to militant political activity," not a particularly negative thing. He did not mention that these people were devoted to Welch's views. Regarding Welch's position on Eisenhower, Buckley diplomatically criticized Welch while avoiding offending members of the organization: "I have never met a single member who declared himself in agreement with certain of Mr. Welch's conclusions."[93] Nevertheless, Buckley was not willing to make a total break. Barry Goldwater relied on JBS members for support at the grass roots, as did many anticommunist politicians in the early 1960s. A complete break did not come until the following year, when internal difficulties in YAF prompted Buckley to remove Welch from the mainstream conservative movement.[94]

The allegation of Birch Society influence in YAF emanated from two places: first, YAF board member Scott Stanley had close ties with Fred Koch, a Birch Society board member and a prominent industrialist. Stanley was himself considered a Birch member.[95] A second source of suspicion was a presentation on YAF before a National Association of Manufacturers meeting in December 1961 at the Waldorf–Astoria Hotel in New York. Cotter, Phillips, and Stanley all spoke at the meeting and allegedly criticized YAF and Marvin Liebman's financial handling of the organization.[96] Scott Stanley denied publicly criticizing YAF; instead, he said, the appearance was organized to gain support for the organization from businessmen.[97] The connection between this meeting and Birch Society influence stems from the fact that two leading NAM members, who were also on the board of directors of JBS, were favorably impressed with Stanley and recommended him to Robert Welch. Welch met with Stanley and asked him to handle the editorial duties for *American Opinion*, at the time one of the highest-circulation magazines on the Right. Stanley was flattered and took the job. At no time, according to Stanley, did Welch ever bring up YAF or using Stanley to "bore from within" and take over the organization.[98]

Nonetheless, the allegations of Birch Society influence were enough to cause Buckley some concern.[99] In January 1962 he acted to kick Robert Welch out of the conservative movement, a campaign begun a year earlier.

In the midst of this effort, Marvin Liebman had offered his resignation to YAF. Although Liebman claimed he was motivated in this act by a belief that the organization "was in a relatively sound position in terms of finances and a membership base," he also was compelled to resign because of slurs he believed came from Caddy and his faction.[100] The resignation was also prompted by Liebman's opposition to YAF's giving an award to Gen. Edwin A. Walker, a prominent member of the JBS and a Korean War hero. Walker, a southerner, was outspoken in his defense of segregation and had engaged in efforts to indoctrinate soldiers under his command in Europe in anticommunist extremism. Walker was controversial, and the knowledge of YAF's giving him this award drew a great deal of press coverage. When finally forced to withdraw the invitation to Walker in February, Liebman, who was blamed for his opposition to the award, was attacked by anti-Semitic groups accusing him of using YAF for his own purposes.[101]

The attacks on Liebman appeared in February in *Spotlight,* a publication of the Liberty Lobby. They were subsequently reprinted in the *Rockwell Report,* the publication of the American Nazi Party. Entitled "Jew-Led Kosher Konservatives," the article featured Jewish caricatures of Liebman, Goldwater, and columnist George Sokolsky leading YAF, Buckley, Welch, and Walker off a cliff into the "patriot's bone yard."[102] Liebman claimed that the publication of such a vituperative smear and the problems with the Caddy faction were interrelated, that "the JBS member on YAF's national board" [Scott Stanley], with Caddy's acquiescence, had endorsed such an attack.[103]

On this point there is some room to criticize Liebman. First, although Caddy admitted to having problems with Liebman's role in YAF, he had just returned from the service when Liebman resigned in January 1962. His problems did not stem from any personal differences, much less any crude anti-Semitism, but rather from the tumults of the previous autumn when Rusher and Liebman tried to remove Caddy from his office.[104] Second, if Caddy's faction was responsible for anti-Semitic attacks against Liebman, as he claimed, why would two Jewish members of the faction, Howard Phillips and Robert Schuchman, go along? According to William Cotter, the idea that anti-Semitism played any role at all in these disputes was ludicrous.[105] Finally, Liebman offered no proof then or later for his claim. His opposition to General Walker's receiving a YAF award was well known, and that opposition was probably enough to get Liebman attacked by the extreme Right. Such groups did not need the help of Caddy or anybody else to engage in such smears, and according to the evidence they did not have it.

Liebman's accusation that a John Birch Society member on YAF's board had plotted the attack is also wrong. First, there was no such member. Second, the Birch Society, for all its faults, was not a racist or anti-Semitic organization. It may have been conspiracy prone, but it admitted any member who accepted its platform.[106] Liebman's accusation implies that he was uncomfortable with Birch Society influence in YAF and in the conservative movement generally. In a document written in reaction to Buckley's efforts against Welch, however, Liebman defended the right of JBS members to speak, regardless of one's views of those remarks. He further claimed that "it would be both futile and injurious to banish right-wingers from the movement who may offend us either semantically, politically, or philosophically."[107] This seems a strange position to take in light of the threat he saw emanating from Caddy's faction and the tie-in he made with the Birch Society. How did these two views square?

Liebman seemed sincere in his belief that JBS members had a role to play in the developing conservative movement. He accepted the old adage, *pas d'ennemis à droit,* which had strengthened the conservative movement in the face of adversity over the years. As the movement developed and became more mainstream, however, public statements that were anti-Semitic, racist, or intolerable to the majority of conservatives needed to be repudiated. The Liberty Lobby and Nazi Party smears clearly fell into the latter category. Therefore, Liebman could claim that those who acquiesced in such attacks should be criticized or ignored, which they were. But Liebman wanted to have it both ways and used these attacks as weapons with which to attack the Caddy faction. The battle over who would control the national board of YAF took a lurid turn in early 1962.

In a February memorandum to YAF's board, Liebman outlined his claims against the Caddy faction. "For the past two months, I have heard reports and received correspondence which are based on the premise that YAF is my personal fief; that I have, in effect, been 'looting' the organization's treasury; that I am directing the policies of YAF so as to 'hamstring anti-Communism' whenever I think I can get away with it. Although I find this type of talk distasteful, I am more concerned about its reflection on YAF."[108] He also placed blame squarely on Caddy, Cotter, and Scott Stanley but offered no proof of how they were to blame. Liebman admonished the board to look into the charges and "clean house" if YAF were to survive.[109] Caddy responded to the charges by writing Liebman's protégé and YAF supporter former New Jersey governor Charles Edison. In his letter Caddy reported Liebman's charges and threatened court action if the slander continued. He also inquired about what position Edison would take on the matter, finally ending by threatening to withhold a YAF award from Liebman at the upcoming March 7 rally.[110] Edison supported Liebman, but not overwhelmingly, and although Liebman resigned from involvement in YAF, he still received the award.[111]

In the midst of this internal mess, the second YAF rally, entitled the Conservative Rally for World Liberation from Communism, was held in New York. The rally drew more than eighteen thousand people into Madison Square Garden to hear Barry Goldwater. Awards were bestowed on novelist John Dos Passos, Herbert Hoover,[112] Strom Thurmond, Charles Edison, John Wayne (who did not attend), Richard Weaver, and Marvin Liebman. The keynote address, given by Goldwater, was entitled "To Win the Cold War." L. Brent Bozell, Buckley's brother-in-law and an editor at *National Review,* warmed up the crowd for Goldwater by speaking on the cause of liberty. Bozell enjoined: "To the Joint Chiefs of Staff: prepare an immediate invasion of Havana. To the Commander in Berlin: tear down the wall. To our chief of mission in the Congo: change sides." The crowd, patient through the balance of Bozell's overlong speech, exploded in approval over those phrases.[113]

The rally received good coverage by the press and was featured on the front page of the *New York Times* the next day along with a picture of Goldwater addressing the crowd. The *Times* reported that receipts from the rally neared eighty thousand dollars and commented on the patriotism of those in attendance. But the story also concentrated on the groups picketing outside the Garden, including the Americans for Democratic Action, the American Nazi Party, and several left-liberal groups.[114] That same night a counterrally was held across town, featuring speeches by Senator Hubert Humphrey and actress Shelley Winters. This rally drew a fraction of the numbers of YAF's rally but still gained coverage in *Time* magazine.

The major attention of the media centered on YAF's rally. *Time's* editors commented on the "busloads of well scrubbed, well dressed young conservatives" who poured into New York. "It was just like a political convention. There were flags in the rafters and a theme song for each speaker. Balloons floated on high and spotlights picked out the celebrities." As the editors of *Time* pointed out, "what would give any politician pause was the fact that a substantial majority of the conservatives in the Garden were under [thirty]."[115]

Internal difficulties within YAF diminished the media's warm reception of the event. On March 8 the YAF national board met to discuss Liebman and other issues. At the meeting a vote was taken concerning the removal of Scott Stanley from the board, but it failed to gain the necessary two-thirds support, and Stanley stayed on through the summer.[116] Although the board failed to throw out Stanley, developments at the meeting encouraged Rusher in his efforts to build YAF's church. The emergence of Robert Bauman as a power in YAF was one result of the meeting.[117] Bauman had been active in YAF since the beginning. A friend of both Caddy's and Franke's, Bauman was a law student at Georgetown and a longtime clerk in the Republican House cloakroom on Capitol Hill. His political connections to leading conservative politicians were well established and his knowledge of parliamentary procedure was a positive factor for future internecine battles on the board.[118] Bauman, along with the majority of those on the board, could be counted on as supporters of *National Review*'s faction, strove to eliminate the Caddy faction. By the end of the summer a final push would be made, and all members of the Caddy clique would be removed from the organization.

Caddy tried one last-ditch effort to preserve his influence in YAF. In July 1962 he wrote Barry Goldwater claiming that YAF was in financial difficulty. This encouraged Buckley, who traditionally recused himself from YAF politics, to intervene with Goldwater and soothe the senator's fears. Audits of the organization's finances had been conducted both in 1961 and 1962 because of allegations, presumably from Caddy, of the misuse of corporation funds (presumably by Liebman). Buckley wired Goldwater and followed up with a letter stating that "there are no financial irregularities within YAF; there is merely a terrible and internecine factionalism."[119] Goldwater was convinced by Buckley's argument and investigated the matter no further.

Caddy's efforts to discredit YAF with Goldwater represented the last straw. After Caddy removed YAF financial records from the office (ostensibly to conduct his own audit), Rusher, along with sixteen or seventeen members of the national board (out of twenty-seven) felt it was time for Caddy to go.[120] In a letter to one of Caddy's supporters on the board, Rusher outlined his objections: "Doug has charged that YAF was being mishandled financially; he had no legal or moral authority to remove [financial records] from the office," and he had embarrassed the organization with his participation in the Liebman accusations the previous year.[121] What was most worrisome was the damage Caddy was doing to YAF as a "result of Doug's unwarranted accusations." In closing his letter, Rusher reasserted that he did not desire to control YAF, as Caddy had long claimed, but rather that he wanted only to ensure YAF's survival as an effective conservative organization.[122]

YAF would survive, partly through the efforts of the national board elected at YAF's first national convention, held in New York City the weekend of September 27–29, 1962. Robert Bauman was overwhelmingly elected the new national chairman to replace Schuchman, who by this time was working in a Wall Street law firm. The board still reflected the organization's East Coast bias, with eleven of the twenty members from the east, but this was beginning to change. The election of David Jones to the board signified the South's emergence in YAF (Jones and his one-time student Randall Teague would both eventually become executive directors of YAF, succeeding Viguerie in that capacity).

Bauman planned several new activities in order to revitalize the organization. These included the establishment of a national legislative service, which would alert YAF members to important bills before Congress; a YAF news service; a national speakers' bureau; an expanded series of rallies; participation in the 1964 World's Fair in New York; and a YAF radio and television program. Also, the *New Guard* was to be expanded and YAF's headquarters moved from New York to Washington, D.C. This move, Bauman believed, would effectuate YAF's cooperation with legislators and other conservative groups in the nation's capital.[123]

If Bauman's election, as well as the election of the new board and the ousting of Caddy and his faction, did not solve all the internal problems in the organization, it did at least give the impression that YAF was heading in the right direction, with new programs and activities designed to recruit conservative cadres. YAF had survived a wrenching internal squabble. It now remained to be seen whether the new board would be able to lead the organization and to what degree YAF would prosper under that leadership.

3

Of Camelot and Communism, 1961–1963

There was a great deal of patriotism among the kids in YAF. You
have to have some motivating factor when, as an eighteen, nineteen,
or twenty-year-old student you give up beer drinking and partying to
make signs, go to caucuses and demonstrate in the streets.

—Robert Bauman

The Liberal Establishment now takes the conservative movement
very seriously, and they will use any device, any stratagem, in order
to divide and frustrate the proponents of our cause.

—Robert Schuchman

Many young people in the early 1960s were captivated by John
F. Kennedy's offering of glamorous possibilities for change and renewal.
Kennedy's charm and magnetism were hypnotic, and his call to bear any
burden in pursuit of justice and freedom, romantic; the very air of Washington was filled with an optimism and creativity not seen in that city since
the halcyon days of the New Deal and World War II; there existed an
excitement, a commitment to solve social problems such as poverty and
racism, and a real chance that America could fulfill its idealistic promise and
become, in Abraham Lincoln's immortal words, the last best hope of Earth.

For young conservatives, however, the Kennedy administration was an
unmitigated disaster. Expansive, intrusive, and weak regarding the Soviet
threat, Kennedy's presidency symbolized not the heroic majesty of King
Arthur's Camelot but rather the putrid sterility of the last Russian czar.
Although involved in serious and disruptive infighting regarding the future
of their own organization, individual YAF members and chapters began to
take an active role in pointing out the misplaced idealism of the New
Frontier, focusing more on foreign policy than domestic reform. Because

of their success in doing this, YAF, by the end of 1963, would be a strong and vital element in the conservative movement's struggle for political power within the GOP.

YAF members never developed the sustained critique of New Frontier or Great Society liberalism that their counterparts on the Left offered during the early 1960s. There were no attempts to work to solve the problems of poverty in urban areas and no effort to assist in the civil rights movement. Young conservatives had their own causes that they believed merited attention and those they believed warranted opposition. Anticommunism and a hawkish stand on the Cold War represented the former, while opposition to an expanded liberal state (including civil rights issues) demonstrated the latter.

Throughout most of the 1960s, YAF was content with publicizing the work of older conservatives who were attacking the welfare state liberalism of Kennedy and Lyndon Johnson. Rather than develop their own intellectual critique of liberalism, YAF members focused on developing conservative cadres who accepted the intellectual tenets of this counterrevolution against the liberal ideas behind the welfare state.[1] In this sense YAF members focused on what they could control (building their own opposition to liberalism) rather than on the activist assumptions of liberal reformers and the utopian dreams of the New Left regarding domestic policy. Never having accepted the premises of welfare state liberalism in the first place, young people on the Right were not let down by its failures; instead they relished them. Their hearts were not broken by the limits of welfare state liberalism but rather uplifted toward the possibility of its eventual rollback.

This does not mean that YAF members were incapable of demonstrating themselves the weaknesses they believed inherent in liberal policy. Lee Edwards spent the majority of his two years as editor of the *New Guard* highlighting deficiencies in the Kennedy administration's policies. "The first six months of the Kennedy administration," Edwards wrote, "have been characterized by an increasing dependence upon Federal activity to solve the problems of the nation. . . . Because there is no organized opposition in the Congress or in the Press, the trend toward Federalization will continue. . . . The cost of [such] bread and circuses will be something called independence."[2] The editors also reiterated that "we cannot look to Washington, D.C. for an answer [to our country's problems]. . . . As young Americans . . . we have faith in ourselves to solve the problems of this country and of the world. We ask only that the Federal government let us rather than it begin to do the job."[3] To Edwards and others in YAF asking "not what your country could do for you" meant simply that. Although Edwards and other YAF critics offered few alternative solutions to the problems addressed by the New Frontier, they did provide a vocal and consistent opposition to the Democratic administration.

Rather than just criticize New Frontier (and later) Great Society, liberalism, Edwards and others within the conservative movement focused their attention on liberalism within the Republican Party. On several occasions Edwards criticized the Republicans for failing to maintain an opposition to the administration, believing, as many conservatives did, that little distinguished New Frontier liberalism from the domestic policy of the Eisenhower years.[4] Some Republicans in the early 1960s found much to like about Kennedy's rather moderate approach to domestic policy, but conservatives saw Kennedy as a continuation of big-government liberal policy, which was not only a threat to limited government and individual liberty, but its antithesis. Even though the Massachusetts Democrat dragged his heels on civil rights, pursued a rather conservative relationship with business, and was aggressive in his rhetoric regarding the Cold War, conservatives found much to dislike about Kennedy's interference in the domestic economy and his failure to roll back Communist advances in Cuba. The GOP, content with a moderate approach to the above issues, was all too happy to go along with much of the New Frontier (and later the Great Society), drawing the ire of the Republican right wing in the process.[5]

The similarity between New Left critiques of Kennedy and later Lyndon Johnson—branding them corporate liberals hostile to democratic reform—and the conservative critique of the GOP during the early 1960s is striking. Many in the early New Left were children of the Democratic Party; many felt compelled to action by the idealistic rhetoric of Kennedy himself and felt betrayed by the president's policies, specifically regarding civil rights (and later Vietnam).[6] At Port Huron, Michigan, in 1962 (ostensibly the founding conference of Students for a Democratic Society), Tom Hayden, drawing on the intellectual mentorship of sociologists Paul Goodman and C. Wright Mills, criticized American society (and implicitly liberalism as well) for contributing to economic abundance (which was maldistributed) and spiritual poverty. YAF members, many of them primarily children of the Republican Party, seemed troubled with the GOP's moderation over similar issues. In typical youthful insouciance, both groups yearned for authenticity among the parties, one fighting for a participatory democratic vision seemingly wrapped in American civic republicanism,[7] the other for a pure opposition centered around America's constitutional order of limited government and maximum freedom for the individual. The young people both in YAF and in SDS saw liberalism as a natural enemy, but it was the liberalism within the GOP that really infuriated the majority of the conservative youth.[8]

The one issue that was of little concern to YAF members was the burgeoning civil rights movement in the South. For many reasons, the civil rights movement never appealed to conservative young people as it did to liberal or radical youth. This had little to do with particular racial attitudes conservatives may have held toward blacks, but much to do with their belief that certain segments of the civil rights leadership were tinged with Communism. What little coverage of the movement made it into the pages of the *New Guard* generally supported the idea, not altogether false, that leftist organizations and individuals were the powers behind the throne.[9] YAF members also echoed the sentiments of FBI director J. Edgar Hoover regarding civil rights organizations. Hoover believed that the civil rights leadership, co-opted by Communist advisors, was engaged in exploiting racial injustice rather than addressing a real need for racial equality.[10] Many young conservatives accepted Hoover's arguments too uncritically.

There were other reasons why YAF members never jumped on the civil rights bandwagon. First, YAF was overwhelmingly white and, in the early 1960s, primarily northern. Many members came from ethnic Catholic backgrounds, where there was no strong tradition of civil disobedience against the government. Southerners in YAF during the 1960s did not join the organization because of its position on civil rights or because conservatism represented segregation, but rather because of YAF's focus on the Communist issue in American politics.[11] The civil rights issue, as several YAF members related, never appealed to them.

The central problem YAF members had in supporting civil rights initiatives had nothing to do with the objectives of the movement *per se*. The majority of YAF members were not segregationists, and the few articles on the movement that appeared in the *New Guard* excoriated those who would deny liberties to blacks.[12] Rather, YAF resented the direct federal intervention in the affairs of the southern states, a policy opposed by conservatives in the early 1960s.[13] YAF members venerated the Constitution and considered themselves defenders of the principles of a federalist tradition, which recognized the legitimate interests of individual state power. The civil rights movement threatened the rights of the states, in YAF's view, and upset the balance of federalism in state and national jurisdiction. To conservatives in the early 1960s, the rights of blacks in the South took a back seat to constitutional tradition, even though the full equality of those same citizens was already defended by both statute law and by constitutional amendments. That the southern states were blocking the constitutional mandate was never an accepted position within the conservative movement.

Finally, YAF members clung to the issue of personal association. When Barry Goldwater voted against the Civil Rights Act of 1964, he argued that the government should not coerce individuals and private business to support measures that were unconstitutional. Titles II and VII of the act, which offered federal protection to blacks against discrimination in facilities and in hiring practices, respectively, were, to Goldwater, "a very grave threat to the very essence of our system of government, namely, that of a constitutional republic in which fifty sovereign states have reserved to themselves and to the people those powers not specifically granted to the central or federal government."[14] There is a strong case to be made for this position. Goldwater had been a longtime member of the NAACP and was not against civil rights, but he was against state power being employed *in favor* of certain groups. Goldwater "had been instrumental in desegregating Arizona's National Guard, public schools and airport restaurants."[15] If segregation was illegal or immoral, might not redressing the wrongs of segregation through the power of the federal government also be wrong? If the Constitution was color-blind, as Supreme Court justice John Harlan had uttered in his famous dissent in the 1896 case of *Plessey vs. Ferguson,* did not that suggest that matters of redress were also color-blind? Few conservatives in the early 1960s would have objected to such a stance.

Young conservatives resented the fact that the federal government, in establishing freedom for one group, was diminishing freedom for another. That southern whites had historically trampled the freedom of Negro citizens hardly mattered. For the majority of YAF members, echoing Goldwater's stand on the tenth amendment, federal intervention on behalf of one group diminished the liberties of all groups by threatening the constitutional balance between the national government and the states. Support for the civil rights movement, under these conditions, never had a chance to catch on within YAF. This did not mean that young conservatives were unconcerned, however. One YAF member argued, "Because it is simply not in the cards for the conservative movement to be enlisted in the vanguard of the Negro movement, or to gain substantial increases in the Negro vote, conservatives do not have to 'count noses' before acting in behalf of the Negro. This allows a certain freedom, and a moral favor higher than that bestowed merely by political reward."[16]

Rather than focusing on civil rights, YAF turned its attention to campus issues, which, along with anticommunist activities, represented the primary focus of the organization in its infancy. YAF took a leading role in resisting the liberal and radical positions drawn up by the leaders of the National Student Association (NSA). The NSA was founded in Chicago in 1947 to promote the interests of college students by mobilizing the common efforts of student body leaders on campus. NSA was designed as a liberally oriented organization, taking stands on the promotion of peace and democracy, supporting academic freedom during the McCarthy period, promoting nondiscrimination on the basis of race and creed, and generally following a left-liberal agenda.[17] Under the leadership of Allard Lowenstein in the early 1950s, the organization pursued an anticommunist agenda while avoiding the more heinous antics of McCarthy, which Lowenstein believed threatened individual civil liberties. In 1952, seeing the importance of having a student organization as a weapon in the Cold War, the Central Intelligence Agency began secretly funding the organization, which was perpetually in debt and in need of cash. Throughout the 1950s, the NSA generally supported the Eisenhower administration's foreign policy; but by the end of the decade it began to waver: it pushed referenda at its annual conventions seeking a unilateral end to atmospheric nuclear testing by the Americans, issued statements supportive of the Cuban revolution led by Fidel Castro, supported the sit-in movement in the South, and called for federal intervention there to protect blacks.

To young conservatives, NSA was proving to be a worrisome organization. Carol Dawson, one of YAF's founders, had opposed NSA for some time as a student council member at her small Catholic women's college in Washington, Dunbarton of the Holy Cross. She saw the organization as accommodationist on Communism, because NSA had passed resolutions praising Castro's Cuba and had called for the abolition of the loyalty oath in the National Defense Education Act and because of its position on unilateral disarmament.[18] Howard Phillips, the student council president at Harvard University, also reported critically on certain positions, such as unilateral disarmament and support for Castro, adopted by the "elite" who ran NSA. Phillips asked an entirely appropriate question: "Do most American students support this?"[19]

According to both Phillips and Dawson, few did. At the thirteenth annual meeting of the NSA Congress, held in Minneapolis during August 1960, with over three hundred student leaders attending, a loose straw poll conducted by Dawson, and certainly not verifiable anywhere else, concluded that about 60 percent of the delegates supported Nixon in the 1960 election. One could conclude that student positions within NSA were fairly mainstream if Dawson's poll results can be believed. However, the subcommittees that determined NSA policy positions repeatedly opposed hearing alternative viewpoints. Dominated by activists whose political positions were far more liberal than those of the majority of delegates, the leaders of NSA, as Dawson and Phillips accused, refused to allow dissenting viewpoints.[20]

YAF's opposition to NSA became integrated into the organization's programs as the Committee for a Responsible National Student Organization, headquartered in YAF's New York offices.[21] Phillips took an active role in anti-NSA activities, as did YAF chairman Robert Schuchman. In August 1961 Phillips printed a summary of a letter from SDS president Al Haber to the liberal caucus of NSA that called for a restriction of conservative expression at the upcoming Fourteenth NSA Congress scheduled to meet in Madison, Wisconsin, that month. Haber claimed that "YAF was associated with 'racist, militarist, imperialist butchers' " like the JBS and that the liberal caucus should aim for adopting the role of NSA "as a radical lobby and action force on the campus and nationally for educational reform."[22] As much as possible, this liberal caucus should " 'counter the propaganda of YAF and the conservative caucus.' "[23] The Young Republicans had voted at their annual convention to disassociate from the NSA if reform of the representative nature of the organization were not achieved. The formation of the YAF-backed coalition, the Committee for a Responsible National Student Organization, and a YR-dominated group, Students Committed for Accurate Representation, led by Northwestern student and YAF founder Kay (Kolbe) Wonderlic, pointed out the concern the Right had with the unrepresentative nature of the NSA and its "arrogantly leftist and undemocratic" platforms.[24]

Phillips had provided for some two hundred YAF delegates to attend the August NSA convention in Madison, raising money from YAF contributors for this purpose. The organized presence of hundreds of conservatives could not, however, prevail to change the organization. Conservative students, a minority of the membership in NSA, simply did not have the votes to reform its structure.[25] The *New York Times* reported that NSA was dominated not by leftists, as YAF and other conservatives had claimed, but by moderate Rockefeller Republicans and Kennedy Democrats.[26] A search through the Americans for Democratic Action papers reveals a coordinated organizational campaign designed to thwart YAF's efforts at Madison.

Howard Wachtel of Campus ADA wrote friendly media commentators and professors about the YAF threat, including in his attack on the group names of several board members affiliated with the John Birch Society.[27] Though the editors of the *New York Times* could claim that the "hard left" communists were a small portion of the delegates and that only the right wing remained as a threat to democracy, the liberal study group did have as its end "an organizational program for the democratic left" that included support for the Peace Corps, migrant workers, civil rights, and Cuba and condemnations of fraternities, loyalty oaths, and HUAC.[28] An article in the *Nation,* no friend of conservatism, argued that YAF's charges concerning the lack of representation in NSA "were true, and nobody really disputes it. . . . The people who come to the Congresses, where NSA policy is formed, are not representatives of their student bodies, nor are the five national officers and about ten staff men who 'execute' policy."[29] YAF reiterated that it did not want to take over NSA but to make it more representative of student opinion.

After the congress YAF turned to an attempt to undermine NSA's credibility as a national student organization by petitioning schools to drop their support for the organization. Kay Wonderlic went on a nationwide tour sponsored by YAF that sought to pressure student councils to end their affiliation with NSA. As a result of this pressure, more than one hundred universities, many of them in the Midwest, did just that.[30] YAF further endorsed a policy at its 1962 annual convention to "oppose NSA . . . until such time as NSA adopts democratic reforms." The Fifteenth NSA Congress, held in Columbus, Ohio, moved to adopt some reforms in NSA representation but still was met with little satisfaction from conservative young people who believed the organization was still radically oriented and did not represent all opinions.[31] These students called for the formation of another student organization, the Associated Student Governments of the United States, which was organized and formed in 1964 as a nonpolitical group dedicated to addressing the common needs of student councils across the country. Although YAF and the YR played some role in the creation of this separate organization, it was not led by YAF.[32] By this time YAF was fully engaged in the presidential campaign of Barry Goldwater and moved quietly away from NSA as a prominent issue; nevertheless, a newer committee, simply entitled Stop-NSA, would keep up the pressure for reform for the next several years.

Why were young conservatives so concerned about the influence of the NSA, an organization of which the vast majority of college students were probably not aware? The answer may lie in the beginnings of campus conflict over the direction of university life and the growing politicization of the campus. Young students on the Right always felt themselves to be a minority on campus. Facing liberal faculty and even more liberal—or apathetic—students, young conservatives fought an uphill battle to maintain power in student government and in campus debates. Several members of YAF were prominent campus activists: Howard Phillips served for two years as Harvard Student Council president and Robert Schuchman was active at the Yale Law School. Phillips recalled campus politics being a rather placid scene until his opposition to NSA became widely known. Only then, as he recalled years later, did he become public enemy number one at Harvard.[33]

A second reason for conservatives to resist NSA was its growing political involvement in activities outside of campus life. Although NSA had always been concerned with a rather liberal domestic agenda, by the late 1950s this agenda was becoming much more radical, with platforms passed criticizing American nuclear tests and calling for unilateral disarmament, supporting Cuba in the face of American opposition to that government, and supporting sit-ins and other forms of civil disobedience in the South. These were positions that could well be argued by NSA delegates, but they did not come up for full discussion. Rather, a small number of NSA activists dictated the policy and platforms of the organization. Why should conservative students support such positions, which they believed were antithetical to America's leading role in the fight against Communism?

Finally, as NSA came under wider attack, it was soon revealed where the organization received its funding. Phillips had long criticized the organization for not fully disclosing where the money came from and how it was used.[34] When it became known that since the mid-1950s some of NSA's budget was secretly supplied by the CIA, a scandal in NSA led to the organization's quick demise.[35] Ironically, it was not YAF who broke the story concerning CIA influence, but the Left, which by 1967 had turned against the Vietnam war and saw little purpose in a student organization that had originally been formed to serve as a weapon in the Cold War.[36]

For these reasons, YAF fought to oppose what they saw as growing radical influence in NSA. There is no evidence to show that YAF was interested in taking over the group (they would never have possessed the resources to do so), but clearly NSA had moved far beyond its original purview. In some small way, YAF's opposition to the leadership of NSA represented the first shot fired in the 1960s campus wars between Left and Right.[37]

Yet YAF was not content with being just a campus organization, and although the campaign to reform NSA was important, it never became the sole focus of the organization. Rather, the Communist threat and the Kennedy administration's weakness in dealing with it became the raison d'être for YAF activism.

YAF focused its criticism of Kennedy's handling of foreign policy in two directions. First, YAF members took to the streets to protest specific Kennedy policies. During the Bay of Pigs invasion and the Cuban Missile Crisis, YAF members picketed the White House in favor of a hard-line policy. Other chapters, for example, those in Florida, marched in favor of hard-line measures against Cuba. The Florida YAF chapter grew in influence because of the Cuban issue, sponsoring talks by former veterans of the Bay of Pigs landing, such as Enrique Llasa, organizing marches against Castro, and sponsoring a course, "Communism vs. Americanism," which became a required course in Florida public high schools.[38]

YAF also passed a resolution on Cuba at its first national convention in 1962, calling for "an immediate armed blockade of the Cuban coast" because of "Communist subversion in the Western hemisphere" in violation of the Monroe Doctrine.[39] *New Guard* editors took the view that what was involved in the missile crisis was "not a few nuclear missile sites . . . but the protracted conflict between the Soviet Union and the United States." YAF praised Kennedy for heeding his advisors who recommended a quarantine against Cuba and a hard-line policy against Soviet missiles on the island. Yet, *New Guard* editors were silent on how the conflict ended, neither praising nor criticizing Kennedy for averting worse conflict.[40]

Another foreign policy issue that YAF focused on was the problem in the newly independent central African state, the Congo. Though Africa remained on the periphery of Cold War concerns for the Kennedy administration, the problem in the Congo reached crisis proportions in early 1960 when the founding premier of the new Congo state, Patrice Lumumba, a revolutionary with ties to the Communists, was overthrown after instigating a campaign of terror against his rivals in the government. During the fracas, Belgium returned troops to Leopoldville to protect its citizens still in the capital. Lumumba called for United Nations troops to intervene to protect him from the Belgian intervention, and the UN sent troops into the country. For the next year, in violation of its charter, UN troops shielded Lumumba from his rivals in the government and protected his faction, with the support of the Kennedy administration.[41]

One Congolese province avoided the anarchy—Katanga. Moises Tshombe, a nationalist Katangese rebel and dedicated anticommunist with ties to Belgian mining interests, wished to remain independent from the larger Congolese state because of fears concerning the Communist ties of Lumumba and other government leaders. Tshombe also favored continued Belgian influence in Katanga, believing that European expertise and markets would serve to enrich the Congolose people. The United Nations soon became embroiled in the Katanga situation, with UN troops being dispatched to prevent secession. The UN, first under the leadership of Dag Hammarskjold (who was killed in 1960 in an airplane crash in the Congo) and then under Burmese diplomat U Thant, sided with the Congo against separatist Katanga. Conservatives supported Tshombe, who was more sympathetic to Western interests and to capitalism than Lumumba, and pushed for the right of Katanga to separate from the Congo. But the Kennedy administration stood firmly on the side of the UN in this dispute, drawing the ire of conservatives who saw the UN violating its charter and siding with a procommunist leader in Lumumba.[42]

YAF began focusing attention on the situation in central Africa in 1962; they seized upon Tshombe as an African leader who resisted Marxian nationalism in favor of cooperation with the former colonizing regime.[43] The West, far from discouraging such cooperation, should aid it. YAF members were particularly discouraged when the United States voted along with the Russians to support UN operations in maintaining the territorial integrity of a united Congo. Moises Tshombe "could not understand the US position. Katanga is a natural friend of the US. . . . He was very bitter" regarding the UN vote "which supported the Russians."[44] When YAF planned to invite Tshombe to receive a freedom award at its 1962 Madison Square Garden rally, the Katangan leader was denied a visa.[45] YAF members took to the streets to protest administration policy, but to no avail. Tshombe would be denied administration backing; instead, UN troops funded in part by the United States put down Tshombe's army and forced him to surrender.[46]

With the Katanga situation out of the news, YAF members turned to other Cold War concerns. In particular, YAF played a significant role in opposition to the Limited Nuclear Test-Ban Treaty in 1963, which would end atmospheric nuclear testing in the atmosphere.

In the wake of nuclear tension and fear engendered by the Cuban Missile Crisis the previous autumn, the administration desired détente with the Soviets. Accordingly, in the winter the administration pursued a wheat deal that would allow surplus American grain stocks to be dumped in the Soviet Union because of poor Russian harvests. A hot line was also installed between the White House and the Kremlin in order to avert future crises. But the most controversial part of Kennedy's détente, for conservatives, was the Limited Nuclear Test-Ban Treaty, which became the first arms control agreement in the Cold War.

Atmospheric nuclear testing had played a major role in U.S.-Soviet relations since the Soviet bomb explosion in 1949. In part, it was a recognition of a practical need—to test and gain more knowledge of nuclear weapons—but it also represented a prime propaganda element in the Cold War. Bigger explosions of more powerful weapons became a staple of this superpower game throughout the 1950s, as each side attempted to outdo the other in explosive power and efficiency.[47]

Eisenhower's defense strategy relied on the development of a credible deterrent. Without continued testing, "a bigger bang for the buck" was difficult to achieve, thereby weakening the president's strategy and showing a lack of resolve in achieving supremacy in nuclear weapons. Testing also permitted the development of more efficient "clean" weapons, designed to limit radioactive fallout.

Kennedy's decision to seek an end to atmospheric testing was based on information that such testing was polluting the atmosphere. Peace groups publicized the dangers of radioactive fallout getting into milk supplies throughout the upper Midwest. It was believed that strontium-90, a radioactive isotope, caused cancers, leukemia, and birth defects in children throughout the world because of the increased frequency and power of both Soviet and American tests in the late 1950s.[48] As the antinuclear movement developed in strength and influence worldwide, politicians were under intense pressure to end testing. The United States and the Soviets agreed to a voluntary cessation of tests in October 1958, but by the end of Kennedy's first year in office, the Soviets had resumed testing.

Within the administration, particularly after the Cuban Missile Crisis, there was a growing consensus to seek a test-ban treaty with the Soviet Union.[49] Kennedy had accepted the views of test-ban advocates, such as Norman Cousins, who argued against testing in the atmosphere because of radioactivity-related illnesses. Kennedy's scientific advisor, Glenn Seaborg, favored a treaty, as did the majority of the foreign policy establishment.

Kennedy worried about nuclear proliferation and believed a test ban would limit the number of nuclear players. The military, for the most part, opposed the treaty. Most of the public seemed indifferent, and the president was baffled at how a treaty could be arrived at that would benefit American interests.[50]

One of the most vociferous critics of the ban was physicist Edward Teller, a Hungarian refugee from fascism and a dedicated anticommunist known as the father of the hydrogen bomb. Teller believed that American nuclear strength was decaying in the late 1950s even with Eisenhower's reliance on these weapons as a main part of his defense strategy. Teller told Senate hearings on the treaty in July 1963 that the Soviets had reached a tenfold increase in nuclear explosive efficiency and had succeeded in developing the capacity of missile defense (something the United States had not yet learned from their respective tests). He also argued that banning testing, rather than ending proliferation, would in fact have no effect because underground tests were allowed. Finally, he believed that the ban would weaken America's ability to develop better and more efficient weapons by placing too much reliance on "brawn over brain." In Teller's view, the treaty would be disastrous for U.S. interests and would help accelerate the arms race.[51]

Teller's eloquent commentary and expert knowledge of nuclear issues were enough to convince the YAF leaders that the test ban was harmful to American interests. (Teller was also a member of YAF's national advisory board.) To counter the ban, YAF sponsored the only nationwide petition against it, had members contact their congressmen's offices, marched in support of testing in Washington, D.C., wrote prominent senators such as Minority Leader Everett Dirksen, and published Teller's testimony in the *New Guard*.[52] YAF believed that the Soviets would break any treaty they signed and that the Senate should reject the treaty. YAF fully supported Teller's arguments, rejected the views of peace groups as "hysteria," and chided them for appealing to "mass fear."[53]

Unfortunately for YAF, by the time it paid adequate attention to the test ban, in the August issue of the *New Guard,* the treaty was already negotiated and in the Senate for ratification. Although YAF entered the debate late in the game, this was the time when enough public pressure could stop a treaty. YAF tried valiantly to elicit that pressure but in the end failed to change the debate. Robert Bauman, who testified against the treaty in Senate Foreign Relations Committee hearings, argued, "President Kennedy is right that this treaty is the first step. But it is the first step toward ultimate surrender, or war on terms most disadvantageous to us."[54] Although Bauman's appearance signified a place in the limelight for YAF, and his words were ominous, particularly to fellow conservatives, they went unheeded. Indeed, Bauman's testimony was harshly questioned by Foreign Relations Committee Chairman J. William Fulbright (D-Ark.), and Senator John Sparkman (D-Ala.) compared him at one point to Soviet delegate Andrei Gromyko for his doom and gloom philosophizing.[55]

On September 24 the test ban was ratified eighty to nineteen (fourteen votes more than the necessary two-thirds). The same day, on the steps of the Capitol, Bauman and Senator Strom Thurmond, a Democratic critic of the treaty, presented YAF's petition, which contained more than fifteen thousand signatures, to the media. Thurmond praised YAF effusively in remarks later submitted to the *Congressional Record*: "I am proud that the high caliber membership contained in this organization has seen fit to oppose the nuclear test ban treaty, even though it may not be the popular thing to do. . . . I feel that this organization is rendering America a great service."[56]

The test-ban debate had three main effects on YAF. First, it showed that the organization could have a voice in a major political debate. The fact that Robert Bauman, representing a youth group, could testify before a Senate committee on so vital an issue indicated that YAF was well thought of in some places on Capitol Hill. It also showed that the organization was concerned not just with youth issues, but with vital questions of foreign and national security policy usually beyond the purview or interest of young people.

Second, YAF stood its ground, as Thurmond argued, on an unpopular issue. YAF members believed that the test-ban treaty was harmful to American interests regardless of what nuclear testing might be doing to health and the environment (arguments YAF members never accepted in the first place). Eventually, as the administration convinced the American people that such a treaty would benefit their interests, YAF found itself on the minority side of the issue.

Finally, the debates over the ratification of the treaty had a pernicious effect for conservatives opposed to the ban. Whereas in the past it was relatively simple for anticommunist arguments to hold sway in a debate over security interests, the test-ban treaty signaled the beginning of the end of that consensus. Opponents of the treaty were castigated as warmongers and extremists for their defense of American security interests. Goldwater, who delivered an impassioned plea in opposition to the treaty, recognized that testing had negative side effects but thought it was a necessary evil in the continued Cold War with the Soviets. Never once did he advocate nuclear war, yet during the 1964 campaign his vocal opposition to the treaty would form a major part of the Democratic effort to discredit his approach to national security affairs. Quite simply, as the country's concerns with the threat of fallout and accidental nuclear war—partly induced by the specter of nuclear conflict emanating from the Cuban Missile Crisis— superseded their concerns with Soviet weapons development, the anticommunist consensus began to crumble, even before the Vietnam conflict further ripped it asunder.[57]

The treaty's ratification represented a major shift in the political culture of the 1960s. For the first time since the Cold War began, the anticommunist consensus had broken down. Partly, the breakdown was because of fallout from the tensions of the Cuban Missile Crisis. The administration desired to seek détente with the Soviets in the wake of that crisis, signifying a new chapter in U.S.-Soviet relations, much heralded by the media and prominent liberals.[58] In other ways, however, the administration signaled its willingness to engage American troops in places like Vietnam, ostensibly in support of anticommunist causes. Once involved there, policymakers found it very difficult to withdraw, dividing liberals who believed Kennedy's movement toward détente with the Soviets indicated a possible end to Cold War tensions.

Conservatives remained the only anticommunist bloc willing to denounce Kennedy for his policy toward the Soviets while supporting him for his efforts in Vietnam. In the short run, this position was disastrous, for conservatives were depicted as both warmongers and extremists when it came to issues of national security and possible nuclear war. In the long run, however, the conservative vision of foreign policy, which stipulated that détente was harmful to U.S. interests and that the Soviets could not be trusted to live up to their agreements, would be the foundation upon which conservative activists in the 1970s could construct a case for a renewed Cold War.[59]

Although YAF failed to stop the test-ban treaty, members were not discouraged. Rather, they felt exhilarated as the autumn waned and the preparations for the 1964 campaign loomed ahead. At YAF's 1963 national convention, held in Fort Lauderdale, Florida, the weekend of November 9–11, more than six thousand delegates heard speeches by Strom Thurmond, John Tower, and William F. Buckley exhorting the young activists to turn their attention to Goldwater and the upcoming campaign. Although

Goldwater would not announce his intention to seek the nomination until January 2, 1964, by the end of the summer it was becoming clear that he was leaning in that direction. The national board, recognizing this reality, passed a resolution endorsing the senator for the nomination.

In YAF's own campaign, Bauman easily won election outright as national chairman; new persons joining the board included Jameson Campaigne, Jr., from Chicago and Alan MacKay of Boston. MacKay had been at Sharon and had been active in the YAF club at Harvard while attending law school. Employed as a lawyer for the Cabot Corporation, MacKay returned to an active role in YAF at this time even as he balanced a career and a family. He would be elected YAF national chairman in 1967 and serve in that capacity for two years.[60]

Campaigne's election to the national board was based more on his skill at cards than his name within YAF circles. Although he had been present at Sharon and active in establishing a conservative club and a YAF chapter at Williams College, he was not widely known. He attended the convention as a delegate from the midwestern region, which was dominated by the College YR. According to Campaigne, there was going to be a purge of the YR and when "they discovered I was a poker player and they needed a fifth, and when they got assurances from me that I was not loyal to the College YR's, they slated me as a board candidate. That's one of the reasons I ended up on the board, because I played poker."[61]

This type of political horse trading, as Campaigne called it, was not uncommon in YAF conventions throughout the decade. Most of the delegates were unaware of the behind-the-scenes politicking that occurred at national meetings. The majority of delegates attended in order to hear and meet their intellectual and political heroes, as well as to renew acquaintances and have a good time. Many came because they believed in conservative principles and were interested in "saving America." They were idealistic, but like any membership organization, conventions "are run by people behind closed doors. Delegations that were well controlled by a state chairman would be able to deliver their bloc of delegates to a candidate in return for some quid pro quo, perhaps making [him] a director."[62]

YAF members left the convention primed to participate in the upcoming election year. Barry Goldwater believed that he could make a serious run against his friend Kennedy in the upcoming campaign, and Kennedy, who personally respected Goldwater, looked forward to an election campaign where ideas, rather than personality, would play a prime role. Then, on November 22, Kennedy was struck down by an assassin's bullet in

Dallas, a conservative southern city that had been quite hostile to the young president. At first, right-wing elements were blamed; then Lee Harvey Oswald, a rather strange and controversial figure who worked for the left-wing Fair Play for Cuba Committee in New Orleans, was arrested and charged with the crime.

Conservatives, like everybody else, were stunned by the assassination. YAF ran Goldwater's favorable comments about JFK and the effect his death had on the nation in the *New Guard*. The editors also ran an article on the killer, depicting him as nothing more than "a Left-wing fanatic."[63] The whole conservative movement breathed a collective sigh of relief when it was revealed that Oswald was not a representative of some right-wing extremist organization. By the end of the year, the conservative response to the assassination, and Goldwater's very real grief over the loss of his friend, helped moderate the public image of conservatives.

But the moderation would be shortlived. As conservatives attempted to pull off one of the most stunning coups in American political history—the draft of Barry Goldwater as the GOP presidential nominee—the exposure they would receive from the media over the next year would be enough to raise public fears that the conservative cause was a threat to continued prosperity and a peaceful world. Nothing the conservatives would do over the course of the year could cleanse them of the charges of extremism placed upon them by a hostile media and the recklessness of some of their public statements. When Barry Goldwater announced, at his Phoenix home, his decision to seek the nomination, his ability to win had already been diminished, if not destroyed, by a lone gunman in Dallas.

4

Going with Goldwater, 1963–1964

The GOP should have one image nationally and stick to it, and the designer of that image, in my opinion, can't be found in Albany.
— Richard Viguerie

The Goldwater movement is in the nature of an attempted prison-break. It is supremely urgent that the effort be made, gloriously encouraging that we are mobilized to make the attempt: but direfully boring to proceed on the assumption that we will succeed.
— William F. Buckley, Jr.

The 1964 presidential election, in which a badly overmatched Barry Goldwater faced the political dynamo Lyndon Johnson, virtually unbeatable after JFK's assassination, may prove to be one of the more important *losing* campaigns in American political history. Despite the Republican Party's devastating electoral defeat that year, by 1966 and 1968 it was the GOP that stood on the threshold of majority party status and the Democratic Party was in disarray. What explains this tremendous shift in voting patterns, demographics, and political behavior has been thoroughly explored.[1] For the purposes of this investigation, the 1964 campaign was a proving ground in which to test the mettle of the growing conservative political movement. It was not so important that the conservatives failed the test as that they put into practice lessons learned from the defeat. By doing this they would contribute to changing American politics in a fundamental manner.

As one of the main activist groups on the Right during the early 1960s, YAF played a key role in bringing about the candidacy of Goldwater. The strong organizational presence of a grassroots Right during the early 1960s, comprising groups such as YAF, the John Birch Society, and myriad other committees and single-issue forums, paved the way for a conservative capture of the GOP.[2] What conservative activists wanted was for the Republican Party to represent "a choice, not an echo." The liberal wing of the GOP had consistently betrayed what conservatives, then a minority within the party leadership, believed the Republicans should stand for— limited government, the pursuit of victory over Communism, and free market economics. Conservatives realized that if these principles were ever to be embodied in the political process, they needed to heed Goldwater's injunction to them at the 1960 convention to "grow up" and take over the Republican Party, which was "the historic home" of conservatives. Activists on the Right, therefore, plotted the restoration of principle over politics and chose the senator from Arizona as the embodiment of that principle, the man who could lead conservatives from the desert of Sinai to the promised land.[3]

Goldwater had been the conservative Moses since the late 1950s.[4] After his impressive showing during the 1960 Republican convention, at which the Youth for Goldwater committee made some of the more impressive displays, conservatives in the GOP sought to foment a Goldwater boom that would culminate in his being the GOP nominee for the 1964 presidential campaign. Goldwater's growing national recognition during the early 1960s helped increase the chances that he would represent the future of the Republican Party. His reelection as head of the Republican Senatorial Campaign Committee, which gave him exposure throughout the country, contributed to his reputation as a national figure.[5] He gave hundreds of speeches during the crucial 1962 midterm elections; he was minority head of the Senate Rackets Committee during its investigation of organized crime; and his bestselling book, *Conscience of a Conservative,* went into twelve printings by 1962.[6] Other leading figures in the GOP showed little interest in being taken seriously in 1964. Richard Nixon was little threat in 1964, having lost a California gubernatorial bid in 1962; and Nelson Rockefeller continually waffled about his future plans within the GOP, believing he was a shoo-in for the nomination. As Nixon sulked and Rockefeller awaited his coronation, grassroots conservatives acted, eventually drafting Goldwater to run for president in 1964.

The story of the Draft Goldwater Committee has been well told;[7] what has not received full consideration is the role of young people in the buildup and eventual candidacy of Goldwater.[8] Conservative young people, who not only coordinated many of the activities between 1960 and 1964 in favor of Goldwater, but also benefited from them, made significant strides in the Goldwater movement. For young conservatives, who were looking for ways to make a difference on the national political scene, the Goldwater campaign provided the best opportunity to test their strength, consolidate their forces, and expand their horizons.

YAF's leadership indicated the direction the organization was heading in 1963 by running a portrait of Goldwater on the cover of the December 1962–January 1963 issue of the *New Guard* with the caption "Can Goldwater Win?" below the smiling, self-assured visage of the senator. Inside, the editors spelled out the possibilities of a Goldwater victory in 1964. What was needed was money, some "$3–5 million" to offset "the Rockefeller millions"; organizational men in every state and congressional district; publicity; the help of professional politicians; and grass roots support "to counteract the certain indifference and hostility which the American press will exhibit toward Goldwater." But more important than all of these factors, to the editors of the magazine, was the need for "the youth of America, which was becoming increasingly conservative, to express their enthusiastic support in concrete terms." If Goldwater were to run and win in 1964, then young people would have to be in his vanguard.[9]

YAF members played a crucial role in some of the activities of the national Draft Goldwater Committee, organized in February 1963. Although Goldwater did not initially support the effort to draft him for the GOP nomination, he did little to stand in the way of the organizers. He continued to appear at YAF functions, including a March 15 YAF rally at Indiana University that drew three thousand people. Goldwater spoke at the rally and indicated his belief that "Kennedy can be beaten and beaten heavily."[10] Also present in Bloomington was former U.S. Senator William Jenner, his son, Bill, Jr., who was a member of Indiana YAF, and Tom Charles Huston, a longtime political activist and later national chairman of YAF.

In May 1963 the Youth for Goldwater committee was organized. James Harff, a twenty-three-year-old YAF member at Northwestern University and former national chairman of the college YR, was named national chairman of the organization. Assisting Harff was Carol Bauman, who served as executive secretary.[11] Other YAF members active on the board of Youth for Goldwater included Robert Bauman, Fred Coldren, William Boerum, Donald Shafto and Morton Blackwell. Only one member was not in YAF, William Gebelin, who was in the Young Republicans.[12] Youth for Goldwater may have played more of a role in rallying young conservatives than YAF had done up to that time. Although the majority of the activists in Youth for Goldwater could not vote, their activities on behalf of the senator, which involved attending campaign rallies, organizing crowds at airports when Goldwater was due to arrive, and the door-to-door grunt work of canvassing, were extremely important not only for the success of the Goldwater campaign but also for YAF. For students on the Right, the Goldwater campaign served as a point of entry into politics and activism.[13] After the campaign, as young people hungered to stay active, organizations like YAF benefited from the membership influx from Youth for Goldwater clubs established the previous year.

The most impressive display of growing conservative influence was the July 4th rally held in Washington, D.C., at the National Guard Armory. YAF advertised the rally in the *New Guard* and organized for busloads of young conservatives, mainly from the East Coast, to attend. Well over ten thousand people showed up, a huge number for any event in the nation's capital in July. Although Goldwater was not present, having gone to Arizona to participate in holiday festivities there, numerous conservative politicians, including John Tower, did address the crowd. All of the trappings of a convention atmosphere were arranged, including red, white, and blue bunting, balloons, and other paraphernalia. Seventy-five coeds dressed in white blouses, blue skirts, cowboy boots, and hats with "Goldwater for President" sashes draped across their torsos, served as usherettes for the event. The "Goldwater Girls" as they were dubbed, would become a prominent feature at almost every campaign event during the next year. Carol Bauman was in charge of the coeds, and Donald Shafto was in charge of the rally.[14] The program was a spectacular success for the Draft Committee. As Lee Edwards and others have claimed, the rally went a long way toward convincing the reluctant Goldwater to accept the inevitable and run for the presidency.[15]

Another symbol of growing conservative power was the Young Republican national convention held in San Francisco over the weekend of June 25–27, 1963. YR conventions, biannual events, were good indicators of trends within the Republican Party.[16] In 1961 James Harff had defeated a moderate challenger at the College YR convention, but conservatives lost the chairmanship of the YR National Federation to a liberal Republican from Minnesota, Leonard Nadasdy.[17] Determined to avoid that outcome in 1963, conservatives had organized to build their strength in the YR and were counting on prevailing in San Francisco. The Youth for Goldwater organization and Goldwater's fiery speech at the convention helped Ohioan Donald "Buz" Lukens narrowly defeat his challenger, the Rockefeller-backed Charles McDevitt, a thirty-one-year-old lawyer from Boise, Idaho.

The convention was not a nice affair, though (foreshadowing treatment conservatives would receive from liberal Republicans the following year), with labels of extremism hurled at Lukens and with outgoing YR chair Nadasdy abusing his parliamentary authority as convention chairman by refusing to let conservatives speak from the floor.[18] The liberal Republicans also prevailed during the College YR convention, with Ward White from Kansas defeating a conservative challenger.

Two weeks after the convention, Rockefeller (who was not present) labeled Lukens's victory as an example of "the radical right lunatic fringe" taking over the party. Conservatives charged that McDevitt had paid fifty thousand dollars to fund his YR campaign, money said to come from Rockefeller coffers.[19] Others defended Lukens and the young conservatives in San Francisco, claiming that the chair of the convention (Nadasdy) acted reprehensibly and that though the tone of the meeting was conservative, it was not radical as Rockefeller claimed.[20] Rockefeller continued to attack Goldwater throughout the summer, hoping to stem the tide of the Goldwater draft. It only convinced the Arizonan to throw his hat officially in the ring.[21]

Throughout the fall YAF continued to fight for the Goldwater draft. At their national convention, held in Saint Petersburg, Florida, on November 9–11, "Goldwater mania" was in full display even without the senator's presence. Speeches by Strom Thurmond, John Tower, and other conservatives all pleaded for Goldwater to accept the will of conservative activists. The newly elected national board sponsored a resolution demanding that Goldwater declare for the presidential nomination.[22] Robert Bauman easily won reelection as national chairman, with David Jones, who had been appointed executive director of YAF by the board in April, continuing in that important post. Richard Viguerie was reelected to his post as executive secretary, although he was exclusively engaged in fund-raising activities. Tom Huston received a promotion to midwest regional director and Jack Cox became director of the western region, which was undergoing extraordinary growth in membership, particularly in California.[23]

Tom Charles Huston and David Jones would become important leaders in YAF after the election. Huston had been a conservative activist since the summer of 1960 while enrolled at Indiana University. He founded the Indiana University Conservative League, the first independent conservative club on any campus in the state. In the fall of 1961 Huston was elected YAF state chairman at a conference held at Wabash College. Always a strong believer in grass roots activism, Huston helped organize dozens of

YAF chapters throughout the state while pursuing his studies and preparing for law school. He succeeded James Abstine as a national board member in 1963 and was subsequently elected YAF's national chairman in 1965.[24]

David Jones, a young high school teacher in Saint Petersburg, Florida, had been organizing YAF chapters after discovering the group through a syndicated newspaper column written by George Sokolsky. Jones taught at Northeast High School and with the aid of several bright students, including future YAF executive director Randall Teague, formed a chapter there in 1961. Jones developed a high school course, "Communism vs. Americanism," which school districts throughout the state would adopt as a required course. The highly charged Cold War atmosphere in Florida, particularly during the Cuban Missile Crisis, made YAF recruitment a fairly simple task; by the end of Jones's tenure as state chairman, there were twelve YAF chapters operating in the state. Because of this, Jones was called to Washington in 1963 and named YAF's executive director, a new position created to spearhead national membership activities, run the affairs of the organization, and support the elected leadership.[25]

YAF members left the convention determined to fight for Goldwater. On January 3, 1964, conservatives heard the news they had been waiting for when Goldwater announced at his Phoenix home that he would seek the presidential nomination. Two years of work to draft the unwilling senator for the nomination had paid off.

The key question facing Goldwater was how to beat Lyndon Johnson, the man who ascended to the presidency after the assassination of John F. Kennedy. For young conservatives, idealistic and optimistic, practical questions of that sort did not matter much. *Their* man was running for the Republican nomination, offering a real alternative to the eastern liberalism of Rockefeller. Like the radical antiwar students of 1968, when both Eugene McCarthy and Robert Kennedy challenged the hated Johnson and Hubert Humphrey for the Democratic nomination, the young people in YAF were too excited to see the likelihood that Goldwater could not win in November.

In early 1964 YAF members and young conservatives generally were well poised to play an active role in the campaign for Goldwater's nomination. Article after article appeared in the *New Guard,* informing young people about things they could do. One of the better pieces was Marilyn Manion's "What You Can Do in 1964," which appeared in the February issue. The daughter of Clarence Manion urged realism about what young people could accomplish. Wearing "your Goldwater sweatshirt to the beach" and possessing "a red, white and blue Goldwater button" clearly showed who you were for in 1964, but it might not be enough. Manion suggested that young people start with their own families and friends and ask them for support. Then, look around in the community: if there is a Goldwater club, join it; if not, organize one. Students could form a club at their high school or write letters to the editor on a controversial issue. All these things could have an effect in a community even though the junior Goldwaterites might be too young to vote or be active in the regular party.[26] Manion's practical political tips may seem juvenile in retrospect, but few young people, even in groups like YAF, had much, if any, political experience. Manion suggested that they take the first step in gaining that experience and organize in the manner that best fit their limited resources.

Some of the ways YAF members responded to Goldwater's decision to run could be quite effective, and some of them reflected the political pageantry then in vogue in presidential campaigns. One member from Mississippi sold Goldwater bumper stickers from his station wagon, with the appeal "Honk and I'll pull over" draped over the back of his car; the Astoria, New York YAF sold Goldwater stock shares as a way to raise money from young people for the effort; a homecoming parade float in the shape of a ship built by the Iowa YAF was pasted with the slogan "Drown the Hoosiers in Goldwater," a reference to the upcoming football game between Iowa and Indiana.[27] Advertisements in the *New Guard* sold Goldwater buttons, bumper stickers, record albums, soap, aftershave, cologne, stamps, and crayons.[28] Every issue of YAF's magazine in 1964 featured some type of campaign paraphernalia designed to appeal to young Goldwater backers.

In more serious ways, YAF members contributed to the Goldwater boom by organizing mock conventions in conjunction with YR groups throughout the country.[29] YAF members were active participants at rallies and were ever present waving "YAF Backs Barry" placards and signs at numerous campaign stops. A picture in the *New Guard* even featured a YAF presence at the elite Phillips Exeter Academy with Goldwater greeting a young supporter during the New Hampshire primary campaign.[30]

YAF even featured its own singing group, "The Goldwaters," made up of four clean-cut, guitar-strumming, fraternity-looking lads from the Nashville, Tennessee, YAF chapter. The Goldwaters wrote folk songs "to bug the liberals." To the tune of standard folk songs, with changed lyrics, the Goldwaters played at political rallies, mixing in "jokes with driving songs extolling the virtues and predicting the victory of the man whose name they have borrowed." Though they were no threat to Phil Ochs or Bob Dylan, the Goldwaters did release an album which YAF plugged in the *New Guard*.[31] Other chapter activities on behalf of the senator included Fort Lauderdale YAF's bikini-clad "YAFettes," who, sporting Goldwater buttons, had beachgoers sign Goldwater for President petitions to the accompaniment of strumming banjos and guitars. These "attractive hijinks" were aired on CBS television's *Eyewitness* program in August 1963.[32]

It is interesting that young conservatives would resort to such strategies for gaining support. The political use of folk music, for example, though perceived as a leftist tool for advancing social change, was not the property solely of radical students during the 1960s. YAF members never developed an affinity for countercultural activities and only rarely included rock bands and folk music in their rallies or programs, but they were part of the youth culture that was changing American society during the 1960s. Accordingly, young conservatives needed to respond to the cultural changes that were occurring throughout the decade.[33]

The national board encouraged local chapters in their support for Goldwater. Lee Edwards, who had joined the Goldwater campaign as director of information, wrote in the March 1964 *New Guard* that "conservative youth organizations are performing brilliantly with excellent organization and plenty of hard work at turning out crowds at airport rallies, motorcades and speeches." Participation by YAF members in mock political conventions organized by YR chapters throughout the nation galvanized support for Goldwater during the primaries. Everywhere the senator traveled, particularly in the key primary states of New Hampshire and California, YAF members supported him with signs, pickets, and youthful enthusiasm.[34]

This activity on behalf of the senator boiled over at the GOP San Francisco convention in July. YAF was an active force at the convention, holding rallies, sponsoring speeches, and demonstrating on behalf of Goldwater. Some YAF members, such as Robert Bauman, had roles to play at the convention itself. Bauman was one of six delegates for Goldwater in the Maryland Republican delegation. Morton Blackwell, a twenty-four-year-old YAF member from Louisiana, was the youngest national delegate to the convention. Two other YAF members also were slated as delegates, and several others were alternates.

YAF's activities at the San Francisco convention were the result of hard work and planning. Bauman and David Jones arrived on July 8, one week before Goldwater's nomination, and coordinated YAF activities there with Western Regional Chairman Jack Cox. The three set up headquarters on the fourteenth floor of the downtown Hilton Hotel, coordinated a system of volunteers (who did everything from driving delegates from the airport to downtown hotels to distributing fliers and free copies of the *New Guard*), and planned the logistics of YAF's five-day blitz on behalf of the senator.[35]

On July 15 Goldwater arrived in San Francisco and, as so many times before in the primary campaign, he was greeted by hordes of YAF members waving signs and banners with "YAF Backs Barry" painted across them. More than four thousand people were at the airport to greet the senator. Over the weekend, wherever Goldwater appeared, YAF was there, showing support by waving their banners and screaming their adulation. YAF's enthusiasm even drew a wry comment from Walter Cronkite when he told his CBS audience, who were witness to a YAF demonstration in front of the Cow Palace, "They're the Young Americans for Freedom, but I don't know what *kind* of freedom."[36]

The Republican Party platform was the symbolic key to conservative efforts over the previous four years. Although most party platforms are of interest only to political historians, the 1964 platform stated tellingly just how far conservatism had permeated the Republican Party. Buz Lukens had argued that the Republican Party should adopt the Declaration of Republican Principle and Policy, agreed upon at a Republican National Committee meeting in 1962, as the basis for the 1964 platform. This document stressed the goals of individual freedom, limited government, victory over Communism, and a free market economy as governing principles for the party.[37] Agreed upon by conservative Republicans such as John Tower as well as liberals such as Jacob Javits, the 1962 declaration was the only way to ensure that the Republican Party would respond to demands that it offer Americans a choice in 1964.

On Thursday, July 9, Robert Bauman testified before the platform committee. He asked that the committee "reject any compromise on principle that was a symbol of the 1960 platform." John Tower, a strong supporter of YAF and the chair of the committee, treated Bauman with respect and cordiality during his testimony, a far cry from the treatment Bauman had received from William Fulbright a year earlier.

But the platform committee hearings became the battleground of a divided party. The hearings were the sole remaining chance for liberal Republicans to stem the Goldwater tide. Goldwater was excoriated for voting against the Civil Rights Act of 1964 and for his comments, made during the New Hampshire primary, that he would allow NATO field commanders more control of battlefield nuclear weapons in the event of a

Soviet attack on Western Europe. Because of the acerbic comments made against his views, Goldwater appeared before the committee itself upon his arrival in San Francisco and addressed charges that he promoted extremism. He stated that as president he would support the laws of the land, including civil rights legislation he personally did not believe in, and he also defused charges that he was a warmonger.[38] The platform conveyed the sense of the 1962 Republican document. Far from being extremist, or even conservative, it was, as Lee Edwards claimed, "a platform on which any Republican could run."[39]

Although Goldwater had the necessary delegates to be nominated as well as the support of the platform committee, moderates and liberals within the party still attempted to sidetrack his nomination. Governor William Scranton of Pennsylvania, whose nephew James Linen IV was on YAF's board of directors, wrote an angry letter to Goldwater on Sunday, July 12. The Scranton letter stunned the Goldwater camp with its savagery. Scranton accused Goldwater of "too often prescribing nuclear war as a solution to a troubled world, too often allowing the radical extremists to use you, and too often standing for irresponsibility in the serious question of racial holocaust."[40] Scranton condemned Goldwater's philosophy as dangerous and wrong for the majority of Republicans. After regaling the candidate with his diatribe, Scranton had the temerity to suggest that Goldwater debate him before the convention, as if the delegates who had campaigned for Goldwater and were elected as his supporters did not represent the true feelings of the GOP that year.

Goldwater was livid, and rather than offering the olive branch to the liberals within the party, he followed his instincts and attacked them in his acceptance speech on July 16 with the infamous charge, "Extremism in the defense of liberty is no vice . . . and moderation in the pursuit of justice is no virtue." The Goldwater campaign slipped off its moorings with that one statement, which conjured all the negative images of extremist radicals taking over the GOP. Although Goldwater had defeated the liberals within his party at the convention, his inability to heal the wider rifts in party unity would damage his chances during the remainder of his campaign.

While all of this was taking place, YAF continued its activities on behalf of Goldwater and conservatism in general. Teams of YAF members went to every delegate's hotel room and passed out copies of the *New Guard*. YAF members also distributed literature on behalf of the Committee of One Million as well as special convention editions of *National Review*. On July 12, almost two hundred YAF members met William F. Buckley's plane at the airport; they greeted him with a Dixieland band playing "Won't You Come Home Bill Buckley" and screamed at the top of their lungs for their intellectual mentor. Bauman led the crowd in a cheer for Buckley and then escorted him to a waiting limousine, arranged by YAF, which rushed him off to his downtown hotel.[41]

On Monday, July 13, the *Freedom Special,* a train hired by the Youth for Goldwater committee, arrived in San Francisco, bringing YAF members from all over the country. Chartered planes flew in from the Midwest carrying hundreds of YAF members.[42] Other members came from far away places, including David Franke, who hitchhiked to the downtown hotels after taking a military ferry flight from his army base in El Paso, Texas. Franke, who arrived at the convention without any money, and in uniform, had the literal good fortune of running into Buckley in the hotel lobby. From him he obtained a meal, and from Marvin Liebman, whom he encountered outside the hotel, he obtained a job on the Miller for Vice President committee for the remainder of the week. Within two hours, he said, "I had a place to stay, something to eat, and money in my pocket."[43]

That evening, as the convention opened with a keynote address by Oregon governor Mark Hatfield, the Youth for Goldwater committee presented a rally attended by thousands of young conservatives. Presided over by chairman James Harff, the meeting featured speeches by Buckley and Congressmen Bill Brock of Tennessee and Ed Foreman of Texas. After the rally YAF sponsored a cruise on San Francisco Bay. The two-hour sail on the SS *Young Conservative* featured more speeches by guest William Rusher, as well as Bauman, Dave Jones, and former national chairman Robert Schuchman. Adding to the entertainment were YAF's own troubadours, the Goldwaters, who delighted the assemblage with their renditions of folk tunes.[44]

On Wednesday, the day of Goldwater's nomination, YAF sponsored a rally outside the Cow Palace where a well-known actor-turned-politician named Ronald Reagan spoke to the crowd from the back of a flatbed truck. Reagan enjoined the young conservatives to continue working hard for Goldwater after the convention. "You were at this long before many," he told the gathered throng, "and God bless you for it." After the rally Reagan and the other delegates in the crowd headed inside for the floor demonstrations and the nomination of the man they had worked for since 1960.[45]

The demonstrations that evening were impressive, and once again behind their success was Donald Shafto. Gold foil was released from the rafters and a massive "Goldwater for President—655" sign (representing the number of delegates needed to nominate Goldwater) appeared almost from nowhere out of the roof. On the convention floor the assembled delegates whooped it up for Goldwater and voted when the roll call of the states began. At 10:35 P.M. California time, on the first ballot, South Carolina's delegation put Goldwater over the top.[46] A roar swept over the crowd as confetti dotted the Cow Palace. It was the culmination of an arduous two years of work on behalf of Goldwater, and the young conservatives in YAF had played a crucial part.

The next day, the final day of the convention, William Miller, a little-known congressman from upstate New York, was chosen as Goldwater's running mate. YAF members played a role organizing for Miller's selection as well, passing out "Miller for Veep" buttons as early as Monday, July 13, and forming the Miller for Vice President committee, headed by Viguerie, Franke, Campaigne, and Lamott Copeland, Jr. On Thursday, almost every demonstrator allowed on the floor to support Miller's candidacy was a YAF member. Many YAF members remained on the floor through Goldwater's acceptance speech that night. Campaigne recalled being cornered by novelist Norman Mailer, who was covering the convention for *Esquire* magazine. He told Mailer, in answer to a query from the novelist, that Goldwater was much braver than Mailer's hero, "that bandit" Fidel Castro. This almost led to an altercation between the two men, but Mailer dismissed the young man as a "punk" and went away.[47]

Goldwater's acceptance speech, remembered as one of the most notorious addresses in American political history, was an anticlimactic ending to what had been an inspirational week for the young conservatives. Although many Republicans in the regular party obviously shuddered at Goldwater's invocation, the young conservatives, idealistic and driven, were not so appalled. Bauman, who was on the floor as a delegate, screamed his approval but also wondered why Goldwater failed to offer the olive branch to the party and actually try to win the election.[48] Campaigne was worried, not so much because he felt that Goldwater's vituperative comments were wrong, but rather because he believed Goldwater fell right into the trap set for him by the Rockefeller forces within the party and by the media.[49] Regardless, the one comment, written by Harry Jaffa, "Extremism in the defense of liberty is no vice . . . and moderation in the pursuit of justice is no virtue," placed in the minds of the party and the American people (an estimated 90 million of whom watched the address) the belief that Goldwater was an extremist. That word had ominous implications because of media coverage and documentation of John Birch Society activities throughout the early 1960s, and much of the favorable press coverage that Goldwater had received throughout his career in the Senate disappeared after he uttered that line.[50]

After the convention the Republicans, some bitter and resentful, others joyful and ebullient, returned home to begin preparations for the campaign. Goldwater met with Lyndon Johnson a week after the convention to discuss the president's policy in Vietnam. Goldwater, ever the patriot, made a promise not to use the Vietnam conflict as an issue in the campaign. In August, after the destroyers *C. Turner Joy* and *Maddox* were fired upon by North Vietnamese patrol boats, Johnson requested a congressional blank check to fight Communism in Vietnam. Goldwater, keeping his word, voted for the Tonkin Gulf Resolution.[51] He would continue to refuse to make the Vietnam situation an issue in the campaign. Unfortunately, the nation was deprived of a debate over Vietnam during a presidential campaign because of Goldwater's placement of patriotism over politics.

The Johnson campaign and the national media certainly needed to learn lessons about principle during the campaign. Bill Moyers, Johnson's young press secretary, orchestrated one of the most vile television campaign advertisements in the short history of that medium. The famous "daisy ad" in which a young girl plucked the petals of a daisy while she counted to ten, with her voice soon replaced by a sinister countdown leading to a nuclear explosion at the end of the commercial, was aired only once as a paid ad but over and over again as a news story.[52]

The media themselves feared Goldwater Republicanism and branded it as extreme, yet they practiced their own form of extremism against the candidate. From the pages of *National Review,* Buckley kept his eyes on press statements. The Republican convention drew much ire from the media. The *Saint Louis Post-Dispatch* stated, "The Goldwater coalition is a coalition of Southern racists, county-seat conservatives, desert rightist radicals and suburban backlashers." The *New York Herald-Tribune* editorialized, "The Republican Party now does face a clear and present threat from the Know-Nothings and purveyors of hate and the apostles of bigotry." Several prominent liberals were less than liberal in their denunciations of Goldwater. Former baseball star Jackie Robinson complained, forgetting the nominee's Semitic roots, "I believe I know how it felt to be a Jew in Hitler's Germany," and columnist Drew Pearson extemporaneously added, "the smell of fascism is in the air at this convention." California governor

Edmund "Pat" Brown seconded Pearson's notion, remarking, "All we needed to hear was 'Heil Hitler.' "[53]

After months of vilification, Buckley struck back by attacking the press, particularly a book published during the campaign by Arnold Forster and Benjamin Epstein entitled *Danger on the Right*. The two authors, funded by the Anti-Defamation League, ironically engaged in a bit of defamation themselves. Epstein and Forster defined the beliefs of "extreme conservatives" so broadly that they included just about any conservative, or even nonconservative American: an extreme conservative "considers American domestic policy socialistic and dangerous, and foreign policy as prone to softness and appeasement." Buckley countered by offering two examples of extreme conservatives according to the authors' definition.

> Now it is true that extreme conservatives believe that we are embarked on the road to socialism. That makes Norman Thomas an extreme conservative. He believes we are doing just that, has often said so, and rejoices in that fact. And that we have unnecessarily appeased the communists? That is the judgment of, for instance, George Meany and Sidney Hook, respectively a Liberal and a socialist. Are they therefore extreme conservatives?[54]

The examples that Buckley pointed to throughout the campaign displayed for conservatives the fact that they would not be welcomed by the mainstream press. Although it was acceptable for Goldwater to be the conservative voice of many Republicans, it was not okay for him to be the GOP's standard bearer. The difference in press coverage between 1960, when Goldwater made his first appearance as a prominent national figure, and coverage in 1964, was astounding.[55]

YAF members prepared for the upcoming presidential campaign but also for their own national convention the weekend of September 9–11. The convention was held in New York City, and a side trip was taken to Sharon on the last day for an anniversary celebration. After four years, YAF was healthy with growing membership, sound finances, and national exposure during the Goldwater campaign.[56] But some worried about YAF's "permanent value" and concentrated on "building for the future" during a furious fall membership drive that would coincide with the campaign.[57]

The meeting in New York proceeded much the way previous YAF conventions had. Perennial speaker William F. Buckley appeared. But his address was a little different. Buckley had telephoned Bauman before the convention and asked what the reaction would be if he informed the young conservatives that Goldwater would be defeated. Bauman thought they would be stunned and recommended that, instead, he give a motivational address about the upcoming campaign. Although Bauman finally relented to let Buckley do what he wanted, he thought that the speech would be used against Goldwater and came at the wrong time during the campaign.[58]

Buckley also informed Rusher of his intentions during the summer. Rusher argued with Buckley, telling him that experienced politicians in YAF already knew Goldwater was going to lose, so why make it worse for them? But, as Rusher related, "just seeing what [Bill Buckley] could get away with and still remain an icon to the conservative movement is a large part of what Buckley is all about."[59] When Buckley rose to give his speech, Rusher recalled, "his face, his forehead were beaded with sweat. His hands were trembling a bit. This was a big, defiant scandal he was about to pull off . . . and it all flew over without a single peep except for Richard Viguerie's wife who broke down and cried."[60]

Buckley spoke of "the impending defeat of Barry Goldwater." He continued, after the initial shock wore off:

> The beginning of wisdom is the fear of the Lord. The next and most urgent counsel is to take stock of reality. . . . It is right to take thought, even on the eve of an engagement, about the potential need for regrouping, for gathering together our scattered forces.

After speaking metaphorically of King Henry's victory at Agincourt, Buckley offered sage advice for the young conservatives:

> To those who remark the danger of demoralization in mid-campaign by talk about an impending defeat, it is necessary to talk about the dangers of demoralization after the fourth of November. I fear that the morale of an army on the march is the morale that is most easily destroyed in the unanticipated event of defeat. There are weeks and months and years ahead of us, and I do believe that Senator Goldwater would be the first to deplore the rise of any spirit of synthetic optimism which might result in a national demoralization of the conservative movement the day after the campaign ends. . . . The point of the present occasion is to win recruits . . . not only for November the third, but for future Novembers: to infuse the conservative spirit in enough people to entitle us to look about us, on November 4th, not at the ashes of defeat, but at the well planted seeds of hope, which will flower on a great November day in the future.[61]

Buckley's performance was masterful. He gently reminded the young audience that not all causes are fought for the present, that conservatism, if it teaches anything, teaches patient veneration of tried principles. Although the speech was a letdown to some gathered at the Commodore Hotel, for many others it served as a clarion call for future activity. If it did anything, the speech forced YAF to look past the election.[62]

Although YAF members helped in any way they could, the Goldwater campaign, hindered partly by visceral attacks on the senator's character by the press and partly by a lack of coordination and poor planning by the campaign staff itself, floundered miserably through the fall. On the day of reckoning, November 3, 1964, Johnson gained the biggest electoral win in history to that time. By wide margins, the Republicans were defeated not only for the presidency but also for Congress and state and local offices. Nevertheless, 27 million people voted for Goldwater in 1964, and a good part of the South, for the first time in history, went Republican in a presidential election. Although it was a tremendous rout, conservatives had learned many lessons they would apply in future Novembers.

For YAF, the defeat of Goldwater, who had been the organization's raison d'être for four years, far from disheartening the young politicos, gave them renewed vigor to work for the future. As if Buckley's address had some powerful hypnotic effect on those who heard it in September, YAF board members worked to organize new chapters and sign up new membership on a scale unprecedented in its short life. In October alone, twenty-five hundred new members joined YAF; after the campaign five chapters were chartered in one day over the telephone. Thomas Phillips, who had the task of membership recruiting, attributed the jump in membership to the frequent discussion of conservatism during the campaign and the formation of Youth for Goldwater clubs on campuses that YAF had yet to reach. It was a natural crossover from supporting Goldwater's presidential drive to YAF membership.[63]

David Jones had a great deal to do with YAF's organizational work that fall. His goal as executive director was to increase national membership to forty thousand members. How to do this in the wake of Goldwater's resounding defeat? Jones believed YAF would be able to capitalize on conservative leadership already present in local communities through the organization of leadership conferences, and by encouraging more effective development of regional and state chapters, providing a speaker's bureau, and developing community and high school chapters.[64] Jones argued that membership retention was important for the success of future conservative candidates, whether at the local, state, or national level. Therefore, political activity became more focused and included local forums designed to instruct community chapters on political action for conservative causes.[65]

YAF members also wished to explore wider options and linkages with the conservative movement as a whole. On December 19, 1964, the American Conservative Union (ACU) was formed as a "graduate YAF" for conservatives who had reached or were nearing YAF's upper age limit of thirty-five. Aside from being a place for former YAF members to turn, the ACU was also intended to serve as an assembly where the intellectual resources of American conservatism could be used on behalf of public policy. It was not a think-tank where conservative academicians and policy gurus charted the future course of American society and government, but rather an organization that kept conservative ideas in the forefront of public debate and supported conservative politicians for office.[66]

The ACU was explicitly modeled on the liberal Americans for Democratic Action (ADA), an organization founded in 1947 in order to preserve the New Deal conceptions of social welfare and to give an anticommunist orientation to liberalism. The conservatives behind the ACU believed, not altogether accurately, that the ADA represented an effort "to help other liberals achieve positions of power and influence in government to work for a socialist America."[67] Observant conservatives noted that one of ADA's founding members, Hubert Humphrey, was the newly elected vice president. Surely, the ACU could achieve the same result over time.

The leadership of ACU was vested in a chairman, Congressman Donald Bruce from Indiana. John Ashbrook was named vice chairman and later in the year succeeded the acerbic Bruce; Robert Bauman was named secretary and Frank Meyer, treasurer. Lammot Copeland, Jr., of YAF served as a director, and several YAF members and alumni, including Richard Allen of Indiana YAF, Lee Edwards, and David Jones, were on the advisory board. An estimated budget of $252,000 was required in order to launch the activities of the organization, which included task forces on conservative principles and candidates, and support for grass roots initiatives and conservative organizations.

One of the problems ACU had in its first month of operation was its failure to gain the backing of Goldwater. Shortly after the election, William Baroody, Sr., one of Goldwater's advisors from the American Enterprise Institute—a think tank in Washington, D.C.—and Denison Kitchel, the candidate's longtime friend and campaign manager, formed the Free Society Association. This organization, designed to gain adherents to conservatism through the publication of pamphlets and newsletters, was headquartered in Phoenix. It included no prominent conservative intellectuals on its advisory board. Both Baroody and Kitchel had worked to exclude prominent conservatives such as Buckley from the Goldwater campaign, and it appeared that they wished to do the same afterward. But ACU's more recognizable advisors held sway over Goldwater's group, and within a year the Free Society Association folded.[68]

For an individual grown weary of youth politics, the ACU was a new organization on which to hang one's hat. Throughout its history, YAF members have played leading roles in its development as an organization. (Bauman, and later David Keene—both YAF national chairmen—have served as ACU's chairmen for more than half its history.) As one example of conservative organizational effort after the Goldwater campaign, the ACU showed that youth politics in the Goldwater campaign was having a repercussive effect on the conservative movement, and not just for YAF. As the movement grew and consolidated its power after the campaign, organizations like ACU were a necessary logistical development for conservative activists.

After the campaign YAF was well poised to begin the most activist period in its history. With the campaign behind them and membership growing, YAF's leadership sought out issues of concern to protest and expose with greater regularity and renewed confidence. Lyndon Johnson's expansion of the war in Vietnam was one such issue; growing protest and radicalism at home, another. For the remainder of the decade, YAF members were consumed, like many of their radical counterparts, with the Vietnam War and the effect it was having on American society. Applying lessons of protest learned from the Left along with organizational methods and strategies employed during the Goldwater campaign, YAF set out to promulgate a conservative alternative for American society. In doing so, without being fully cognizant of the fact, YAF would help transform American politics. In the cultural and political wars of the sixties, YAF would hold its own against the voices of protest from the Left, and in the process offer its own vision of what America should represent.

PART II

Revolt on the Campus

5

Why Not Victory?

YAF and Vietnam, 1965–1968

The gauntlet was down and our job was to support our country and its efforts . . . and to show that the protestors weren't the only people that had an opinion.   —Tom Charles Huston

Because SDS and the Leftists were against the war in Vietnam, [Lyndon Johnson] effectively got Republicans and conservatives to back him in waging it.   —David Franke

I was told that if I voted for Goldwater, we were going to war in Vietnam. Well, I did, and damned if we didn't.   —popular joke

"Perhaps at this late date," Ronald Reagan intoned in a 1988 Veteran's Day ceremony at the Vietnam Veterans Memorial, "we can all agree we learned one lesson: that young Americans must never again be sent to fight and die unless we are prepared to let them win."[1] In examining the lessons of Vietnam, conservatives have been apt to describe a situation where the forces of Communism, aided by the antiwar movement at home, impaired America's ability to win in Southeast Asia.[2] For the majority of conservatives, echoing Reagan, the defense of South Vietnam was a "just and noble cause" in defense of freedom. "If you believed that Communism was really a threat, then the national security state . . . and our commitment to Vietnam were justified," according to David Keene.[3] For the members of YAF, arguments on behalf of opposition to Communist totalitarianism made a compelling case for supporting America's involvement in Vietnam.

The Vietnam conflict represented the high point of YAF's activity on behalf of anticommunist causes. Even though YAF had failed to stop the test-ban treaty's ratification, young conservatives stayed true to their anticommunist course.[4] In seeking victory over Communism, YAF maintained its allegiance to the principles of the Sharon Statement and also to Goldwater's injunction in *The Conscience of a Conservative* that "war [against Communism] may be the price of freedom."[5] YAF's arguments for victory in Vietnam were consistent with the organization's intensely held belief that Communism represented the biggest threat to American interests and to the security of the world.

The YAF support of victory developed in two basic forms. The first involved the vocal defense of American policy in Vietnam. YAF members organized rallies in support of the war and protested against antiwar pickets on numerous occasions. The organization did not necessarily agree with Lyndon Johnson's policies but supported American involvement while recommending that further offensive actions be taken against North Vietnam. To further their goals in this regard, YAF leaders expanded contacts with worldwide anticommunist organizations, particularly in Asia, for the purpose of giving support to nations under threat from Communism.

The second type of support involved stopping American corporations from trading with Communist nations. For YAF, the war in Vietnam represented a struggle of global proportions against the Communist world, not, as in the antiwar view, an unjust intervention on behalf of a corrupt puppet state in South Vietnam. YAF's globalist view therefore preconditioned a strategic rethinking of America's relations with other Communist regimes—one that would rule out American trade with nations allied to North Vietnam and reject improved relations with the Soviet Union. It also, however, put YAF and conservatives in general on the side of regimes that were not exactly democratic in their rule. To defend South Vietnam as an ally was one thing; to defend it as a democracy was another.[6]

In the early years of Johnson's escalation of the war, YAF possessed some leverage in the debate over the efficacy and extent of American involvement in Southeast Asia. Throughout 1965 and 1966 it was still possible to hold meaningful debates over controversial issues on campus without fear that one's opinions would be ridiculed or condemned as "fascist" by radical students. The placid years of mid-decade seem almost generations away from the divisive and violent era of the late 1960s. For the members of YAF, growing in confidence and ability after the Goldwater campaign, these years would see a great variety of activity on behalf of the anticommunist and provictory cause.

YAF had given little exposure to Vietnam and Southeast Asia before the Goldwater campaign in 1964. A few articles about Vietnam had appeared in the *New Guard*, several of them written by Robert Harley, a YAF board member who had traveled extensively in Southeast Asia during the summer of 1961. In September 1961 Harley participated, as an official representative of YAF, in the founding of a short-lived worldwide anticommunist youth group. The group's platform articulated that young people should "fight with all weapons at our command the forces of international Communism." It also appealed to "the youth and youth organizations of the world to support . . . and to establish a world-wide organization to abolish Communism."[7] Harley also reported that the Chinese community in Saigon provided the key for a successful defense of South Vietnam. Working in conjunction with the Asian People's Anti-Communist League (APACL), Harley toured the Chinese enclave of Cholon, home to the majority of Saigon's ethnic Chinese; he toured the remainder of the area surrounding Saigon with Tran Tam, the Vietnamese representative of the APACL. Harley argued in terms then considered moderate even within the Kennedy administration that defending South Vietnam represented a first line of defense for the remainder of Southeast Asia.[8]

In similar ways, YAF addressed the global implications of a Communist victory in Vietnam. "If the communists win South Viet Nam, Laos will fall and the rest of Southeast Asia with it. . . . should [the Soviets] succeed in this, the communists will have little difficulty in taking so-called neutralist Indonesia and India. The Communists must be stopped. Ngo Dinh Diem needs our full-scale help. There is no alternative."[9] This editorial, written in 1962, may sound unduly alarmist today, but consider the situation in South Vietnam that year: a growing Vietcong insurgency, a weakening regime hurt by dissent, and corruption within the Army of South Vietnam (ARVN). YAF members were pleading with the administration to bolster its efforts in Southeast Asia rather than cutting and running, a policy that would be recommended by the Left. Employing rhetoric no worse than any mainstream liberal at the time, YAF members urged Kennedy to stand firm in Southeast Asia.

A subtle shift in tactics occurred after the coup d'état and the assassination of South Vietnamese president Ngo Dinh Diem in November 1963. YAF argued that the assassination of Diem, a "democratically elected" leader, represented an amplification of "the Kennedy Administration's . . . appalling . . . record of appeasement." The January 1964 *New Guard* featured an article that attacked the war in Vietnam as a symbol "of the failure of contemporary American liberalism. . . . Our leaders no longer view power as a means of winning back freedoms taken from a people." After a strong analysis of the problems involved in defeating the Vietcong insurgency, the author recommended what would define YAF's strategy toward Southeast Asia for the remainder of the war: "This nation must first commit itself to total victory in South Vietnam."[10] One article stressed that the West could prevail in Vietnam and other Third World conflicts if the United States organized guerrilla forces modeled on those of the Communists. But this would take time—a factor that the American people ultimately were not willing to grant in the Vietnam conflict; the emphasis on anticommunist guerilla conflict would later be implemented, with mixed results, during the Reagan administration.[11]

For YAF the matter of Communist aggression against an independent and free South Vietnam was always the issue during the Vietnam War. Little else mattered except that the regime be defended. Imbibing a view of the Cold War that saw defeat after defeat (a mordant view strikingly at odds with the optimistic conservatism of the 1980s),[12] conservatives sought a victory in Vietnam. This zero-sum game worldview (where a loss for the United States was a victory for the Communist world), YAF believed, should guide American policy. The implementation of such a strategy involved, for YAF, somewhat of a reactive posture to counter those on the Left who believed the Cold War policies of the previous twenty years had been unproductive and downright dangerous for the health of democracy. YAF's support for a victory in Vietnam was contingent on a victory at home.

YAF implemented the first phase of its victory strategy early in 1965 when chapters nationwide scheduled counterprotests against antiwar pickets. In New York, Washington, D.C., and Cleveland, YAF members, waving signs and banners supporting South Vietnam, walked alongside protestors from the Student Peace Union and Students for a Democratic Society who carried placards calling for peace and negotiations. Several other counterdemonstrations took place throughout February 1965, including a rally organized to protest a well-attended antiwar picket in New Haven, Connecticut.[13]

On many occasions over the next year YAF chapters were embroiled in efforts to counter antiwar protests with marches in support of the war. Robert Bauman called for "the overwhelming majority of the young people in America who support President Johnson's policy in Vietnam to make their support known. We must not let it seem for one minute that the small cliques of pacifists, left-wing extremists and beatniks calling for retreat speak for our generation."[14] At one such picket in New York, a group of hunger strikers demonstrating against U.S. policy were greeted by YAF members carrying banners emblazoned with "better fed than red" as they stuffed food in their mouths.[15] Other chapters organized food and clothing drives for war refugees and paperback book drives for servicemen. Most unusual was a "wash-in" where soap was purchased and sent to men in Vietnam.[16] At numerous antiwar events and marches YAF members were there to voice their support for American policy.

In January 1966 YAF sponsored a nationwide series of rallies dedicated to supporting America's efforts against Communism in Vietnam. Thousands gathered to attend ceremonies and rallies commemorating fallen American soldiers and to hear speeches supporting victory over Communism in Asia. In Saint Louis more than fifty-five hundred people attended a rally held in "Joe Louis" arena. Speakers included Phyllis Schlafly, Maj. Gen. Thomas Lane, James Drury—television star of *The Virginian*—and Cardinal outfielder Lou Brock. YAF members in New York City lit a torch of freedom at the Statue of Liberty on a frigid, windswept day. Other rallies had folksingers such as Vera Vanderlaan sing in support of freedom in Vietnam. All in all, although far less well-attended than comparable antiwar marches, YAF's scattered rallies were successful. They showed that not all Americans, and specifically not all young people, were against the war.[17]

More important than the marches in favor of American policy was the effort the national board made to support other anticommunist causes throughout the world. The instigator of this activity was Tom Charles Huston. Huston had been elected YAF's national chairman at the 1965 convention to replace Bauman, who left YAF to work for the American Conservative Union. In his inaugural address, which YAF published and distributed as a pamphlet, Huston chided conservatives for harboring extremists "who abuse the truth, who resort to violence and engage in slander, who seek victory at any price without regard for the broken lives . . . incurred by those who stand in the way."[18] Huston's speech was an unmitigated attack on the John Birch Society and other extremist beliefs (even a tacit admission that conservatives had erred in supporting McCarthyism), which represented an effort—that Huston had long endorsed—to put forth a responsible conservatism capable of offering society an alternative to liberalism.[19]

Huston's excoriation of extremists in the wake of the Goldwater campaign offered hope to those on the Right who believed that conservatism could be transformed into a ruling political ideology. It also served to give the movement greater credence in the battle against Communism, particularly in Vietnam. Huston was obsessed about the Vietnam issue. He had been interested in Asian affairs since learning about a missionary uncle who had been killed by Chinese Communist forces before World War II. The month after he won election as YAF's chairman, Huston attended the annual meeting of the Asian Peoples' Anti-Communist League in Manila.[20] Founded in 1954, the league, with the help of Marvin Liebman, coordinated anticommunist efforts as "a type of anti-Comintern" throughout Asia.[21] In December, under league auspices, Huston returned to Southeast Asia to speak to soldiers during the Christmas season.

Huston's actions on behalf of the APACL resulted in the establishment of the World Youth Crusade for Freedom (WYCF), an organization designed to work in conjunction with anticommunist groups throughout Asia. An organization like this had been under discussion for some time (the short-lived group that Robert Harley endorsed during his 1961 Asian trip was a predecessor), and with Marvin Liebman's support, the group was founded the previous autumn, 1965, at the Manila meeting of the APACL. Huston was involved from the start and seemed the perfect choice to head up the organization, because of his visits and interest in Asia. The WYCF was affiliated with YAF but was not an official YAF project, as Huston told the board of directors at a March meeting. Rather, the WYCF, much like other YAF-dominated front groups, was set up as "a separate incorporated group committed to the defeat of Communism."[22]

Huston outlined the purposes and program of the WYCF for attending delegates at a founding meeting held in Hong Kong on May 8, 1966. The WYCF would sponsor a Freedom Corps, modeled after the Peace Corps— a program YAF had condemned earlier—comprised of ten or twelve American students who would spend July and August in Asian countries, ostensibly "to study local conditions . . . and talk with individuals and groups about the United States and its position in world affairs." They would then use that knowledge to participate in some "work project, such as teaching, working with organizations of local youth, etc."[23] The participants would be selected under a "harsh training process" that included a week-long seminar at Yale on political and economic problems facing Asian nations. David Rowe, an anticommunist professor at Yale, would lead the seminar.

Delegates from Asian countries attending the Hong Kong conference were enthusiastic, particularly because the WYCF would raise the funds to send the selected students to Asia. Little remained for the host nations to do but plan the itineraries and prepare their guests for meetings with anticommunist officials and organizations.

By June, enough money was raised through donations from benefactors to send Freedom Corps representatives to Asia, and nine people attended Rowe's seminar at Yale the second week of June. The most prominent among the nine was David Keene, a first-year law student at the University of Wisconsin and a YAF board member. Keene and Richard Wright (a fellow Wisconsin student) had the distinction of being chosen to go to South Vietnam, the most prestigious destination because of the war. Three other volunteers were sent to Taiwan, while one each worked in Australia, Singapore, India, and the Philippines. The Philippines drew the lone woman in the Freedom Corps, Toby Solovioff.[24]

Participation in the Freedom Corps and the WYCF helped Keene's YAF career immensely. Although Keene had been an active conservative since the Goldwater campaign and had been an editor of *Insight and Outlook,* a publication of the Conservative Club at the University of Wisconsin, it was his participation as a vocal exponent of victory in Vietnam that brought him to the attention of national YAF and especially its chairman, Tom Huston.[25]

Throughout the summer of 1966 the Freedom Corps volunteers sent monthly reports back to WYCF headquarters in New York. The three Taiwanese volunteers reported conflicts with Peace Corps representatives who considered the WYCF volunteers "fascists," but apart from that, the students found "no serious weakening of the will to resist or the desire to return to the Mainland among Chinese youth." Keene and Wright met with youth and student leaders in Saigon and reported—alarmingly, given the situation in their war-torn nation—that "Vietnamese youth are not much different than young people anywhere else. Many use every means possible to stay out of the armed services of their country; others carp about government bureaucracy and corruption; still others have been indoctrinated by the communists." In the countryside, the two volunteers found a different story. "The Vietnamese people outside of Saigon have seen the real face of Communism. They fear it and are prepared to fight to the death against it." After several meetings with American servicemen, Keene and Wright traveled north to work in South Vietnamese villages.[26] In each nation visited by the Freedom Corps volunteers, people were found willing to resist Communist encroachments and desiring nothing more than to live in freedom and peace.

WYCF activists parlayed their experience into productive tasks upon their return to the United States. David Keene formed a WYCF spin-off group, the Student Committee for a Free China (SCFC), which was designed "to inform American students of the realities of Red China and to mobilize student action against any appeasement of the Peiping regime." Keene believed that the formation of such a committee was necessary because "there is one thing we all learned in the Freedom Corps: the greatest single enemy of freedom in Asia is Communist China."[27] The SCFC was not designed to be a membership organization but was to work in conjunction with other groups on campus to prevent the Left from monopolizing the debate on China. By the fall of 1966, sixty-seven SCFC campus representatives, many of them YAF members, had volunteered for service in Keene's group.

In an age when American students waved Mao's "little red books" and rather uncritically accepted the propaganda lines emanating from Beijing concerning American imperialism in Vietnam, the SCFC seemed like a good idea to conservatives. But like many such letterhead organizations of the day, its impact was limited. Since Taiwan represented the cornerstone of the free world in Asia, SCFC made efforts to send anticommunist students to Taiwan on six- to eight-week study tours. While gaining college credit, students would attend lectures and seminars on Communism in Asia and the response to it by free nations. When they returned they would be better prepared to debate pro-Mao leftist students on campus. Although this was certainly a limited program and had only marginal success, given the changing debate over China's role in world politics, the summer courses did encourage young people to defend the regime on Taiwan as a bulwark of freedom in Asia and prepare them to confront radical students on campus.[28]

YAF leadership was aware that, in supporting groups like SCFC and the Freedom Corps, the anticommunist foreign policy consensus was under challenge. Student groups on the left as well as peace organizations such as Women Strike for Peace and Clergy and Laymen Concerned about Vietnam were challenging the very foundations of American policy in Southeast Asia in a way that seemed treasonous to many young conservatives. Although YAF members shuddered at Johnson's strategy in Vietnam, they were even more afraid of the alternative in Southeast Asia if the Vietnamese people were merely left to their fate. For YAF members the desire to support Johnson's war, however limited, was balanced by the continuing need to resist Communist expansion wherever it might occur. Although some of them, like their leftist brethren, were growing skeptical of the government's rationalizations for war, the majority nevertheless believed that defending South Vietnam's freedom was worth American lives and treasure.[29]

The second element in YAF's victory strategy had to do with American trading relations with Communist nations. The Kennedy administration's $200 million wheat deal with the Soviet Union opened Pandora's box as far as YAF was concerned, luring private enterprises to trade with Soviet bloc nations. YAF chapters had protested the wheat deal vigorously throughout 1963 and fought for restrictions on further trading with the Soviet Union. Chapters organized letter-writing campaigns and pickets against the wheat deal. By February 1965, when the first major article appeared in the *New Guard* regarding trade with Communist nations, several chapters were already well prepared to act.[30]

The first opportunity for action occurred in the spring of 1965 when the Firestone Tire and Rubber Company announced plans to build a synthetic rubber plant in Romania. Partly, this move reflected State Department efforts to woo satellite nations away from the Soviet Union. Since Romania was a major Eastern European producer of oil, and its leader, the harsh dictator Nicolae Ceauşescu, seemed amenable to American overtures, Romania was a logical place for such an investment. Upon hearing the news of Firestone's intentions, a Pennsylvania YAF chapter began a seemingly isolated picket of Firestone offices in downtown Philadelphia. Within weeks, pickets followed in several other cities, including Cleveland, Brooklyn, and Providence, Rhode Island. John LaMothe, the YAF chapter leader in Philadelphia, argued that Romania was supplying Communist China with heavy trucks. In turn, China was supplying heavy equipment to North Vietnam. By building a plant in Romania, Firestone would be facilitating trade with an American enemy.[31]

This slippery slope argument put a great deal of pressure on Firestone's corporate board. YAF claimed Firestone's board was worried that continued picketing of retail chains would have an effect on business. Contributing even further to Firestone's nervousness, the Goodyear Tire and Rubber Company decided to spurn contracts to build plants in Communist nations. A Brooklyn YAF chapter circulated a petition praising this decision. The climax of the campaign came when Indiana native Jameson Campaigne suggested that YAF threaten a demonstration at the well-attended Indianapolis 500 auto race over Memorial Day weekend. Sometime during the race, a plane would fly over the grandstand towing a banner that said, "The

Viet Cong ride on Firestone," mimicking a popular Firestone advertisement campaign. When word of this reached Firestone in April, the company announced that it was going to break the contract with the Romanian
government.[32] YAF had succeeded in pressuring a corporation to change
its trading policy.

The reaction in the press was mixed. A May 12 *Washington Post* editorial
castigated YAF for its "slashed tires caper," concluding that "United States
relations with 'westward-moving Romania' certainly must not be governed
by what these self-styled patriots think is best for America."[33] The rather
conservative *Richmond News-Leader* praised YAF's efforts, stating that "the
YAFers were right to show Firestone the fallacy of strengthening the
dedicated enemies of our system."[34]

The matter was not finished, however. In reaction to YAF's success, J.
William Fulbright, the powerful chairman of the Senate Foreign Relations
Committee, condemned the organization in a speech on the Senate floor.
Fulbright believed the deal was instrumental to American interests and
labeled YAF a "vigilante group" for blocking it.[35] Strom Thurmond rose
to defend the organization, but Fulbright's political point had the desired
effect. In reaction to the speech, Johnson ordered a State Department
investigation into why the Firestone deal fell through.[36]

Fulbright's speech and his charges that YAF had used Goodyear to
pressure Firestone to break the contract possibly led to a change of policy
for YAF. In reaction to his charges, the national board adopted an official
policy regarding its position on trade with Communist nations. In the
future YAF would "concentrate our efforts against those trade deals which
plainly give aid and comfort to the Communist enemy by building up their
military power"; second, the organization intended "to form an official
advisory committee of noted experts on the matter of strategic trade"; and
finally, YAF pledged "not to engage in boycotts" but rather to pursue an
informational campaign against companies intent on trading with the enemy. With American policy dedicated to stopping Communism in Vietnam, YAF found it "sheer absurdity to undermine this stand by trading
with the enemy through the back door of Romania or any other Red
nation."[37]

YAF's opposition to American corporations trading with Communist
nations resembles left-wing tactics used during the 1960s to keep corporations from trading with South Africa because of that nation's apartheid
policies. Later in the decade, leftist groups were able to protest successfully
against corporations that exhibited little concern for a healthy environment

or practiced discriminatory hiring practices against minority workers.[38] If opposition to corporate policy was a justification for the Left to protest against business, how could an organization of presumably probusiness conservatives justify this activity?

For members of YAF, the action against Firestone had little to do with the right of a particular corporation to make profits. The Sharon Statement argued that the market economy was the "single economic system compatible with the requirements of personal freedom." Firestone's actions violated, in YAF's view, the interrelationship between free trade and trading with enemies of the nation. To YAF, Firestone's intention of trading with a Communist nation smacked of treason. Although most YAF members considered a free market important, the Sharon Statement also spoke of the fervent belief that international Communism was the greatest threat to American liberties and that "freedom can only exist when free citizens defend their rights against all enemies."[39] By trading with Communist nations, even nations with which we were not in any technical sense at war, America put its own freedom in danger, and more importantly, risked the lives of American soldiers fighting against Communism in Southeast Asia. The market economy was the sine qua non of Western freedom, but the threat of Communism and the necessity to retain a bulwark against it outweighed the rights of corporations to trade with those nations. As M. Stanton Evans queried, "if you are in a struggle where someone is trying to do you in, do you then give them the wherewithal to do it?"[40]

YAF members restricted themselves to persuasive and relatively polite tactical protests against corporations trading with Communist nations. Like the Left, conservatives felt that pressure on private businesses could compel them to change their policy. Unlike the left, YAF's protests never dissolved into questioning the very basis of a corporation's right to profit, nor did YAF use violence to further its goals.

For example, radical student protests against the Dow Chemical Company, the maker of napalm, a jellied gasoline used to obliterate Communist positions in Vietnam, were at first well-disciplined marches against the corporate headquarters similar to civil rights demonstrations against segregation earlier in the decade. But as the anger of protestors expanded, other tactics were tried, including boycotts of Dow consumer products such as Saran Wrap, the disruption of Dow's efforts to recruit on campus, and even the destruction of the corporation's personal property.[41] Eventually, the hostility that students felt toward Dow as the symbol of death and destruction in Vietnam boiled over into violence.[42]

Young people throughout the 1960s were beginning to realize the potential strength of their generation's consumer power. If businesses failed to respond to their demands, as both Firestone and Dow initially did, they would face an escalation of protest, and perhaps even boycotts, of their products. Although conservative students never wished to interfere with a corporation's right to profit from what were seen by them as legitimate enterprises, the very fact that they would endorse these strategies for countering unpopular corporate policies showed that they understood the power of public exposure of the policies.[43]

The foreign trade issue continued to draw the most attention from YAF members over the next two years. YAF activity in this regard culminated in the Stop-IBM campaign in the spring of 1968, YAF's most public, but ultimately least successful, effort to stop trade with enemy nations.

The momentum for the Stop-IBM campaign emerged from YAF's efforts against American Motors Corporation the previous autumn. The details of the effort are rather murky, but they involved a statement that appeared in a November 27, 1966, *Chicago Tribune* article claiming that AMC intended to sell cars in the Soviet Union.[44] The Valparaiso, Indiana, YAF chapter began a picket of its local AMC dealer and pressed for clarification of AMC policy on this matter from the company's Detroit headquarters. In December Tom Huston wrote Michigan governor George Romney, who had recently been president of AMC, to pressure the corporation to stop the proposed deal. Huston argued that the "trade deal . . . would indirectly give aid to Communists in North Vietnam." David Jones further clarified YAF's policy: "The selling of autos to Russia will most definitely aid the Soviets' support of the war in Vietnam. This will result because it allows the Reds to divert metals, rubber and other materials away from their domestic market and into their military industrial efforts." By the end of December, almost a month after the original story broke, AMC backed down and reneged on arranging a deal with the Soviets.[45]

Whether YAF was ultimately responsible for pressuring AMC's board of directors to change their minds or not was unimportant; YAF members believed they had succeeded. In their confidence they were able to organize and implement one of their most public efforts to put an end to trade with enemy nations, the Stop-IBM campaign.

The IBM effort began in July 1967 when California YAF chapters organized marches against IBM's Los Angeles offices because of the corporation's trade in computer products with Eastern European nations. When pressed by YAF members, IBM had admitted to engaging in such trade but denied that this technology transfer was with the Soviet Union, stressing that the computers were for Eastern European nations. What concerned YAF members most was the Soviets' gaining sensitive computer technology that would allow them to modernize the guidance systems of their nuclear missile forces or to use for espionage against the West. A California YAF position paper outlining the reasons behind the pickets stated: "It seems rather illogical that an industrial giant in our nation should be seeking means to aid the same political structure . . . that is murdering hundreds of American soldiers every week in Southeast Asia."[46]

Unlike Firestone and American Motors, however, IBM did not buckle to YAF's pressure. By early 1968, the YAF board transformed the local pickets against IBM into a national campaign. Marches against IBM offices in various cities continued to be quite successful, as were letters written to protest IBM policy, but new tactics were employed as well. The purchase of one share of IBM stock by the national organization allowed YAF representatives to attend the corporation's annual stockholders' convention in Boston in April 1968.[47] Other measures, such as the printing and distribution of thousands of computer punch cards with YAF's arguments against IBM's actions printed on them, were successful in galvanizing opinion behind YAF's cause. David Keene also spoke before policy committees at both the Republican and Democratic 1968 conventions, pleading with delegates to support planks requiring tougher measures against trade with Communist nations.[48]

Some of this activity had the desired effect on IBM's stockholders. A letter acquired by *New Guard* editor Arnie Steinberg, from the A. C. Nielsen Company in Chicago, displayed the pressure some IBM customers were under because of YAF's "bombardment" of their offices with literature regarding trade with Communist countries. Arthur Nielsen, director of the company, wrote IBM chairman A. K. Watson, "If I am substantially correct in my understanding of Communism . . . your company has apparently been making a very serious mistake." Nielsen encouraged Watson to make a change in IBM policy regarding trade with Communist nations, arguing that "such a change would set a fine example which would undoubtedly be followed by other producers in the free world—and perhaps even make the difference . . . between victory and defeat in the world struggle of free men against the threat of enslavement by Communism."[49]

Steinberg kept Buckley and other conservatives informed of the issues regarding IBM throughout 1968. As a result, Buckley wrote a column in *National Review* that YAF's contact inside the corporation admitted had a positive effect for YAF's purpose.[50] Letters from new national chairman Alan MacKay to senators such as William Proxmire also drew a response from State Department officials attempting to justify trade with Communist nations.[51] One such letter to Proxmire stated that the Export Control Act "prohibits the export to the USSR and other Eastern European countries of goods or technology that would make a significant contribution to their military or economic potential in a way which would prove detrimental to United States national security and welfare." In speaking about IBM's trade in computers, the State Department argued that "these computers are not designed for use in space programs" and that "the small volume of our trade with Eastern Europe makes no contribution to its military production and aid to North Vietnam."[52]

On April 22, MacKay and Steinberg met with three of IBM's top executives before the stockholders' meeting that day. On condition that YAF not picket the meeting, MacKay was granted ten minutes to argue his case. IBM executives presented MacKay and Steinberg with reams of evidence that the computer technology they were selling to Eastern Europe was not suitable for defense purposes and also told the two young men that all information that IBM received from doing business with these nations was forwarded to the CIA. Steinberg queried whether the Soviets understood this and therefore were being duplicitous when it came to what they were telling IBM officials. Not one of the three executives could answer.[53]

Later that day MacKay was escorted to a prearranged seat at the stockholders meeting where Albert Watson, Jr., head of IBM, would call on MacKay when the time came. To Steinberg, "IBM's efficiency in the whole operation was truly frightening." When MacKay spoke, he told the assemblage, "By trading with Communist nations, we save them from their own economic failures, thus perpetuating regimes that are repressive and form part of a system which, taken as a whole, poses the greatest threat to human freedom in our time." After MacKay's short speech, Watson thanked MacKay and YAF for their statesmanlike handling of the affair and then proceeded to reiterate IBM's desires to "build bridges" between the United States and Soviet bloc nations. The State Department line was enough for IBM stockholders to accept continued trade in computers with the Soviet satellite nations.[54]

Though MacKay and some of the other leadership of YAF were quite statesmanlike in their handling of the matter, the national board could not control everybody. Ron Docksai, a precocious, intelligent young member of the New York YAF and a student at Saint John's University, wrote a piece in his YAF campus paper, "The Western View," stating that Albert Watson's father (who also had been CEO of IBM) was decorated by the Nazis in the 1930s. "Now, Tom Watson was hardly a sincere Nazi! He simply felt it was kosher to trade with the enemy, that IBM and the fruits of American business could, no less, even dissuade Hitler from acting upon his psychopathic pronouncements."[55] Docksai accused Watson's son, now IBM chairman, of doing the same thing with the Soviet Union.

The article drew a fiery reply from Watson denying that IBM had traded with the Soviet Union as Docksai had stated and also defending his father's efforts to build bridges with Hitler in the 1930s. "Clearly, along with everyone else, his efforts in the 1930s to contribute through business toward a basis for preventing war were a failure. But it certainly does not follow that the United States should forever abandon any attempts to encourage peaceful international commerce. By using trade with selectivity and intelligence, we may someday break up the Communist monolith."[56]

Docksai's misguided article, which, to be fair, repeated charges *Newsweek* magazine had made that same week, marked the end of the IBM campaign and perhaps represented a frustrated last gasp on the part of local chapters that had worked hard to stop IBM. The campaign still dragged on throughout the summer of 1968, but national politics and growing radicalism on campus now drew the attention of most YAF members. MacKay's August 4 appearance on Clarence Manion's radio program, *The Manion Forum,* signaled changes in YAF's policy on East-West trade. No longer would YAF confront a specific corporation's trading policy. Although MacKay evinced pride at the efforts YAF had made against the $35 billion IBM Corporation, future efforts, he hinted, would be aimed at changing the government's policy on trade with Communist nations. This was even more ambitious, but it also signified that YAF was withdrawing from the battleground of protesting unfavorable corporate practices.[57]

The final effort YAF made to construct a case for victory in Vietnam involved a "trial" of Communism. Lee Edwards, who had left his active role in YAF before the Goldwater campaign, helped plan the trial in conjunction with several YAF chapters and other anticommunist organizations. Plans had begun in January 1967; originally the goal had been a trial date in November, to coincide with the fiftieth anniversary of the Bolshevik revolution, but delays pushed the date forward to February 1968. William Roberts, a director of the Institute of International Law and Relations at Catholic University in Washington, was to be the prosecuting attorney; witnesses included prominent conservatives and anticommunists such as Frank Meyer, Stefan Possony, Phillip Abbott Luce, and John Dos Passos, who could all speak to the crimes of Communism. Though the trial was for show, Edwards believed there should be a defense. He refused to allow Communist attorneys to organize the defense, however, since they would attempt to grab all the headlines rather than address the charges.[58]

In January Edwards mailed a court summons to fifteen Communist nations through their embassies in Washington. Fourteen American Communists, including Gus Hall, Herbert Aptheker, and Dorothy Healey, were "subpoenaed" to appear to defend Communism, but none of the fifteen nations sent representatives and none of the Americans replied. The trial, therefore, relied on the witnesses for the prosecution. On Monday, February 19, Eugene Lyons testified about the costs of Communism, citing the figure of 45 million deaths caused by Communist policies over the previous fifty years. Other witnesses, such as former Progressive Labor leader Phillip Abbott Luce, told of the illegal trips he and other students had taken to Cuba in 1963 and 1964. Luce spoke of the lies he had heard about living conditions in Communist countries versus the realities he saw when in Cuba.[59]

For three days, testimony on the crimes of Communism echoed through the auditorium at Georgetown University. Hungarian freedom fighters told of torture at the hands of the invading Soviet armies; a Romanian Jew turned Christian evangelical minister disrobed to show the scars of torture at the hands of the secret police; Taiwanese representatives spoke of horrible conditions in China; and Herbert Philbrick told of the conspiracy in America involving the American Communist Party and its ties to Moscow. The defense, appointed by the court a week before the trial began, presented their case, and the court released a verdict two weeks later. Not surprisingly, international Communism was found guilty of crimes against humanity.[60]

The impact of such a trial was, of course, purely symbolic, but many conservatives must have wondered if anyone was paying attention. The event drew very little media coverage, except for the conservative press, and did little to rejuvenate a shattered anticommunist consensus.[61] Except among conservatives, Communism lacked the appeal it had once had to stir emotions.

Of what worth, then, had been YAF's anticommunist and provictory activities over the period 1965–68? The protests against East-West trade, the support for the war in Vietnam, and efforts like the trial against Communism all had little effect on membership recruitment and fund-raising.

YAF certainly was not alone in supporting anticommunist efforts during the 1960s, but it was the most capable and the most vocal of conservative organizations in its denunciation of Communism and its support for the U.S. war effort in Southeast Asia. As the decade drew to a close, YAF's activities in support of victory in Vietnam, though not winning over the American public, did point to the fact that not all Americans felt the war was unwinnable or immoral. As the trial of international Communism showed all too clearly, to allow South Vietnam to fall under the sway of the Communist North was a more heinous moral position than the antiwar movement's tacit support for the North Vietnamese.

Regardless of YAF's anticommunist efforts, on campus the antiwar position remained strong. Concerned about what radical students were doing to the war effort, as well as to American society, YAF members dedicated themselves to confronting a new enemy—the New Left. For the next several years, as the antiwar movement escalated the "war within" concerning Vietnam, YAF turned away from anticommunist activity to deal with the new danger they saw emanating from the campus. In doing so, YAF began the most active, but also the most disruptive, period in its history. YAF would survive the tumults of that era, unlike its counterparts on the left, but its future usefulness to the conservative cause as an activist organization was forever tarnished by the experience.

6

Up against the Wall
YAF and the New Left, 1968–1970

The New Left is simply a movement that has pushed the premises of
relativist ethics and coercive economics to their logical (or illogical)
conclusions.   —M. Stanton Evans

My God, America needs vocal students and young people who will
re-establish the national reputation, which nowadays rests on a
Catherine wheel's production of pot-smokers, betelnut chewers, clam
juice fanatics and others strung out on left ideology.
                                          —William F. Buckley, Jr.

YAF would find its greatest impact as an organization not so
much directly supporting a provictory strategy for Vietnam but indirectly
in its battles with the antiwar forces of the Left. Ultimately, it was not even
the issue of the war that brought the two sides into combat, but rather the
issue of unlawful and disruptive campus protest. YAF chapters throughout
the nation battled the New Left on campus, seeking to stem the radical
tide while restoring some measure of order to campuses thoroughly politicized by the war and racial issues. The national board, which had done so
much in the past to coalesce YAF chapters around the issues of anticommunism and support for conservative politicians, waffled over the idea of
resisting the Left on campus; the board went so slow, in fact, that local
chapters were compelled to force its hand, in the process turning YAF into
the main organization of the antiradical resistance. Only then, and with
some success, did YAF move against disruptive—and increasingly violent—
left-wing activity.

Although young conservatives and left-wing radicals were in evidence
throughout the whole decade, the two largest student activist groups on
campus in the late 1960s, YAF and SDS, would have little conflict with

each other until 1968.[1] Only then, and with growing frequency thereafter, did the two poles come into contact.[2]

Through most of the decade, YAF members did not worry much about the threat to American society from the Left. Even during the much publicized Free Speech Movement at the University of California at Berkeley during the fall of 1964, YAF and student radicals did not confront each other. One YAF member at Berkeley, without support from the national office, played a disruptive role in the negotiations between the free speech participants and the university administration, but he also participated with great vigor in the so-called "filthy speech movement" that followed.[3] From the national office's perspective, and from the perspective of many conservatives, the Free Speech Movement was only peripherally concerned with free speech and overwhelmingly concerned with student power on campus.[4] By middecade, therefore, the conflict between left- and right-wing students, however ambiguous before that, was growing.

Other situations in which radicals and conservatives came into conflict had to do with Vietnam. David Franke, who became the *New Guard*'s editor after the Goldwater campaign, wrote disparagingly about the May 15, 1965, National Teach-In, concluding that it was "no convocation of open minds" and suggesting that "what the country needs is a good anti-Communist teach-in."[5] Franke also argued later that year, far earlier than would be feasible on campus, that "curbing the New Left is the business of organizations like YAF. The task is to isolate the New Left; to render it impotent."[6] It would be several years before this became the official policy of the organization, but Franke was recognizing a growing urgency to solve a problem at home that bore upon victory in Vietnam.

The situation was compounded by the growing radicalism in America during 1968. First, the student Left, partly in reaction to the assassinations of Martin Luther King and Robert Kennedy, was losing patience with the political process. The riots at the Chicago Democratic convention would be the last straw for groups who believed the system could be changed from within. The largest student radical group, SDS, was coming apart over the issue of violence and revolution, with certain factions splitting away to further their revolutionary goals. Other radical groups, including the Oakland-based Black Panther Party, drew public (and governmental) attention because of their confrontational style as well as their success at self-promotion within the radical Bay Area community.[7]

A second reason for conflict had to do with the failure of YAF's hopes throughout 1966 and 1967 to further the cause of victory in Vietnam. The

Tet Offensive of January 1968 had shown the weakness of the government's strategy in fighting the war. Even though Tet was a military victory for the Americans, it was a stunning political setback, coming as it did within weeks of Johnson's reassurances that the war was being won. When Johnson called for negotiations with North Vietnam and an end to the bombing, any hope of gaining victory seemed to vanish. If victory against Communism was not to be sought on the battlefield, perhaps it could be achieved at home by confronting (and hopefully marginalizing) the antiwar movement.

YAF's activities on behalf of anticommunist activity were having little impact, as shown by the failure of the Stop-IBM campaign. Few Americans were worried, it seemed, over this issue. IBM refused to back down, even after Soviet tanks crushed Czechoslovakian dissenters in Prague during the summer of 1968.[8] YAF changed its policy from confronting corporations to attempting to persuade high government officials and congressmen to stop trade with enemy nations. But such activity took time, and YAF moved away from serious anticommunist political activity in order to provide chapters with ample time and energy to combat the Left.

Finally and most importantly, the Left's antics provided the most direct reason for action. Growing radicalism on the campus, such as the siege of Columbia University and the University of Wisconsin's "Dow Days" riots during the spring of 1968, pointed to a need to resist student activism.[9] A breakdown in authority and the fear of revolution gripped the air as classes resumed in the fall of 1968; the campus was more politicized than ever before, and a hard-core active Left was making inroads among formerly apathetic students disenchanted about the war, the draft, and the growing oppressiveness of American society and government. For the next several years, YAF would turn to combat the Left on campus.

Throughout the spring of 1968, the board discussed YAF's purpose in relation to issues such as the New Left, racial turmoil, and Vietnam. The only consensus was to continue fighting for victory in Vietnam. A resolution adopted at the April meeting of the board stipulated that Johnson's negotiation strategy played into the hands of the enemy and represented "criminal negligence with respect to the American armed forces there." Other issues, such as race problems and even the New Left, could not be addressed by the board without disagreement. Jameson Campaigne argued against involving YAF too exclusively in direct resistance against the Left, that "YAF's responsibility was to beat the drums for well thought out ideas." Campaigne, always more interested in developing intellectually sound YAF members, won out (temporarily), with future activity confined first to "issues papers" before the organization would sponsor direct action against the Left.[10]

While the national board debated, local chapters acted. One of the more popular ways to confront the Left was to form coalitions with other anti-radical students. At Columbia University, graduate student John Meyer (Frank Meyer's son and a member of YAF) joined a coalition of anti-SDS students called Students for a Free Campus (SFC) who supported "open recruiting" by potential employers on campus, which SDS opposed because of the university's contracts with Defense Department research agencies. A campuswide vote taken on this issue showed that open recruiting was supported by 67 percent of Columbia undergraduates. SDS, ignoring the results of the student vote, still protested when Dow and other defense-affiliated corporations came to recruit on campus.[11]

Apart from supporting open recruitment, the SFC specifically resisted SDS's protests against the construction of a new gymnasium between Morningside Heights and Harlem. Radicals saw this as a racist move by the administration that would further isolate the university from the poor black neighborhoods of Harlem. On April 23, 1968, SDS called for a demonstration at Low Library, which Meyer and the SFC protested. When SDS, propelled by its radical leader Mark Rudd, decided to "liberate" Low Library, SFC intervened, blocking the path of radical students in "a long, tense, but nonviolent confrontation." SDS backed down and occupied Hamilton Hall (a classroom building), where they held a dean hostage. That evening the Student Afro-American Society (SAS), an organization supported by Harlem neighborhood activists, kicked Rudd and the others out of Hamilton Hall. SDS returned to Low Library, broke in, and successfully occupied the university's main administrative building for the next six days.[12]

The SFC organized a vigil outside Hamilton Hall and succeeded in getting the dean released on April 24. SFC demanded that the administration take action against the radicals, and anti-SDS students flocked to Hamilton and other occupied buildings to protest the university's inaction. The majority of these students were fraternity members and athletes at first, but after three days of inaction, other student groups fed up with radical antics showed up outside Hamilton.[13] In reaction to the swelling of their ranks, SFC leaders formed a "majority coalition" that attempted to persuade the administration to clear out the radicals. On April 28 the antiradical coalition blockaded Low Library, demanding that the university act to expel the students from the building. By dawn the coalition's strength had grown "with athletes now firmly in the minority" of the students present.[14] The following day, after SDS rejected a faculty committee's last plea to compromise, the police, who had intervened between Low Library and the antiradical blockade, attacked the building with the endorsement of Columbia's administration, forcing the radicals out of Low and Hamilton (with 148 injuries). The use of police against the students was unpopular, except with original supporters of the SFC, and within a year the Columbia administration, under continued pressure from the student body, had caved in to radical demands concerning the gymnasium and recruiting on campus.[15]

Although antiradical resistance ultimately failed during the Columbia siege, it did succeed in pressuring the Left just enough to force its hand. It also showed that if antiradical students organized with moderate students, they could effectively pressure the radical students to adjust their tactics. Accordingly, other YAF chapters applied the lessons of coalition-building to their respective campus situations. In May William Steel, who was a member of the national board and a student at the University of Southern California, formed the Free Campus Movement among interested groups in the Los Angeles area. The purpose of this organization was "to effectively coordinate students of the Right . . . to take preventive and direct action against Radical takeovers of various schools." With the recent Columbia University siege much on his mind, Steel recommended that in similar situations antiradical students should "surround the affected buildings, disrupt facilities Radicals us[e] (cut off electricity, cut off plumbing, prevent passage of food, by adding a 'powder ex-lax' in what food we allow)" as well as "provid[ing] leadership for counter demonstrations and rallies and demand[ing] immediate action from administration and trustees."[16] Representatives from several Los Angeles area colleges attended the founding meeting of the FCM and endorsed Steel's methods. Since a small minority of the membership of the Free Campus Movement consisted of fraternity members and athletes, Steel suggested it was up to those groups "to contact their "brothers" on the affected campus and induce them into direct action against the left.[17]

At Indiana University, R. Emmett Tyrrell, Jr., a graduate student in history, helped organize a conservative political party to take back the student senate from radical students. "Radicals at Indiana," Tyrrell argued, "controlled student government, they had conducted sit-ins, threatened strikes, and some even taught classes." But an organized student resistance had developed, and on April 3, 1968, "Indiana University became the first university to toss out the New Left." A student conservative party, Impact! which Tyrrell advised, defeated the leftist Progressive Reform Party and won all but one of the university senate seats and regained the office of student body president. Tyrrell concluded that Indiana owed its success to the fact that moderate students were finally compelled to act to resist the radicals. At Indiana, at least, Tyrrell concluded, "the New Left is burning itself out."[18]

If there was one person who represented YAF's shift to direct action against the Left, it was Tyrrell. He had been a Republican from birth, he claimed, but had come to his conservatism through his participation in intercollegiate athletics. A swimmer for the powerhouse Indiana University program, Tyrrell learned conservatism through competitive sports, where one developed the attitude of winning through hard work and training. The conservative movement, according to Tyrrell, did not possess these attributes. Conservative intellectuals, such as Russell Kirk, were fatalists— they expected, because they were conservatives, to lose. For Tyrrell, who was getting up every morning at five to work out in the pool, this attitude was misplaced, to say the least. He sought to change conservatism's fatalism by applying the lessons of winning through hard work that he had learned in the tank.[19]

Tyrrell was appalled by the New Left. In 1966, he recalled, he found Indiana University dominated by "an expanding crowd of bug-eyed messiahs heralding a New Age wherein war would be passé, workers would have vast stretches of leisure in which to compose poetry or sonatas midst the marijuana fumes . . . and sex would be for our time what religion had been for the Middle Ages and with the same promise of celestial mysteries."[20] Tyrrell's "discovery" of the New Left spurred his conservative activism. Along with other like-minded conservatives (many of whom were members of YAF), he founded *The Alternative: An American Spectator* in the spring of 1968.[21] Funded with support from the Lilly Foundation, The *Alternative* was truly a conservative *student* publication and always reflected the editor's Mencken-like wit and skepticism and his hostility toward the New Left.

Tyrrell had some success with The *Alternative,* gaining the endorsement of conservatives such as Buckley and liberals such as Sidney Hook and Irving Kristol who disliked student radicals. In one sense, Tyrrell's magazine represented the first shot fired in what would come to be called the "culture war" between the Left and the Right, because the main focus of the publication became the condemnation of the New Left and its activities; in another important way, however, by featuring disenchanted liberal scholars like Kristol and Hook, Tyrrell also appealed to a group of intellectuals and policymakers disgusted with liberalism's shift to entitlements and rights and away from personal responsibility.[22] Future neoconservative scholars were attracted by Tyrrell's fusillades against the "New Class"; in this sense, the *Alternative,* a publication edited and published by students, and itself the product of 1960s youth culture, would have profound ideological consequences for the conservative movement's rise to political power during the 1970s and 1980s.[23]

Another prominent YAF leader taken by the tactic of direct action was Ronald Docksai. A student at Saint John's University in New York, Docksai had been elected to YAF's national board in 1968 and was made vice chairman at the 1969 convention. Active in conservative causes since he manned a Goldwater table in Queens, New York, the energetic Docksai believed SDS's methods should be used against the Left. In August 1968 Docksai led twenty-one YAF members in a sit-in at the headquarters of the National Mobilization Committee to End the War in Vietnam (the Mobe) in New York City. Docksai demanded an "admission" from the Mobe's leaders "that their activity [at the recent Chicago Democratic convention] was wrong." After spending the night in the hallway of the office building, the YAF members left the following morning.[24]

In November 1968, building on their previous effort, the Greater New York YAF council "liberated" an SDS office in Greenwich Village. Docksai, James Farley (who was YAF state chairman in New York), and others entered the office and told the secretary that "YAF is hereby liberating this office." John Meyer and seven other YAF members joined them as they called the media and reported the takeover. "By 11:10 A.M., four TV crews, six radio correspondents, and other assembled press reached the location." After a complaint was filed by the building's owner, YAF members vacated the premises. Farley gave a statement "to the effect that YAF is opposed to SDS" and that they "took command of the office as a peaceful protest." TV and radio covered the takeover, but newspaper coverage was sparse.[25]

The Massachusetts YAF pulled off a similar stunt a week later. Led by Don Feder, now a newspaper columnist, twenty-two YAF members occupied the headquarters of the Resistance, an antiwar group in Boston. Inside, eight members of the Resistance "reacted violently to the liberation. One member called the Black Panthers . . . constantly harassed the press . . . [and] in a final rage, [Resistance members] stomped on the California grapes brought by YAF as a snack."[26] In a press release, Feder announced that "because we respect property rights as fundamental in a democracy, no attempt will be made to hold this building for an extended period of time. . . . We want to make it clear to the left that though we abhor its tactics of abrogating the rights of others to make a point, we, too, could do the same thing." After hanging a South Vietnamese flag on the wall and distributing pamphlets exposing North Vietnamese atrocities, YAF members left the office. In contrast to the New York "liberation," there was extensive coverage in the Boston press.[27]

In October the Purdue University YAF confronted an SDS sit-in that challenged the right of Purdue students to interview with the CIA and other recruiters on campus. A rally organized by YAF was held the night before the vote by the trustees on recruitment policy was to be taken, with over four hundred students in attendance. David Keene and Jerry Norton (YAF's director of college operations) flew in to speak to the crowd, as did board member and Hoosier native Dan Manion (son of Clarence Manion). The Purdue administration subsequently voted to support open recruitment.[28]

Some of the most productive, as well as disruptive, YAF action was undertaken by chapters in California. California campuses were a cauldron of radical and racial ferment during the late 1960s, in part because of the hard-line antiradical position taken by Governor Ronald Reagan, but also because California was the place where countercultural elements such as the hippies and revolutionary groups such as the Black Panthers thrived. If the revolution was to come, it would probably start in the Golden State.

Young conservatives in California, by default, were on the frontlines of the campus wars. Radical activity was growing in the state, prompting Phillip Abbott Luce, a defector from the Maoist-oriented Progressive Labor Party (PLP), to describe the situation in the state as "crazy. . . . I doubt that any other state in the nation stands as close to total student anarchy as California."[29] The California YAF reacted to the radicalism by creating the "blue button" campaign. Antiradical students wore plain blue buttons on campus in order to symbolize their opposition to the Left and their affinity for academic freedom on campus.

First worn in the winter of 1969, the buttons signified support for embattled San Francisco State University president S. I. Hayakawa.[30] Hayakawa had resisted student efforts to establish a black studies department at San Francisco State. A prominent semanticist and longtime antiradical, Hayakawa spoke out against black radical students throughout the fall 1968 semester and was appointed interim president following the resignation of the chancellor in the wake of a black-sponsored student strike.[31] After ordering the school to remain in session during the strike, Hayakawa personally confronted leftist students speaking on campus, at one point climbing aboard a truck to dismantle microphone wires. This gutsy action led to further confrontation and a decline in classroom attendance to around 20 percent of the student body. Throughout the winter, San Francisco State was a battleground between the conservative Hayakawa administration (backed by University of California system chancellors and Governor Reagan) and leftist students. After 134 days the student strike finally ended with the administration eventually caving in to radical demands. A black studies department was instituted, as were requirements that "one-third" of entrants be "third-world students." In return, the administration gained an end to the strike and refused to drop charges against arrested protesters and faculty members.[32]

This divisive polarization of the campuses worried California YAF members, who continued to insist that the campus was being used as a political forum rather than a place for intellectual development. YAF chapters responded in different ways to growing radicalism on campus. The Berkeley chapter mimicked leftist "nonnegotiable" demands by insisting that a "college of conservative studies be established immediately" on UC campuses, that "right world students" get preferential seating on university committees, that one conservative faculty member (at least) be hired in every department, and that students get days off for the celebration of Buckley's, Goldwater's, and Nixon's birthdays.[33] At Long Beach State a YAF-dominated coalition led a successful counterprotest against an SDS–Black Student Union plan to shut down the university. "Armed only with blue armbands and determination," the YAF-led coalition defeated the Left's plan to shut down the Long Beach State campus.[34] Finally, at Stanford, a powerful YAF chapter headed by Harvey Hukari, Jr., a charismatic student leader, heckled an SDS march in January 1969, chanting "pigs off campus" and demonstrating with signs claiming "SDS is Revolting" and "If You like Hitler, You'll Love SDS." The march was turned back twice by the antiradical crowd's persistent demonstration.[35]

Other California YAF initiatives were bearing fruit as well. California YAF leadership possessed a strong libertarian intellectual influence and used it to their advantage. Patrick Dowd, a YAF leader from UC-Davis, became state chairman and helped organize a libertarian-dominated caucus within YAF. The leaders of the caucus were all from California and included Dana

Rohrabacher (currently a California congressman) and William Steel. Phillip Abbott Luce, who lived in California, was a frequent contributor to libertarian colloquia held on California campuses but felt that Cal-YAF should not divide into factions and that Dowd and others within the state should work together with more traditionalist elements in order to combat the Left.[36]

California YAF had powerful political and financial backers as well. Governor Reagan endorsed many of YAF's initiatives against campus radicals, as did Senator George Murphy. Actors Chuck Connors and John Wayne were also on Cal-YAF's board of directors. Sometimes this influence was beneficial. A California state legislative subcommittee hearing on campus disorders called state chairman Patrick Dowd to testify on the campus situation. The libertarian Dowd, with recent events at San Francisco State much on his mind, told the committee,

> Radical students have *some* legitimate grievances [concerning black studies departments and the hiring of black faculty] . . . and we wholeheartedly support any legal, peaceful methods . . . to achieve these and other ends. However, we are unalterably opposed to any tactics which abrogate the rights of other students on campus—such as blocking their access to classrooms, physically assaulting them, or trying to halt the educational process by closing down the college.

Dowd recommended that the legislature establish some sort of hearing board for the campuses and recommended that more "open communication" between students, faculties, and administrators be achieved.[37] After San Francisco State, however, as Dowd probably realized, any effort at accommodation between students and college administrations would be unlikely.

In other areas of the country also, YAF chapters resisted radical activism. The Pennsylvania State University YAF chapter sent a telegram to that school's administration demanding that order be maintained on campus in the wake of recent disruptions. The Student Committee for a Responsible University, a YAF-dominated coalition, argued in the telegram: "By accepting our tuition, this university has entered into a contract with us. . . . If the actions of a belligerent minority deny us our rights by disrupting classes, we will bring suit if necessary to have the university live up to its contractual obligations."[38] The idea of lawsuits spread quickly. Activists from Monmouth College in New Jersey filed a suit against their administration. The national board planned to initiate a legal offensive at its 1969 summer meeting, putting more than "100 legal action kits in the hands of attorneys in cities where campus disorders are expected."[39] Though lawsuits showed YAF's resolve in the face of campus disruption, they were unexciting to students who may have joined antiradical coalitions solely for the thrill of confronting student radicals.

Even with the success local YAF chapters were having, board member Jameson Campaigne resisted YAF's drift into direct action throughout 1968 and 1969. Although not averse to such strategies per se, Campaigne believed that an inadequate understanding of conservative principles on the part of direct-action shock troops would vitiate the effectiveness of such action. Most of the individuals turned on by such action were more likely to be opportunists jumping on YAF's anti–New Left bandwagon, not principled conservatives.[40] Campaigne worked to develop the organization's intellectual muscle in combating the Left. He presented an elaborate plan to the national board arguing that "the young left is mindless; there is a danger that the young right drifts in that direction." He believed that a "pro-active oriented conservatism" was necessary, but he thought the Right was in danger of losing its direction. The danger stemmed partly from the fact that those who joined the conservative cause during and after the Goldwater campaign were not well grounded in conservative ideas. What he recommended was that YAF must "spell out why we should be vested with the reins of society, as *the* alternative to the liberal disaster." To accomplish this, he proposed increasing "the intellectual capabilities of our own membership and attracting new membership that has these capabilities."[41] Through article services and rentals of audio tapes and filmstrips, Campaigne believed new YAF members could receive enough basic education in conservative principles to prepare them to beat back leftist influence on campus.

Throughout the autumn of 1968 the national board developed and debated the tactics that YAF chapters should utilize against the Left. The board understood that "our most successful chapters are active and get violently attacked by the Leftists and liberals on campus. YAF chapters need to take an active and controversial role on campus."[42]

Early the next year, the board put forth a policy that combined some of Campaigne's ideas with the direct-action tactics already in use. The Young America's Freedom Offensive was designed to effectuate broad programs for YAF chapters, including the endorsement of direct action, coalition-building with moderate groups, resistance to Communism, high school programming, and education in conservative principles.[43] The most controversial element of the campaign was the effort to build coalitions. On campuses such as Columbia and Berkeley, where there was a well-organized and powerful left-wing presence, the national board believed that YAF chapters should work with other anti-radical groups such as the Associated Student Governments of the United States (ASG) to combat radical influence.

ASG was founded in 1968 as a student organization designed to build a working majority of conservative and moderate students "who are concerned about the present problems on university campuses."[44] YAF actively supported the formation of ASG, as did Tom Huston, who joined the Nixon administration as an aide to the president. Huston often suggested to H. R. Haldeman, the president's chief of staff, that Nixon take a more active role in developing an antiradical student organization on campus that the administration could point to as effectively combating the Left.[45] The president considered YAF inadequate for the task, stating at one point that "they are about as nutty as the militants."[46]

The main problem with ASG and coalition-building in general was that YAF's influence was buried. James Farley recommended that majority coalitions be dropped from the freedom offensive. "YAF members working in such a situation do most of the actual work, organizing and financing and end up with none of the credit." Farley also argued that YAF chapters were not getting credit for "spearheading the anti-SDS drive." If they did, moderate students, rather than seeing YAF as some sort of "bogey man will find that it's not so bad after all, since in most cases it will be the only campus group actively expressing the anti-SDS sentiment."[47] Ignoring Farley's criticisms, YAF continued to form majority coalitions on campus. Farley even formed one in New York that was quite active in encouraging protests against the Left.[48] Individual students who were anti-radical continued to flock to these coalitions, not understanding, perhaps, the role YAF chapters played in their creation. In the short run, YAF membership increased dramatically throughout 1969 and 1970, but after radical activity died down following the Kent State shootings, many of these "joiners" did not remain in the conservative cause.[49]

Nevertheless, by the autumn of 1969, YAF chapters were thoroughly engaged against the Left. The national board had finally come around to sanctioning antiradical direct action, and majority coalitions were flourishing on campus. The election at the 1969 Saint Louis convention of a traditionalist, strongly anti-Communist national board further influenced YAF's position by the end of the year. With antiwar groups prepared to make one last herculean effort to end the war through antiwar marches planned for October and November, YAF chapters began to plan an active campaign to counter the Left.

The Left's antiwar efforts reached a peak when the National Mobilization to End the War in Vietnam sponsored Washington rallies for October 15 and November 15, 1969. An estimated six hundred thousand people marched in Washington in November to protest the war. Young conservatives could never hope to duplicate the sheer numbers of people angered enough to protest against the war, but Ron Dear, who had recently been appointed to head regional and state activities for YAF, began to plan an alternative weekend designed "to tell Hanoi that they have misjudged America's youth." Dear and his staff prepared YAF's retort to the Mobe's protests for the weekend of December 13, 1969, calling their effort "Tell It to Hanoi."[50]

The model for Dear's campaign was a giant rally to counter the planned November 15 Mobe rally. It was held on Veteran's Day at the Washington Monument and coordinated by former YAF member Lee Edwards. A part of what comedian Bob Hope had organized as "National Unity Week," the Veteran's Day march was sponsored by the American Legion and Veterans of Foreign Wars and featured a mixed crowd of "liberals and conservatives, Republicans and Democrats, a Boy Scout for the Pledge of Allegiance, and a beautiful young black girl for the Star Spangled Banner." A crowd Edwards estimated at 25,000–30,000 turned out to "support our fighting men in Vietnam." Miniature American flags were handed out to the throng and were waved on a signal from Edwards—this was pictured on the cover of *Time* magazine the following week.[51]

Dear organized YAF's series of nationwide rallies the same way. Leaving the technicalities to the local and state chapters, Dear and his staff prepared over one million copies of a "tabloid" for distribution at the rallies documenting the crimes of Hanoi and New Left acquiescence in them by their support of the Communists. On more than six hundred campuses, students heard speakers denouncing Communism and North Vietnam. The purpose of the rallies, as Ron Docksai announced, was to show that "we, as young Americans who are beyond ideological puberty will not continue to allow the good name of peace to be monopolized by . . . isolationist students." More than sixty student body presidents signed YAF's petition to "tell it to Hanoi."[52] Turnout was impressive; the Massachusetts YAF drew over twenty-five hundred people to its Boston Commons rally, which received prominent coverage from the Boston area press.[53] Teach-ins were also sponsored by the organization that weekend, and "hundreds of thousands of signatures" on petitions were sent to the North Vietnamese delegation at the Paris peace talks.[54]

YAF's "alternative weekend," despite the fact that the organization could not claim the large turnout of antiwar protests, was successful in pointing out that young people were divided on the issue of support for the war. Not all college students were against the war, and there were tens of thousands who agreed that North Vietnam should be resisted and American troops supported.[55] Furthermore, although the October and November moratoriums were peaceful, New Left and countercultural violence throughout the fall was quickly turning public opinion against the protesters. The antics of the Weathermen in the October Days of Rage, the shocking murders of film star Sharon Tate and four others by young cult members following the "bug eyed messiah" Charles Manson, and the murder of a rock festival attendee at the hands of the Hell's Angels motorcycle group in Altamont, California (hired as "security" by the Rolling Stones) showed too clearly that many young people had lost their moorings and that law and order were needed to return the nation to the straight and narrow. YAF, building on its successes from the previous year in countering the Left, would thrive (ironically) in the radicalized atmosphere of the early 1970s.

Throughout 1970 YAF continued to combat the Left. The freedom offensive was redesigned to support a more active organizational push against radicalism on campus. Legal action remained the fulcrum of the offensive, but YAF expanded its activities on campus to include a "boycott of paying student funds until [college] administrations balanced speaking programs, the protection of private property from attacks by radicals, the protection of recruiters on campus, instruction in free market economics, and the support of conservative candidates for student government positions."[56] The freedom offensive continued to emphasize action against radicals by local YAF chapters, but more frequently the national board was dictating what type of action YAF chapters should take. After 1970 there were fewer and fewer campus protests and fewer YAF actions taken against the Left. Even in the wake of events like Nixon's invasion of Cambodia and the Kent State shootings in May, YAF's response to heightened campus protest was mild.[57]

The organization did take some action after the shootings. The national board finally sanctioned a full court press in its legal offensive against university administrations unwilling to rein in protest on campus. At Adelphi University in New York, the YAF chapter filed a court injunction to reopen the school after it closed because of protests; at Wayne State University in Detroit, a restraining order was sought against the university's president in order to reopen the doors for classes. In June, Ohio State YAF members won a court injunction against radicals who had closed down the university. At the University of Wisconsin, Richard Wright, a YAF alumnus, filed a federal lawsuit "accusing the school administration of denying students the right to pursue an education." Randall Teague also sued George Washington University requesting reimbursement for tuition expended by students for canceled classes.[58]

In most cases the lawsuits were successful in pressuring administrations (at least) to keep school doors open. A pamphlet drawn up by the national board to support the legal offensive stated YAF's position clearly:

> We urge campus administrators to take disciplinary action against students who violate the rights of others by disrupting classes or meetings, or by preventing access to campus buildings. . . . We favor free and unrestricted picketing and demonstrations . . . but only so long as the freedom of other students is not suppressed. . . . We reject the trend toward requiring the university to respond *as an institution* to political and social problems. We do not agree that the classroom is a proper place for such politicization.

Finally, the board argued that "it was improper to cancel classes [unless] it is in recognition of a near unanimity of opinion." This did not exist in the wake of recent protests and disruptions on campus.[59]

YAF's arguments were compelling and offered a contrary opinion to the growing tendency of universities to be arms of radical and social change. It was eminently clear that some of the young people in YAF understood as conservatives that universities were not social laboratories but rather places for thought and quiet study: "a place for academic leisure and reflection, not for action," in the words of YAF advisor Russell Kirk.[60] But students, bored by an educational establishment that did not educate, were prompted by intelligent but "emotionally immature" ideologues to strike back at the culture that they abhorred, according to Kirk.[61] Thus, the politicization of university life.

Shocked by growing campus violence, Nixon ordered Pennsylvania governor William Scranton to head a commission to "study dissent, disorder, and violence on the campuses." David Keene, YAF's national chairman, testified before the commission, giving his account of radicalism at his campus, the University of Wisconsin. Keene reiterated how protests had developed "not overnight" but over the course of his by then seven-year tenure on campus, because of the indifference shown radicals by an administration led by historian Fred Harvey Harrington. In 1969 things were so bad at Madison that "the underground newspaper, *Kaleidoscope,* urged students to 'take up the gun' and advised them specifically to use 12-gauge shotguns because they give the user the opportunity to 'kill several at one blow if done at close range.' "[62] Keene also lucidly discussed the threat to academic freedom such threats of violence engendered.

Keene was no stranger to New Left fanaticism. A law student who graduated in 1970, he was in Madison when radicals blew up the Army Math Research Center on the night of August 24, 1970. Authorities hunted for a cabal of two students and two former students held responsible for the bombing. (Three were caught; one conspirator remains at large to this day.) Henry Fassnacht, a postdoctoral researcher and a father of three who was doing research in the building that night, was killed.[63] Two decades later, Keene said in a public television documentary that he had made a bet with a colleague that he could go down to the student union and find someone who would agree that Fassnacht deserved to die because he was in the building. Keene won the bet.[64]

The Scranton Commission's report on campus unrest was released to unfavorable reviews from conservatives and the Nixon Administration during the early fall of 1970. YAF countered its release with an exposé pointing to what the commission was supposed to do but failed to do. Project directors Dan Joy (former *New Guard* editor), Jay Parker (former YAF board member), and Randall Teague joined with Catholic University professor William Roberts in condemning the commission's analysis of the roots of university protest and its endorsement of some of the goals of such protest.[65] Nixon was angry that the commission's recommendations excused some of the radicalism on campus and suggested in a September 16 speech at Kansas State University that "violence and terror have no place in the free society, whoever the perpetrators are and whatever their purported cause."[66]

By the fall of 1970, with radical protests ebbing (SDS had collapsed by then) and Nixon's policy of Vietnamization taking effect, YAF distanced itself from further action against the Left. The organization was now ten years old, having celebrated a decade in existence by returning to Sharon in September 1970, and was becoming much more professional in its dealings with conservative movement luminaries and politicians. YAF had survived—indeed, thrived—amid the tumults of late-1960s protest, an important consideration given the demise of SDS and other radical organizations. Membership was at an all-time high, the financial situation seemed bright, and YAF's leaders were well poised to exert further conservative influence as the new decade began. All of the above, plus the end-of-the-decade public disgust with the Left, poised YAF for a grand future. But YAF entered the 1970s with many weaknesses masked by the more public disruptions occurring on the Left. Philosophical differences between traditionalist conservatives and increasingly radical libertarians almost destroyed the organization at its 1969 Saint Louis convention. The libertarians were crushed, but increasing factionalism and crippling egotisms led to periodic crises on the national board, prompting intervention by elder conservatives and a growing bureaucratization and routine in YAF's affairs. For these reasons, even as the Left waned, YAF could not effectively seize the opportunities for power and leadership on campus brought about by radicalism's demise. The inability to build on such success crippled any chance to make the organization a genuine campus force. YAF would survive as an independent organization, but its influence would increasingly be buried in the machinations and permutations of the wider conservative movement.

7

Trads and Libs

Schism on the Right, 1968–1970

Right-wing libertarians were committed to the rhetoric of *laissez-faire* capitalism, free trade and open markets. . . . they spoke of "Freedom to the Individual" rather than "Power to the People."

—Jerome Tuccille

If the fusionist [conservative] said that freedom was necessary to aspire to a good society and that free people should choose that, the libertarian would say it doesn't matter if they choose it, and the traditionalist would say they damn well better or else.

—David Keene

Vietnam should remind all conservatives that whenever you put your faith in big government for *any* reason, sooner or later you wind up as an apologist for mass murder.

—Karl Hess

In 1969 the conservative movement was jolted by newspaper headlines that revealed that Karl Hess, a speechwriter and former aide to Barry Goldwater, had joined forces with the New Left. Hess disclosed that he was an anarchist and claimed he was "opposed to state authority at every level and in every area. . . . I take my stand with the anti-authoritarians and so does the New Left."[1] Hess, who had been an editor at *Newsweek* for five years and at *National Review* a short time, had grown increasingly critical of the conservative movement's defense of state power in the war against Communism in Vietnam. He told William F. Buckley that "you would not like me now at all, not a patriot, not a believer, no longer even deeply concerned about the difference between *their* imperialism and ours, just concerned that somehow we get on with the business of letting this be a fit and liveable world for people whose enemy is the state."[2]

Hess's decision was not made capriciously. Since the early 1960s, Frank Meyer's concept of fusionism was the preoccupation of an intellectual majority on the right, serving as a philosophical "vital center" for the conservative movement. Meyer and William F. Buckley believed that if the two poles of conservative thought—traditionalism and libertarianism—could be brought together in order to support the war against Communism, the conservative movement could develop into more than just an intellectual salon and would be able to gain political strength. Until the time came when Communism was defeated, support for the state, which both libertarians and a growing number of traditionalists considered an anathema, was justified.[3]

Meyer's philosophy was widely shared by mainstream conservative organizations throughout the 1960s and was much in evidence in Goldwater's speeches and platform during the 1964 campaign. YAF's national board, for instance, fully supported the fusionism of the *National Review* crowd and had imbibed much of Meyer's fusionist influence in the drafting of the Sharon Statement.[4] Yet a minority on the right, and within YAF, rejected Meyer's efforts at consolidation; by the late 1960s, both because of the Vietnam war and because of the decline of traditional values in the face of rising discontent and social protest, radical voices on the right began to decry the conservative movement's fusionist *cri de coeur* and offered their own prescription for a new conservatism.

Challenges to the conservative mainstream had been quite normal throughout the 1960s. Buckley and other conservatives had battled with the John Birch Society, finally expelling its leader, Robert Welch, from the conservative movement. They also successfully marginalized the influence of anti-Semitic and racist influences within the movement.[5] For YAF and the conservative movement in general, the late 1960s presented new challenges. Not only were problems on the left enough to cause concern, but there were also internal factions on the right that would challenge the delicate fusionist balance that had facilitated the growth of the conservative movement during the previous ten years.

Within YAF, these groups included pro–George Wallace segregationists; Catholic ultratraditionalists who supported L. Brent Bozell's journal *Triumph;* and alleged racist and anti-Semitic cliques like the "rat finks," a small sect of the Young Republicans in New Jersey with links to YAF chapters in the Garden State. None of these groups ever achieved much influence within YAF.[6] Indeed, the organization may have shown its immunity to such extremism when the first issue of *Rough Beast,* a conservative Catholic journal whose cover featured a picture of an aborted fetus at the bottom of a garbage can, was sent to state YAF chapters; two chapters returned used prophylactics, rather than money, through the mail to the editors of the journal.[7]

These antics aside, the problems of keeping YAF a fusionist and pro-*National Review* young conservative group were becoming apparent by the late 1960s. Aside from threats from the right flank, radical libertarian influence was growing within the conservative movement and affecting the thinking of many younger people who were just discovering conservative thought. Although libertarianism had always been a healthy dynamic on the right, radical libertarianism had the potential of disrupting YAF. This dogma insisted that the state, in all its functions, including defense, was the main enemy of freedom. In Vietnam, according to radical libertarians, Americans were waging an evil war against the Vietnamese people, largely enriching the state and its benefactors. American conservatives, with their aspirations for power and their determination to wage a global war against Communism, were as much to blame for the ongoing war as were the liberals who began the war.[8]

To Frank Meyer, who espoused a libertarian credo based on protecting individual freedom from the state, radical libertarianism was dangerous. In an article reprinted in the *New Guard,* Meyer argued that radical libertarianism "sharply repudiated the struggle against the major and most immediate contemporary enemy of freedom, Soviet Communism—and does so on grounds, purportedly, of a love for freedom." These radicals, whom Meyer did not name but who would include pacifists like Murray Rothbard, "attack the militantly anti-Communist position of the leadership of American conservatism because it is prepared to use the power of the American state in one of its legitimate functions, to defend freedom against communist totalitarianism."[9]

Radical libertarianism grew in influence out of the anger and protest surrounding the Vietnam War. Although the great majority of YAF members never accepted this philosophy, a growing number of YAF recruits found the arguments of Karl Hess and Murray Rothbard illuminating. Once a dedicated conservative anticommunist, Hess had come to believe the increasing power of the American state was a greater threat to individual liberties than the spread of Communism.[10] Rothbard, a brilliant economist, had been a lifelong pacifist and traced his ideological libertarianism to the

1930s Old Right. He was consistently a defender, then and to his death, of pacifism, laissez-faire capitalism, maximum freedom to the individual, and non-intervention in the affairs of other nations.[11] In the schemata of the post–World War II anticommunist Right, this philosophical creed placed Rothbard in a right-wing minority who had more in common with the pro–civil libertarian Left, it appeared, than with their brothers on the Right.

What bothered some libertarian-leaning rightists, such as New York YAF member Jerome Tuccille, was not Hess's philosophy but rather his defection to and embrace of the New Left. Tuccille, who eventually became a member of the radical libertarian faction of YAF, believed that if one wished to be a true libertarian, it would be impossible to take refuge in the increasingly faction-ridden, Marxist, and paranoid politics of the New Left. In an April 1969 *New Guard* article, Tuccille attacked Hess and exposed the fallacies behind his defection to the Left, pointing out that New Left heroes were Mao Tse-tung, Che Guevara, and Fidel Castro: "Philosophically and emotionally, they are anti-individual, anti-capitalist, anti-libertarian, and ultimately, anti-freedom."[12] Hess defended his decision to join the New Left by calling the New Left the "last bastion of anti-statist individualism" left in the country.[13] Perhaps they were, in Hess's mind, but in the face of growing factionalism (often inspired by Marxist influences), collectivism, and violence on the Left, it was a fantastic statement to make concerning the late-1960s New Left's concept of freedom.

Although Hess's defection represented a blow to the movement, conservatives scored a coup themselves when Phillip Abbott Luce, who had left the Maoist-oriented Progressive Labor Party (PLP) in 1965 and become an informer for HUAC against PLP, joined YAF.[14] From 1968 to 1970, he wrote a regular column in the *New Guard* entitled "Against the Wall," and in 1969 he was appointed YAF's full-time director of college operations, a position he relinquished after six months. Luce had been a prominent leader in the PLP, had edited its magazine, and had gone to Cuba in 1963 as part of a contingent of radical American students. In an interview Luce explained that he "defected not because I was reconciled to the injustices of American society as I saw them, but because I realized that communism would bring infinitely worse injustices."[15] Luce regularly used his column to prod YAF members to take action against the Left on campus: "Let's stop sitting back and acting as if the Left is some-kind-of-pariah. . . . The best YAF chapters in the country are those willing to stand up to the Left and say, 'the hell with you and your concept of political terror.' "[16]

Luce was extremely active in coordinating YAF campaigns against the

Left. Luce observed, as a resident of California, the tremendous growth in YAF chapters in that state, primarily as a result of the growing radicalism on campuses there. Yet underneath the surface, the California YAF was divided. An internecine factionalism, based on personality and philosophical differences, threatened to destroy the gains Cal-YAF had made against the Left in the state. Luce penned a fiery missive denouncing the leadership in the state for engaging in "the politics of the playground. We stand very close to losing our influence on the campus because we have begun to function as a factionalized bunch of children more interested in ego involvements than in the necessity to 'act' as one in the political arena."[17]

The key disputes in the leadership of Cal-YAF revolved around personal and philosophical divisions between traditionalists such as Allen Brandstadter, who was the state's executive director, and a growing libertarian faction led by state chairman Patrick Dowd, Harvey Hukari, Jr., William Steel, and Dana Rohrabacher. For some time the two factions had been able to cooperate effectively on basic issues regarding the draft, the Vietnam War, and resistance to leftist activity on campus. But the more philosophically attuned libertarians were being exposed to radical libertarian views in a recently established journal put out by Murray Rothbard and Karl Hess, entitled *The Libertarian*.[18] The founding of a radical libertarian journal, in combination with a perception on the part of libertarians that they were underrepresented on the YAF national board, led them to form a libertarian caucus within YAF during the spring of 1969.

The libertarians' perception of their weakness may have stemmed from a YAF debate held at Saint John's University in New York in April 1969. Frank Meyer, Tuccille, Hess, and Henry Paolucci (a conservative professor at Saint John's) discussed Hess's defection. Tuccille, the sole source for the debate, described the event as a "three-to-one gang up on Hess." Meyer spoke first, reiterating his fusionist arguments concerning the necessity of supporting the state in the war against Communism. Hess, dressed in work pants and beads, clothes that reflected his recent switch to the Left, argued that it was "inconsistent to preach individual liberty and local government out of one side of the mouth while calling for a vast, centralized military complex through the other." Tuccille offered what he called a "dual message of qualified anticommunism and radical opposition to the corporate state." He certainly did not intend to offend the crowd, but the reaction from the traditionalist crowd was entirely negative, with only Hess's supporters applauding Tuccille's remarks. When Paolucci, the last to speak, offered his indictment of anarchism, he attacked both Hess and

Tuccille, much to the delight of the assembled YAF members: "For a solid three minutes . . . the YAFers rose and demonstrated their appreciation" for Paolucci's argument.[19] Tuccille became an active radical that day, he subsequently claimed, turned off by the "obnoxious" and obsessive traditionalism of the intensely anticommunist YAF crowd.

This one debate was certainly not enough to galvanize a radical libertarian movement within YAF, but the libertarian caucus grew throughout the spring, drawing elements from various YAF chapters around the country. Dowd and Steel were members from California, and Don Ernsberger of Penn State YAF joined as well. In a June memo the libertarian caucus claimed seventy-two members nationwide (this in an organization of over forty thousand members) and made five demands on the board:

> that there be more libertarian members on the national board; that libertarian
> stands on economic, political and moral issues be taken; that there be amend-
> ments to basic programs and committees inconsistent with freedom; that
> there be basic changes in the Sharon Statement to go along with libertarian
> precepts; and that all members of the national board should be elected by the
> total membership, not delegates.[20]

The caucus was organized with the intention of battling traditionalist domination at the upcoming YAF convention in August. There, it was hoped, the libertarian caucus could take over YAF and turn it into "a radical, pro-freedom laissez-faire capitalist movement." The libertarians misperceived their strength, however, when they argued that "the idealism of the New Left is a monument to the failure of the new right to develop after the Goldwater campaign into THE MOVEMENT."[21] Any conservatives they hoped to "turn on" to radical libertarianism would reject that argument outright.

Throughout the summer, libertarians made their demands on YAF's national leadership. In a letter to Jay Parker, the only black member of YAF's national board (and a traditionalist), the radicals somewhat exaggerated their power among YAF members. Claiming again that they were "frozen out" of the national board, the libertarians offered the board one last chance to compromise before the national convention: share power with a competing faction or face a possible split.[22] The notion that radical libertarians had enough loyal adherents to suggest such a share of power was preposterous.

Individual members of the board were at a loss to explain the paranoia affecting the libertarian caucus. Don Feder, head of Massachusetts YAF, claimed that "two things became increasingly apparent" after reading the libertarian demands: "If you take control of YAF there will be no place in it for traditionalists or non-objectivist libertarians [fusionists]; secondly, you seem bent on a course of rule or ruin." Feder argued that the Massachusetts delegation was not antilibertarian but rather, as good conservatives, would vote for individuals "on their merits" rather than for a slate of candidates.[23]

Luce also replied to the caucus's charges. He had recently been appointed as YAF's full-time director of college operations, and as a libertarian he questioned the view that few members of the board were of that persuasion. Randall Teague, who had taken over the duties of executive director the previous spring, had appointed libertarians like Luce to prominent positions in YAF. Luce also denied the other claim that a purge "of forty individuals" was planned at the national convention. He assured the caucus that "no such plan existed." The problem, as Luce saw it, was that the "actions of the 'freeks' [*sic*] is driving a wedge between rational libertarians and the rest of the movement." The writings of Hess and Rothbard and their denunciation of YAF as "fascists" played into the hands of YAF's enemies on the Left.[24]

The rhetoric of the radical libertarians heated up as the YAF convention neared. The Radical Libertarian Alliance (RLA), a group formed during the summer by Rothbard and Hess to unite left- and right-wing libertarians, planned to infiltrate YAF's convention in August and "slice off the left-wing" of the organization.[25] In an attack on YAF in the RLA's August 15 *Libertarian Forum,* Murray Rothbard told libertarians to "leave the house of your false friends behind." He denounced the leaders of contemporary conservatism as a "gaggle of ex-communists and monarchists." He asked: "What has YAF, in its action programs, ever done on behalf of the free market? Its only action related to the free market was to call for embargoes of Polish hams." YAF supported the expansion of state power, particularly its war powers; it supported Mayor Daley's cops in beating demonstrators on the streets of Chicago; and it supported the continuation of the draft. (The latter two accusations were false). Rothbard concluded: "Why don't you leave now, and let the 'F' in YAF stand then for what it has secretly stood for all along—fascism."[26]

In a manifesto called the Tranquil Statement, drafted that same week, some radicals went even further. Karl Hess IV (Hess's son), a leader of a separate anarchist caucus, argued that YAF should "support the student's right to revolution" rather than oppose it; that the United States "represented the greatest threat to the freedom and peace of all men"—a distinctively New Left revisionist view of American power; that YAF should "take the initiative in the fight against American imperialism" and reaffirm the principle of universal freedom; and that YAF should "reemphasize its commitment to liberty" by restructuring the organization and junking the Sharon Statement.[27] According to the young Hess, YAF had become too bureaucratic and too defensive of state interests to fight for the cause of freedom. Although the Tranquil Statement is significant in the sense that it offered a real alternative for debate at the upcoming convention, it was far too radical to be taken seriously by the majority of delegates in Saint Louis. Nothing in the statement was considered in resolutions put forth that week.

Partly in reaction to some of the tumult on the organization's right flank, the national office took steps to solve some major organizational problems. A week before the convention, Patrick Dowd (a libertarian) was removed from his position as state chairman of California YAF, and Allen Brandstadter (a traditionalist) was also removed from his post as the state's executive director. There had been accusations of favoritism made against both leaders, and Randall Teague and Alan MacKay believed that removing them served the best interests of the organization.[28] Teague also promised that the new national chairman would go to California to investigate the situation there and get Cal-YAF back on its feet. No provisions were made as to who would replace the purged leadership of the state.

This action, taken before the convention began, set the stage for a rather tumultuous weekend in Saint Louis. In many ways the 1969 convention appeared, on the surface, to be no different from previous YAF conventions. Speakers included Buckley, Rusher, Frank Meyer, Phyllis Schlafly, and Luce—a rather mainstream anticommunist group; discussion panels included such issues as effective organizing against the Left on campus and how to build new YAF chapters. Over twelve hundred delegates were present and would vote on slates of candidates running for national chairman and national board seats. David Keene, who had been Alan MacKay's vice chairman, was the odds-on favorite to win election as chairman, having support from both traditionalist and libertarian factions; traditionalist conservatives wanted to make sure they held onto the majority of positions on the board.[29] In essence, the convention exemplified YAF's growing success as an organization over the previous four years. Little in the way of fireworks was expected, even with the presence of disaffected elements from the libertarian caucus and other groups.

On the convention's opening day, August 28, however, a rumor swept the crowd that Karl Hess (not a scheduled speaker) would appear and wished to speak before the convention. After some debate, his offer was turned down. An offer by Hess to debate Buckley at the Gateway Arch after the opening night ceremonies was rejected, with Buckley claiming he needed to get back to New York.[30] Tuccille, who remains the best source for the tumult of Saint Louis, also argued that radical-libertarians were denied credentials by those in charge of the convention, preventing them from organizing enough numbers on the floor to push their viewpoints.[31]

The opening address by William F. Buckley was booed by radical libertarians. Buckley, reacting to the crowd's surliness, denounced critics like Rothbard and Hess as "cankerous muse[s]." He told the gathered audience, amid catcalls, that "the historical responsibility of the conservatives is altogether clear: it is to defend what is best in America. At all costs." The radical libertarian alternative was a denial of freedom.[32]

Some libertarians at the convention waved banners and unfurled black flags, calling for an end to the war, chanted slogans calling for an end to the draft ("Fuck the Draft"), "power to the people," and "no more Vietnams." In the end they were unable to drown out the more numerous traditionalist conservatives; despite their vocal denunciations of Buckley and the convention itself, they represented a minority of the delegates present.[33] The traditionalist factions were also better organized and better equipped for some of the convention infighting that took place.[34]

Despite their inferior organization, over three hundred libertarian YAF members went to meet Hess at the Gateway Arch that night, where they debated the formation of a Left-Right libertarian alliance well into the predawn hours. Two positions were decided upon: some conservative libertarians (as distinguished from radical libertarians) should remain within YAF and attempt to fight for libertarian views within the organization. This group, essentially the members of the preconvention libertarian caucus, believed more could be accomplished from inside the organization than from the outside. A second group, numbering no more than fifty people, decided to follow Rothbard and Hess into an alliance with New Left libertarians.[35]

After an uneventful second day, the convention met to vote on candidates to the national board. The libertarian minority was routed by the traditionalists, who retained control of the national chairmanship (Keene was supported by both sides) and the national board.[36] Regarding convention resolutions, the membership also took a traditionalist stance: they voted against the libertarian recommendation of immediate withdrawal from Vietnam, tabled the motion to legalize marijuana, and rejected the call for

active resistance to the military draft.[37] When this last motion failed, Tuccille recounted, the convention turned into bedlam. One YAF member,
Lee Houffman, burned his draft card on the convention floor, which set
off a melee between libertarians and traditionalists. Tuccille described YAF
members attacking Houffman and his radical allies, yelling "Kill the com-
mies." Fists flew and the radicals tried to protect Houffman from being
trampled by the mob. After a half hour of conflict, the two sides separated;
the national board later voted that the action of the card-burner was illegal
and against the best interests of YAF. Houffman was subsequently expelled
from the organization.[38]

The draft resolution, which caused so much consternation at the convention, had developed out of long debate on the issue within the national
office. David Franke had first endorsed withdrawing conservative support
for the draft—on libertarian grounds—in 1967. He gained the support of
a skeptical national board and put together a coalition of conservative
intellectuals, both libertarian and traditionalist, who were against the draft.
In the May 1967 New Guard, a symposium on the draft was organized that
featured essays by classical liberals such as Milton Friedman and traditionalists such as Russell Kirk. Friedman argued that the draft was an inefficient
use of resources and that military manpower "at the present level" could
be achieved under a voluntary system.[39] Russell Kirk argued that the concept of a "mass army" became obsolete in the trenches of World War I
and that the nation would be better served by an "elite, professional
force."[40] Numerous politicians joined in the call for an end to the draft,
including Goldwater, Donald Rumsfeld, and Mark Hatfield. Others on the
Left agreed with Franke's call for ending the draft, including libertarians at
the University of Chicago and members of the Students for a Democratic
Society.[41] Far from reflecting a prodraft stance, YAF for two years had been
fighting to eliminate the draft and install a voluntary military system. This
reflected the fact that defensible libertarian arguments, rather than being
rejected by members of the board, were supported by most.[42]

Nevertheless, moderates in the libertarian caucus were now radicalized,
Tuccille claimed, by the fracas on the convention floor; they recommended
splitting from YAF. In the hotel rooms that night frequent disputes occurred over ideological differences, with some traditionalists verbally taunt-
ing the libertarians by calling them "lazy fairies."[43] More than three hundred radicals left the organization and formed the Society for Individual
Liberty (SIL).[44] Many ex-YAF members from Pennsylvania, California, and
New Jersey joined SIL and other libertarian groups in their states. By the

end of the summer, radical libertarians who remained in YAF were a negligible influence at best.

That influence diminished even further when the new national board met on August 31. The main topic of discussion was the California YAF situation. William Saracino was elected to fill a board vacancy that resulted after board member William Steel broke from YAF at the convention. Saracino had worked in the election campaigns of both Reagan and U.S. Senate candidate Max Rafferty, both of whom were traditionalist anticommunist conservatives. Patrick Dowd, the only other Californian on the board, voted against Saracino's nomination because he believed the appointment of "another traditionalist" to the board would further divide Cal-YAF. Keene and others disagreed, Keene declaring that he would "go to California to work out an equitable settlement of the volatile situation" there. Saracino was easily elected with only Dowd voting against his appointment.[45]

Libertarians, far from accepting their defeat, blasted the new national office as "authoritarian." William Steel published the "California Libertarian Report," which served as an informational report on the activities of YAF in the wake of the convention. It focused on the continuing "purges" of libertarians from the board; executive director Randall Teague was the target for charges of the "national office's heavy-handedness."[46] A postconvention anarchist report entitled "Young Authoritarians for Freedom" claimed that YAF's "fusionism" was nothing more than "social fascism." The report also stated that the successful repudiation of the draft, a resolution endorsed by the convention delegates, was a product of the anarchist caucus.[47] It was not. The anarchists insisted on draft resistance and not an end to the selective service system which the majority of YAF members voted for.

Was there anything to libertarian charges that YAF was now controlled by authoritarian elements hostile to individual freedom? As charges and countercharges continued throughout the fall, several of YAF's national board members attempted to reassure disgruntled libertarians that they were welcome in the organization. Ron Dear, YAF's new director of regional and state activities, answered the charges that YAF members had been "purged" for their philosophical beliefs. He defended the removal of Patrick Dowd as California state chairman on the basis of factionalism within chapters in the state. He also responded that the libertarian charge of "unequal representation" was altogether false. Phillip Luce was college director, Rod Manis and David Friedman had prominent roles in the organization, Arnie Steinberg had been the libertarian editor of the *New Guard* since 1967 (his replacement as editor in 1969 was Californian Ken Grubbs, also libertarian), and there were many libertarians (albeit not radicals) represented on YAF's board.[48] David Keene also spoke to the problem of this split in YAF. He considered himself both libertarian and traditionalist in the manner of Frank Meyer's original conception of fusionism. He had not thought that libertarians should be purged; only when they threatened the continued vitality of the organization should steps be taken to remove them, or anyone else, from YAF.[49]

Throughout the autumn the libertarian-traditionalist split was diminishing the organization's effectiveness on campus. Ronald Reagan, a member of both the national and California YAF advisory boards, worried that the state chapter had gone off the deep end;[50] Luce was concerned that YAF would miss opportunities to confront planned antiwar marches set for October and November;[51] and Ronald Dear worried that recent schisms would diminish YAF's activities on behalf of victory in Vietnam.[52] Continuing factionalism among national YAF leaders only encouraged such perceptions that the organization was headed for disaster.[53]

This perception deepened when Keene, after reviewing the California situation, decided to make Saracino the new state chairman.[54] After that action libertarians such as Harvey Hukari, a well-respected YAF leader at Stanford University, resigned from the organization. Former YAF leaders held a symbolic YAF membership card burning on Stanford's campus, which garnered much local press, and participants at the burning created a Free Campus Movement to replace YAF there.[55] The loss to YAF of leaders such as Hukari proved damaging for the short-term interests of the organization on campuses like Stanford.

Hukari's decision sowed division on California campuses. Although the situation in California had stabilized somewhat by the end of the year, Patrick Dowd claimed that ideological purges had caused Cal-YAF to lose "one-third [sixty-five] of its chapters."[56] The University of California at San Diego chapter had gone "completely objectivist." While Hukari's Free Campus Movement continued to battle the Left at Stanford, other state school chapters remained in YAF but "were pissed off about national YAF's actions."[57] A new organization, the California Libertarian Alliance, claimed more than twelve hundred members (presumably many were defectors from YAF) by the end of the year, and Don Ernsberger's SIL was gaining ground in California.[58] The widening factionalism in California demanded immediate attention, which those disgruntled factions believed Saracino incapable of supplying.

Why did Keene, then embroiled in his own campaign for the Wisconsin state Senate, not show greater earnestness in dealing with the California situation? Why had he broken his promise to check out the situation there firsthand? It appears that Keene's decision to appoint Saracino and risk a revolt from the Left may have been the result of pressure from older conservatives. Reagan's alarm at the state of Cal-YAF and his correspondence with Buckley over this issue may have prompted Keene's actions.[59] Though Keene believed that Saracino could handle the task of reuniting Cal-YAF, the libertarians considered Keene's move a breach of trust. In the short run, it may have been the best decision for the state chapter, but the long-term membership losses in the state and on crucial campuses like Stanford, which Keene believed to be only a temporary result of his decision, would be the price paid for support from the elder conservatives. YAF's relationship with and support from conservatives like Reagan, Buckley, Rusher, and Goldwater was more important, according to most on the board, than losing potential national leaders like Hukari.

Given the history of generational relations during the 1960s, the fact that older conservatives could intervene and effectuate change at the national level without unduly compromising the autonomy of YAF says much about the ability of young conservatives to work with their elders. Far from being an organization that rejected the values of anyone over thirty, YAF relied on the advice and guidance of older conservatives. This averted the factionalism that ruined so many other student organizations in the 1960s. It also showed that YAF would sacrifice short-term interests (power on campuses like Stanford) for longer-term goals such as the creation of conservative cadres for future political battles. By the end of the decade, YAF was increasingly an important and reliable part of the conservative movement's mainstream.

YAF handled the libertarian challenge with relative dispatch. The national board, firmly controlled by fusionists, had endorsed the purges of radicals. One longtime California member and an original Freedom Corps representative, was charged with conduct "detrimental to the interests of YAF" and ousted from the organization. A resolution banned anarchism from the organization as "inconsistent with the Sharon Statement." Dual membership in YAF and SDS, a possibility if one accepted radical libertarian doctrine, was also prohibited. Within a few months after the convention, the new board had become what the radicals had charged—an authoritarian board purging those members who disagreed with their "pronouncements."[60] Though YAF leaders would consistently deny the charge, radical libertarian influence had been crushed by the beginning of 1970.[61]

The libertarian-traditionalist split revealed dangerous undercurrents as YAF began its second decade. First, although it was important that YAF maintain unity on the national level in order to stimulate adequate action against the Left, the rigor with which some leaders pushed for this unity diminished other options that could have strengthened the movement. Randall Teague, whose self-described leadership style was "Machiavellian," argued after the split, "We have cut off a part of that which functions under the conservative umbrella. . . . What this could mean is that, as an organization, instead of widening our appeal, we are narrowing it."[62] The memo, which has an anguished tone to it, was right on target. By insisting on a single fusionist viewpoint, YAF considerably narrowed its political and policy options.

A second negative element was the lack of maturity, something quite common to youth movements. Compromise was lacking on the part of both radicals, who insisted they share power when their numbers did not dictate such an arrangement, and traditionalists, who reacted to radical influence by crushing it *in all cases*. Harvey Hukari, a sensible libertarian, was no anarchist like William Steel or the younger Karl Hess in his radical demands. Rather than deal effectively with reasonable differences, which improve the vitality of any membership organization, both sides struck intransigent poses, thereby widening the breach.

Finally, at a time when greater concentration of action against the campus Left was needed, the split ended coordinated efforts against student radicals. Such action would continue, but the board turned its attention to other matters, often fulfilling the libertarians' prophecy that the new board was authoritarian by engaging in personal squabbles among themselves. Power was the new raison d'être in YAF, and power increasingly flowed from the national office after the 1969 convention.

There were some positive results. With libertarian influence attenuated, YAF members could focus on other issues. The continuing lure of agendas such as support for American policy in Vietnam galvanized young people concerned about the fate of the nation as the 1960s waned. Even with internal factionalism plaguing the organization, YAF's membership was never higher than at that time. YAF's financial picture, always troublesome, also appeared bright. The potential to bring together antiradical students into a conservative coalition was quite strong at the end of the 1960s. Regardless of the internecine battles over control of the national board, the organization seemed in good health as the 1970s dawned.[63]

Yet, after 1970, as the main issues and events of the divisive decade faded, YAF was increasingly in danger of becoming an anachronism. With no student Left to combat, with the war in Vietnam winding down, and with anticommunism as a raison d'être for Cold War replaced by détente, there were few exciting issues with which to support a conservative student group on campus. New leadership emerged, which would continue to lead YAF on the "fusionist" path, but political involvement in student activist organizations ebbed throughout the early years of the me decade. Though YAF would find issues to fight for, increasingly it buried itself within the widely growing adult conservative political movement of the 1970s. In that sense it was a crucial tool for the achievement of political power by the end of the decade, but in this broader coalition, the continuing existence of a separate conservative student organization like YAF proved harder and harder to justify.

PART III

Cadres for Conservatism

8

"We Are the New Politics," 1971–1974

The results of political changes are hardly ever those which their
friends hope for or their foes fear. —T.H. Huxley

The excesses of the radical left made YAF members long for the day
when striking would be replaced by streaking. —Ron Robinson

YAF's preeminence is owed less to its acceptance among young
conservatives than to its ability to convince middle-aged Americans
that it speaks for a "majority coalition" of youth. —Brad Evans

One might think the election of Richard Nixon, committing
the government to someone at least friendly to conservatism and viscerally
associated with it by his enemies, would have brought on halcyon days for
YAF, not to mention job opportunities and connections with power. Some
of the latter benefits did materialize, but by most definitions of conservatism—certainly by YAF's—Nixon was no true conservative. Conse-
quently, his election in reality only caused YAF problems and produced
dilemmas that proved insoluble. The Nixon years would prove unkind to
the youth wing of the conservative movement.

In early 1971 Ron Docksai, who assumed the duties of national chairman when David Keene entered the Nixon administration, raised with the
national board the quandary YAF faced. He argued, "YAF is not the youth
vanguard of President Nixon" and recommended that the board discuss
the matter of "our actual and potential relationship with the Nixon administration."[1] At the next board meeting, Docksai's concerns were addressed,
with Dan Joy (editor of the *New Guard*) arguing that YAF "*un*identify
ourselves with the President. It should be our mission to battle Nixonian-
ism in its present form, presenting the logical conservative views and issues

on which we oppose Nixon." In this way, rather than attacking Nixon when the board disagreed with the administration, YAF would make a vigorous effort to move the president in a more conservative direction.[2]

YAF's disregard for Nixon had long roots in the political culture of the 1960s. Although Nixon had supported Goldwater during the 1964 campaign, when many other notable Republicans jumped ship for Johnson, conservatives were wary about Nixon's candidacy in 1968. William Rusher openly pushed California governor Ronald Reagan as the conservative candidate, but Reagan was diffident about challenging the stronger Nixon (although he did allow his name to be entered into nomination at the Miami convention).[3] YAF also endorsed Reagan at its 1967 convention and in pre-1968 polls, but many in the organization felt, realistically, that he was not widely known enough to be elected;[4] only David Keene and one other board member openly supported Nixon in 1968.[5] Others on the Right were skeptical of Nixon, but with the choice seemingly between Rockefeller and him, it was clear for whom conservatives would be compelled to vote. As the convention neared, some conservatives pushed aside their misgivings and rushed to embrace Nixon as "the one" in 1968.[6]

Although conservatives had been able to influence the convention immensely in 1968, the Nixon administration represented a setback for the conservative movement.[7] Many conservatives had tired of Nixon by 1971 and would work hard against him in the 1972 campaign.[8]

Reasons for conservative disenchantment with the president were legion. First, Nixon's economic approach represented an effort to expand the welfare state through conservative principles. Although proposals such as Daniel Patrick Moynihan's Family Assistance Plan (FAP), which would guarantee a direct federal payment of up to four thousand dollars to a poor family as a way of eliminating the welfare bureacracy, were well received by some on the Right (such as economist Milton Friedman), other Nixon programs led to an expansion in the powers and size of the state. The creation of new government programs proceeded apace, with as many domestic departments and regulatory agencies begun in Nixon's tenure as in Johnson's or Kennedy's.[9] Worse yet, for conservatives, Nixon seemed to lack the incentive to change or roll back the massive spending instigated by the Johnson's poverty programs, even as he followed a policy of "benign neglect" toward them.[10] The administration's monetary policy, particularly the removal of U.S. currency from the international gold standard in 1971, raised conservative ire, as did Nixon's embrace of Keynesian spending policy the same year.[11]

The *New Guard* had focused attention on the growing government throughout Johnson's presidency, particularly critical of Great Society programs as examples of wasteful spending. Yet, young conservatives were more disenchanted with Nixon's embrace of government regulatory powers and its impact on business. Nixon seemed unable to stop the trend toward regulation during the 1970s.[12] The GOP never controlled Congress during his presidency, and liberal forces within the Democratic Party, who insisted on environmental protections and regulation, had won out over business-friendly Democrats. But these political factors did not matter much to the youngsters in YAF who saw their support for Nixon contingent on reforming, if not rolling back, Great Society programs.[13]

Nixon's foreign policy equally troubled the Right. Conservatives were skeptical of the president's "secret plan" to end the Vietnam War but supported the Vietnamization policy and his efforts to get Hanoi to the bargaining table through increased military pressure, such as the Cambodia invasion and the mining of Haiphong Harbor. At the least, since it seemed improbable that any president would implement a victory strategy, Nixon was attempting to get the United States extricated from Vietnam with some credibility. Other Nixon foreign policy initiatives, however, especially the opening to China, the pursuit of an American-Soviet strategic arms limitation treaty, and the signing of the Anti-Ballistic Missile Defense Treaty in 1973, caused concern for conservatives. They could see the logic of withdrawing from a war that politicians were not prepared to win, but they were furious when Nixon attempted to improve relations with the Soviet Union and China. Détente was tantamount to capitulation in the minds of conservatives; it was treason comparable to Yalta.

Finally, conservatives distrusted Nixon as a person. Although Nixon attempted to form a relationship with conservatives during his administration—by calling on Buckley for advice, having Russell Kirk meet with him on cultural matters, and employing young conservatives like Tom Charles Huston and Patrick Buchanan as aides (and appointing Howard Phillips as head of the Office of Equal Opportunity)—conservatives were ostracized from important positions and debates within the administration.[14] Much as Goldwater had done during the 1964 campaign, Nixon relied for advice on a loyal coterie—men he trusted, such as H. R. Haldeman, John Erlichman, Charles Colson, and John Dean. None of these insiders possessed credentials or inclinations as movement conservatives; all indulged the president's paranoia regarding outside enemies and his contempt for the media; none could resist the temptations of cover-up, which would lead to the president's downfall and inconceivable, albeit short-term, damage to the Republican party.[15]

YAF members, particularly those on the national board, dealt with these questions with growing frequency. Ultimately, they served to "professionalize" the organization, moving it away from youth politics and concerns and turning it into a Young Republican–like youth wing of the conservative movement. Issues like campus protest, which had died down anyway after the uprisings of 1970, disappeared from YAF's radar screen as the organization focused more on national politics and what young conservatives could do to effect change on that scene.

During the spring and summer of 1971, at state and regional conferences, Ron Docksai and other board members played up YAF's political theme for the upcoming year: "We are the new politics." This slogan, borrowed from the successful Conservative Party campaign of James Buckley for the U.S. Senate seat from New York, pointed to YAF's emergence as the professional political youth vanguard for conservatism. YAF had joined with leaders from the American Conservative Union (ACU), *National Review,* and *Human Events* to form an alliance to promote conservative policies and politicians. The first meeting of leaders of the four groups took place at the Manhattan offices of *National Review* on May 25, 1971; they discussed conservative responses to Nixon's policies.[16] On July 26, 1971, the "Manhattan Twelve," as they were called, announced a conservative break with Nixon, stating that conservatives "will seek out others who share our misgivings" about the president.[17] Further meetings of these conservative leaders led to the endorsement for president in 1972 of John Ashbrook, a young Republican congressman from Ohio.[18] They also led to the organization of the Conservative Political Action Conference (CPAC), which would meet each year thereafter to hear from and give support to conservative political leaders.[19]

YAF's participation in such activities emboldened young conservatives to criticize Nixon's policies, particularly with regard to Vietnam. YAF had lost its focus on the Vietnam issue, preferring instead to concentrate on fighting against the Left on campus. In 1971, with antiwar protests ebbing, the organization renewed its efforts regarding Vietnam.

In part, the return of Vietnam as a prominent issue in YAF circles began in debates on the board held the previous autumn. Jerry Norton, a member of the national board and a Vietnam veteran, wrote a scathing memo attacking the fallacies of the victory strategy and YAF's hypocrisy in recommending such a strategy when "so many YAF leaders . . . judiciously do everything they can to avoid serving there themselves." Norton argued that YAF's continued endorsement of a victory strategy was helping to further divide the nation; also, no political leader was going to implement such a strategy. Therefore, Norton recommended a "quiet YAF withdrawal from Vietnam" as an issue.[20]

Responses to Norton's suggestions were, not surprisingly, negative. Dan Joy and Ron Docksai both said that "while you make some valid points," it was the Left's antiwar position that endangered America's "noble effort" to defend South Vietnam and led to division at home. "Victory over Communism wherever it threatens our existence and offers us no recourse, is an objective moral necessity. It cannot be measured in terms of student popularity."[21] Docksai further recommended that Nixon's program of Vietnamization offered a hope for victory, *if* American military withdrawal did not mean an end to American aid to South Vietnam.

Nixon's Vietnamization position was supported by YAF members, particularly, as Randall Teague claimed, because YAF "deferre[d] to David Keene's closer contacts with the administration. . . . We started gravitating more and more toward support of the Nixon policy."[22] By the spring of 1971, however, YAF's position had changed. Perhaps fearing that Nixon's efforts to withdraw American troops were based less on winning the war (which, in 1971, meant defending South Vietnam) and more on winning reelection in 1972, Teague attacked the administration and made it clear that YAF's support would continue only "if it means an assured defeat of Communist aggression."[23] Ron Robinson, a new member of the national board from upstate New York, concurred with Teague and recommended that YAF "continue to strive for a foreign policy based on the objective of victory over the communists. . . . *If the North Vietnamese had the leadership we have had they would have been driven back onto their own territory years ago.*"[24]

YAF members within the administration pressured the organization to support Nixon's policies. Former national chairmen David Keene and Tom Huston held important positions as political aides to Agnew and Nixon, respectively. Keene was convinced that Vietnamization was the best way not only to extricate American troops from Vietnam but also to preserve victory there, a goal YAF had pushed since 1965.[25] Huston also believed that "[Nixon] intended to do what he could to get out but also to save South Vietnam and give it a chance to survive."[26] Huston often recommended to White House chief of staff H. R. Haldeman that Nixon try to get groups like YAF to support his policies in order to combat antiwar influence, but few efforts toward this end were ever taken.[27]

Even under pressure from White House staffers, YAF clung tenaciously to its right to criticize Nixon. In preparation for the 1971 YAF national convention, Ron Docksai sent several memos to national board members concerning YAF's relationship with Nixon. Docksai argued in one memo that "disillusionment with Nixon . . . was widespread among YAF members." He listed several alternative candidates whom conservatives could support, including James Buckley, Democratic senator Henry "Scoop" Jackson, and Ronald Reagan, none of whom had much national support. Only the latter name appealed to Docksai, and he recommended that YAF board members start "Young Citizens for Reagan" clubs.[28]

Throughout the summer YAF leaders stressed their differences with the president. Docksai stated that "YAF must take the lead in urging other conservatives to be more critical of Nixon."[29] Teague wrote Buckley encouraging him not to give a speech calling for an endorsement of Nixon at the convention. "YAF membership today is so strongly in opposition to the President, now or in 1972, that a major address before the convention urging them to support the President for re-election would result in the speaker being booed and hooted at, irrespective of who he is."[30] When news of this disenchantment reached Barry Goldwater, he informed Docksai about his hope that "the convention is not prevailed upon to put forth any resolutions aimed at detracting from the strength of the President. . . . He is a Republican, and when I think of the alternatives to him, I shudder." Goldwater also added, in language strikingly similar to his speech at the 1960 Republican convention, that as conservatives YAF should "stay with the President, try to influence him, and at the same time increase our strength in the [Republican] party."[31]

Goldwater's intercession had little effect. Docksai had already planned to support someone other than Nixon in 1972. Partly, Docksai and other conservatives were searching for someone to run against Nixon in the primaries. Preliminary discussions by the Manhattan Twelve led to the decision that a candidate from the Right "would not be selected until mid-fall." It was agreed, however, that Reagan could not possibly be the candidate selected if he was to have any chance to lead the Republican Party in the future. Therefore, Docksai recommended that YAF board members "conspire together so that Reagan is not the final nominee at the mock convention."[32]

The plan worked. At the nominating convention held on September 4, YAF members overwhelmingly chose Spiro Agnew as their presidential candidate, a safe pick that upheld Docksai's injunction to stay away from

Reagan.[33] Many YAF members liked the outspoken vice president because of his attacks on the Left and liberalism, not to mention his support for the organization. In that sense, the selection of Agnew made as much sense as that of any other conservative leader. In another way, though, the choice was futile. Although "personally flattered by the choice," Agnew, as vice president, could not criticize the administration and stated that YAF should come around to support the president.[34]

The selection of a candidate other than Nixon helped advance the convention's main theme, that YAF represented the "new politics." In his inaugural remarks to the convention after being elected national chairman outright, Docksai stated that YAF was not a tool of any political party. "We will use this source of strength and independence to praise, criti[c]ize, and if necessary to condemn those political figures who forfeit principle for the illusory comforts of pragmatic vacillation."[35] He added: "Young conservatives presently feel disenfranchised. The man they helped elect President on a conservative platform seems instead to be carrying out the program of Hubert Humphrey. Young conservatives are not kids who can be satisfied with an occasional lollipop from the administration."[36] Wayne Thorburn, a graduate student in political science who became the new executive director, argued that young conservatives in YAF "are calling for, and participating in, a new politics of conservative principle based on ending big government bureaucracy, protecting individual rights, and preserving the national security. . . . The new politics exemplified by YAF concerns itself with the course of our nation not only for the next two, but also the next 20 to 40 years."[37]

Thorburn's assessment was quite prophetic, but YAF's ability to guide the conservative ship to port would be diminished within the next two years. The plunge into politics was replete with dangers for the young conservatives. First, activity against the New Left had given the organization its highest membership, which peaked at over fifty thousand in 1969. If those who joined YAF to take part in counter-demonstrations against the Left could be turned into movement conservatives, then YAF would have a bright future. Unfortunately, as soon as New Left influence on campus dissipated, so did active involvement in YAF. Much as board member Jameson Campaigne had warned earlier, turning activists concerned about the New Left into conservative cadres was a tricky proposition at best.[38] Membership sank from fifty thousand in 1969 to under thirty thousand by 1971. It would drop even further after that year.[39]

Second, the organization faced recurring financial crises after 1970. As of January 22, 1971, YAF's accounts payable were $189,871, and it had $834 cash in the bank. Teague, in a desperate letter to Buckley, stated that recent elections, a poor economy, inactivity on campus, and poorly organized fund-raising appeals had all contributed to a drought in YAF's funding. Problems in the national office were not mentioned as a cause of the financial crunch, but YAF's "Washington bureaucracy" had been cut back, as were action projects. YAF projects were being cut by $9,000 monthly, including layoffs of salaried employees.[40] By the winter of 1971, the board faced a desperate financial picture.[41]

Once again, however, disaster was averted by another mail solicitation.[42] Rusher wrote Buckley in March, claiming that Teague had been successful in "grossing $274,000 . . . as a result of a [recent] mailing. . . . Between this and other bonanzas, they are out of debt and actually have a $70,000 surplus. Randy assures me they are taking steps not to get back in the same sort of trouble again."[43]

Trouble was never far away from the national office the remainder of the year. Teague's long tenure as executive director, beginning in 1968, had made him numerous rivals and enemies on the board. Though his handling of the financial crisis earned him plaudits from the national board (and a financial bonus), his position was precarious, and at the end of the year, partially because of yet another financial downturn, Teague was removed from his position and replaced by Wayne Thorburn.[44]

Teague claimed he was removed from his office because of his hostility toward Nixon. He had given a speech at summer regional conferences criticizing the Nixon administration's Vietnamization strategy. Teague believes that David Keene's influence on YAF's national board was strong enough to dictate his removal as executive director.[45] Keene later denied this charge, insisting that he had left YAF behind when taking his job as Agnew's assistant.[46] The evidence seems to show that Teague's removal was partly personal and partly political. His insistence on exploring the prospects for a different Republican nominee in 1972 and his continuing criticism of Nixon made him enemies within the administration, particularly Keene. When a second financial crisis developed in October 1971, board members loyal to Keene seized the opportunity to throw Teague out.[47] Personality conflicts may have been the greater reason for his removal. Admitting to his rather Machiavellian handling of YAF matters, Teague, who was a protégé of David Jones, had been involved in the organization's financial affairs for several years. Condemned by libertarians in the 1969 tumult for his "heavy-handedness" in running YAF's affairs,

Teague was left in a precarious position, at best. Removing him was perhaps the result of personality conflicts coupled with myriad financial difficulties.

Teague's expulsion had little effect on policy. The board decided to continue its liaison with the anti-Nixon conservatives and began a campaign to support Ohio congressman John Ashbrook in a challenge against Nixon in the Republican primaries. Docksai and Thorburn met with other representatives from the Manhattan Twelve to endorse Ashbrook for president.[48] YAF backed the shortlived Ashbrook campaign much as it had the Goldwater efforts eight years before. YAF members were the shock troops in New Hampshire and Florida, two states where Ashbrook's campaign staff decided to test the waters. Those efforts were to no avail. Of 118,000 Republican votes cast in the New Hampshire primary, Ashbrook netted only 16 percent, too little to stimulate further campaign efforts.[49]

After Ashbrook faded, YAF still refused to endorse or support Nixon. The decision was made by Docksai and others at national board meetings in February but not finalized until the spring. Instead, YAF members were encouraged to participate in state and local elections as part of the organization's "Politics '72" campaign.[50] Docksai also recommended that since there was "little prospect of young conservatives volunteering energy for Nixon," YAF members might "wage a campaign against the Democrats on issues." That idea, which would lead to the formation of Youth against McGovern (YAM) in the fall, would allow conservatives to support Nixon by campaigning against McGovern.[51]

YAF members were active in YAM but did not control the organization. That distinction fell to YR activists, who looked upon the coalition as a way to build support (indirectly) for Nixon. Nevertheless, YAF members and chapters participated in the anti-McGovern effort, deploying thousands of bumper stickers, buttons, and anti-Democratic leaflets at meetings and campaign sites throughout the country.[52]

In the end, Nixon was reelected in a landslide. Young conservatives took little comfort in this development, but they found much to cheer in the election of Jesse Helms (R-N.C.) and William Scott (R-Va.) to the Senate and the reelection of YAF supporters Strom Thurmond and John Tower. YAF's analysis of the campaign pointed to a much-discussed and important trend in 1972—the inroads made in the South by the GOP. But other victories on the Right were scattered, so conservatives made only modest gains in the 1972 elections.[53]

If YAF members were disappointed with the elections and the condition of the Republican Party in 1972, internal problems added to YAF's malaise after the election. Throughout 1972 YAF's financial woes continued, hampering the organization's ability to mount new action projects. Jim Minarik, a board member from Ohio, wrote Docksai in June of his fear that YAF was about to die: "An operation that has a mailing list, a board of directors, and a national office is not necessarily alive." Minarik complained that for financial reasons YAF dropped programs like chapter services and political organizing, which were its only hope to recruit new members. He complained of factionalism on the board, a factionalism driven by personality clashes rather than ideology. In sum, he thought that YAF had reached a desperate state by midyear.[54]

The financial situation confirmed this. Over a twelve-month period through April 1972, a budget deficit of $150,000 had accrued. In reaction, the national office laid off employees, cut production of promotional materials, pruned the pages in the *New Guard,* reduced travel allowances and perks to board members, and cut back action programs. It was not enough. Unless more funds were raised and expenses further cut, YAF would continue to operate in the red.[55]

Personal conflicts among board members also contributed to troubles within the organization. Individuals were continuing to use YAF as their personal fiefdom. Charges of favoritism in appointments and other factional infighting threatened to diminish—if it had not already diminished—the vitality of the organization. One effort to remove Wayne Thorburn from office contributed to these problems. Ten board members were specifically named by Docksai in a confidential memorandum as potential troublemakers and were threatened by him with expulsion.[56] This type of infighting reduced the prospect for unity at the national level and threatened the very life of the organization.

YAF action projects also continued to lack the sex appeal that could draw students into a conservative student organization. One such project, the Movement for Quality Education, was designed to pressure legislators and educators to improve academic standards at universities while resisting the politicization of higher learning by such actions as the establishment of women's studies departments. How could a student organization bring this about? It turned out that it could not. Quite simply, it was too ambitious a program for an organization of young people, given their lack of political experience and the organization's increasingly perilous financial condition. Though the national office, through its contacts in the conservative movement and on Capitol Hill, could lobby for legislation to curtail these developments in higher learning, members in local chapters could do very little to improve the situation on their respective campuses.[57] This project, with its ambitious design, could not attract increasingly apathetic college students to the organization.

Other YAF efforts had the potential to excite some passion on campus, but their duration as issues proved to be short-lived. At the February 1973 board meeting, YAF declared its reluctance to support the Paris Peace Accords ending the war in Vietnam. The key problem for YAF was not the treaty itself, but a provision being debated by Congress as a condition of its passage—the grant of amnesty to draft resisters. YAF also opposed stipulations in the treaty that would have granted aid to the North Vietnamese government. As YAF members marched on campuses, passed out leaflets, and called press conferences against amnesty, these positions generated some excitement, including a protest meeting held on the steps of the nation's Capitol that drew five hundred people.[58] YAF formed coalitions with other antiamnesty groups throughout the country, perhaps recalling their recent efforts to resist left-wing activity on campus, but by the fall of 1973 antiamnesty efforts had faded from YAF's national program.[59] Resistance to amnesty alone could not stir enough passion and simply was dropped as a program by the national office.

YAF fought for other ideas that would help reshape the conservative movement during the 1970s. Social issues such as abortion, the Equal Rights Amendment, crime, pornography, and busing became springboards for YAF activity. In the past, YAF members had resisted active involvement in debates like these, preferring to concentrate purely on political and economic concerns. But during the early 1970s, with an increasingly active Supreme Court deciding in favor of legal abortions, forced busing, and affirmative action, such issues could no longer be ignored. YAF saw them intertwined with a growing bureaucratic impetus that would diminish individual freedoms. They opposed them out of their continued resistance to an active judiciary, not so much because they were influenced by the morality of such positions or, in the case of abortion, a woman's "choice" to decide.[60]

Yet, the libertarian influence among many YAF members did not allow for a united front on many of the aforementioned issues. David Brudnoy, a bright Ph.D. from Boston University, argued vociferously in favor of individualism throughout his many articles for the *New Guard* on social and cultural issues. Hiding a homosexual and drug-using lifestyle, Brudnoy argued for decriminalizing victimless crimes like pornography and marijuana use and for not settling on preconceived definitions of pornography. Brudnoy's views were rooted in his academic study of libertarianism (he wrote a dissertation on American libertarian Theodore Schroeder, an influence behind the founding of the American Civil Liberties Union), his reading of Ayn Rand's philosophical works, and his lifestyle choices, which he admits were more libertine than libertarian.[61] A prolific essayist, Brudnoy's inability to find an academic teaching position led to his later television and radio career in Boston, where he continues, despite his recent contraction of the AIDS virus, to defend his libertarian conservatism over the radio waves.[62]

Although social issues were important to the developing conservative movement in the 1970s, Communism remained the central concern of most YAF members. YAF continued to identify itself with anticommunist conservatism by recommending continued American involvement in Vietnam, resisting détente with the Soviet Union, supporting the Nationalist government on Taiwan, and fighting for increased defense expenditures, including initiatives like the Supersonic Transport (SST). YAF established a National Security Project designed "to provide information to the general public on strategic defense questions and to aid political action in this area." Heading this project was YAF member Chris Lay, a legislative assistant to Idaho Republican representative Steve Symms, a member of YAF's national advisory board. The project disseminated information on nuclear issues to friendly congressmen and the general public, but its tendency to evangelize the already converted minimized the impact of the project. By 1975 the project faded away.[63] Anticommunism, especially after the end of the Vietnam War, lacked the ability it had once possessed to excite students on campus.

By the end of 1973 YAF was still in financial trouble. The organization's lack of a clear focus hampered fund-raising. During the early 1970s social issues were the main drawing card for conservative fund-raisers, but YAF was ambivalent on these issues. Complicating the fund-raising picture was the fact that YAF's average donor was over fifty years of age. The generation gap between fifty-year-olds who saw social issues as important and the younger, more libertarian-minded conservatives in YAF threatened the organization's future funding.[64] If YAF could not find an appealing focus and find it soon, its fund-raising potential would wither.

A second financial problem involved the organization's purchase of a building to house the national office. Since YAF had moved to Washington in 1962, the organization had paid exorbitant rent on office suites. For several years the national board looked into the possibility of buying a building in the Virginia suburbs, both to alleviate rental costs and to have a place to hold meetings, workshops, and conferences. By the end of 1973 the board had finalized the purchase of a house and eight acres of land in northern Virginia for the sum of forty-two thousand dollars.[65] The purchase of the building (dedicated as the Freedom Center in 1974) made sense as a place to centralize the organization's activities—and to avoid growing rent payments in Washington—but not when finances were tight and membership in decline. However, the building would prove to be one of YAF's most marketable assets in the long run. As property values soared in northern Virginia during the 1980s, the Freedom Center property became increasingly valuable to an organization more and more cash-starved.

A bleak membership picture continued to plague the organization. John Meyer wrote a memo pointing out a serious vacuum in state YAF leadership throughout the country. He claimed that twenty-two states were without state chairmen. Meyer argued, "It is not necessary to have a real state organization, but it may well be necessary to have a state chairman in order to have a real state organization. . . . As long as we are claiming 50,000 members, we had better have those state chairmen."[66] Ron Robinson, who was in charge of YAF membership, replied to Meyer's memo by stating that YAF's board should continue to monitor the leadership vacancies but that the board should also act prudently by "closely review[ing] our appointments." Robinson believed that the organization should make sure whoever it appointed to vacancies was truly conservative.[67]

Nonetheless, Robinson understood that Meyer's memo pointed to a grim reality: YAF was in the midst of a serious membership crisis. Robinson made several recommendations on how to improve membership retention, including increased and better-focused direct mail solicitations, advertisements in college newspapers, and a new speaker's bureau. He also suggested that "in the past YAF's most productive ways of recruiting new members have been by direct person-to-person contact."[68] Growing apathy on the college level contributed to the decline in membership growth.

The numbers were cause for concern. Figures from September 1973 depicted a membership level of 11,526; by February 1974 it had sunk to 8,812 national members. Some states had no members at all, and some, such as Montana, once a well-organized state chapter, could claim only a handful.[69] The implications of declining membership were obvious. Without some major issue that could galvanize young people around conservative issues, YAF was potentially finished as a membership organization.

The Watergate crisis aggravated YAF's problems. At first, the organization did its best to ignore the scandal. There was little coverage in the *New Guard* and no discussion of the issue at national board meetings. However, after six months of televised hearings, compounded by Nixon's actions during 1973, the board suddenly took interest in the question of Nixon's culpability in the affair.

Docksai was the first member to publicly criticize Nixon. At a press conference before the opening of the annual Conservative Political Action Conference (CPAC), held in Washington the weekend of January 25–27, 1974, Docksai was asked his view of Nixon's role. Charging that "Nixon cannot escape being held responsible for the illicit activities of his aides," he recommended that the president "either have full disclosure before Congress . . . or . . . resign his office."[70] Docksai told the reporters that this was his personal view and not an "official position of YAF," but two days later, in a memo to the board, the chairman argued, somewhat disingenuously given YAF's precarious financial position, that YAF "should take risks . . . because we have the resources and administrative ability to service a principled, conservative opposition in American politics. . . . We will therefore have to play the role of standard bearer in a way which we have not in the past."[71]

Docksai's memo was discussed at the February national board meeting. A week before the meeting, Bill Saracino responded to Docksai's suggestion that Nixon resign. First, Saracino believed that "there is no compelling reason for the President to resign. . . . the Watergate 'crimes' measure no larger nor perfidious than the abuses of power by every administration since Roosevelt." Secondly, the call for resignation would ally YAF with "the lunatic left" (groups like Common Cause, ACLU, ADA, etc.). In addition, "the call for resignation would do great harm to the organization. . . . the average conservative-Republican does *NOT* want Nixon to resign. For us to join what is viewed by Republicans as the 'get Nixon' clique would be the end of any hope of YAF and GOP-oriented conservatives cooperating on any project or election."[72]

Saracino's call for a measured response to Nixon's involvement in Watergate had the desired effect.[73] Docksai wrote one disgruntled YAF member (who defended Nixon) that "Watergate and Nixon are not everlasting.

Young conservatives need the support of our elder supporters and advisors. Otherwise, where else would we be?"[74]

Docksai's call for Nixon's resignation had little effect on the president's decision to resign in August. It also did not, as Docksai claimed it might, serve as a ploy by which YAF could take over as a leading force in the conservative movement. Privately, many leading conservatives felt the same as Docksai, but they made no public pronouncements concerning Nixon until the summer, when impeachment was almost certain.[75] But the key questions Saracino raised in his February memo haunted the organization the remainder of the year. What purpose would it serve for YAF to take such a stand? Was this the type of issue that YAF should be spending time on at all?

YAF's activity during the remainder of 1974 clearly showed that it was not. The national board could no longer effectuate policy that would lead to increased membership or develop support for conservative issues. By the mid-1970s the board was hopelessly incapable of furthering a conservative youth agenda or even agreeing on one. Personality clashes on the board hurt the effort to coordinate policy, as did favoritism in appointments and charges of incompetence in the national office.[76] Although YAF would continue to function, it operated as a shadow of its former self and would increasingly be involved in bizarre fights more becoming of Communist sects than conservative ones. What was left of YAF by the mid-1970s was an increasingly bureaucratic national office with little grass roots support, funded by wealthy older conservatives engaged in little more than political campaigning for GOP candidates. One might as well join the Young Republicans, which, by the late 1970s, was proving to be a reliable bastion of young conservatism. The YAF, on the eve of conservatism's ultimate push toward political power, seemed exhausted.

9

Revival and Collapse, 1975–1986

Like those Americans who built our frontier communities through
barn-raising and spelling bees, YAF members are pitching in
whenever less fortunate fellow citizens need help. They are the hope
of America, the leaders of tomorrow.   —John Wayne

Deck the halls with Commie corpses,
Fa la la la la la la la la,
Its the time to be remorseless,
Fa la la la la la la la la,
Wield we now our sharp stiletti,
Fa la la la la la la la la,
Carve the pinks into confetti,
Fa la la la la la la la la.   —YAF song, 1981 convention

In 1986, with YAF mired in debt, Terrell Cannon, who had
assumed the duties of national chairman a year earlier on the resignation of
Robert Dolan, elected to that office in 1983, ended the organization's
contract with its direct mail fund-raiser Response Dynamics and sold YAF's
Freedom Center in Sterling, Virginia. After years of financial problems and
infighting, YAF underwent a quiet death, meriting not one single word in
the conservative or mainstream press. For twenty-six years, YAF had been
the preeminent conservative youth organization, dedicated to building cadres on campus and mobilizing young people for political action. But years
of internal problems, multiplied by the conservative movement's own success at building support for their causes and policies, had left YAF in a
chronically weak state during the very time conservative principles were
enshrined in the White House and Washington. How this happened forms
the last chapter of YAF's history, a story of revival and collapse.

*

YAF had suffered, like the rest of the nation, from a post–Watergate malaise. Membership declined, programmatic innovations ebbed, and anticommunist politics faded from the scene as the nation experienced a collective sense of guilt from Cold War excesses. In the era of the Church Committee, a congressional committee named after Senator Frank Church and charged with investigating the abuses of U.S. intelligence agencies; the War Powers Act (designed to restore congressional suzerainty over the conduct of American foreign policy); the Mayaguez crisis; and the oil shocks; to stand up for America and wave the flag proudly was emblematic of another time, a far distant period that had seemingly disappeared by the nation's bicentennial year. Apathy on campus after years of tumult further contributed to the malaise, but so did a general cynicism regarding politicians and political activity.

YAF did its utmost to weather the defeatist tide, engaging more in direct political activity than at any other time in its history. Primarily through the efforts of executive director Frank Donatelli and national chairman James Lacy, YAF fully wedded itself to the 1976 and 1980 Reagan presidential campaigns, serving as shock troops for the conservative cause and, increasingly, as delegates for the Reagan effort at Republican National Conventions. The buildup for Reagan drew most of YAF's attention in the interim, particularly as Americans confronted renewed foreign and domestic crises and the weakened resolve to face them.

Frank Donatelli was crucial in the push for Reagan in 1976. Donatelli had replaced Wayne Thorburn as executive director in 1973. A longtime YAF activist from western Pennsylvania, a graduate of the University of Pittsburgh and American University Law School, Donatelli worked his way up through the ranks to gain a seat on YAF's national board in 1970. He worked in the national office as part of a faction that included Ron Robinson, Thorburn, Ron Docksai, and eventually Robert Heckman. This Middle Atlantic faction was strengthened by conservative activity in New York and Pennsylvania, including the election of New York Conservative Party candidate James Buckley to the U.S. Senate in 1970 and the successful campaign of former Buffalo Bills quarterback Jack Kemp for a congressional seat in 1972.[1] The New York chapter in particular, with Docksai as national chairman from Queens and with Robinson (from Buffalo) ensconced in the national office, would remain a powerful force in national YAF for the remainder of the organization's history, competing, in many cases, with midwestern and western groups intent on broadening YAF's base and challenging the eastern-dominated leadership.[2]

One example of this regional tension was on display at YAF's 1975 convention, held at the McCormick Inn in Chicago. Ron Docksai, who had served the longest tenure of any YAF chairman, relinquished his post. One of the more promising candidates running to replace Docksai was Fran Griffin, a member of the national board from Illinois. Griffin had long been active in YAF activities in Chicago and had run for a state Senate seat from her south-side Chicago district in 1974. The candidate selected by the national office to oppose Griffin was Jeffrey Kane, who had most recently been northwest regional director of YAF. In early 1974 Kane was ready to quit YAF and move on to other activities when Donatelli and Wayne Thorburn intervened and convinced him to remain in the organization, getting him elected to the national board in the process. Articulate, intelligent, and looking like the good old American boy next door, Kane was the choice of a coterie of YAF national officers, who had flown out to Washington to endorse his northwest organization in January 1974.[3] The core of this group, including the Middle Atlantic faction (except Robinson, who supported Griffin and vice chairman John Buckley), later sponsored Kane for national chairman. He easily defeated Griffin in a landslide election (376–12). John S. Buckley, a distant cousin of William F. Buckley, was elected vice chairman and would replace Kane as national chair in 1977.[4]

The Chicago YAF convention gave the impression of strong activity among the delegates as awards were dispensed to the most active chapters. The *New Guard* ran a photo montage of the award ceremonies, but the small number of delegates voting for national chairman (388 in all) signified a precarious membership situation that belied the optimistic front displayed in YAF's magazine.[5]

Part of the problem in 1975 lay with regional tensions. For some time the Midwest region felt excluded from a prominent role in YAF's national office. Even though Dan Manion, the Hoosier son of YAF advisor Clarence Manion, had been Docksai's vice chairman for two years, emerging talent from the Midwest was consistently bypassed in favor of factions from the East Coast. Jameson Campaigne, who left service on YAF's board in 1974, wrote Ron Docksai about some of the problems facing YAF under his leadership. In a particularly vapid exchange between the two, Campaigne clearly enunciated that in the mid-1970s YAF suffered from weak leadership based on factions and personalities rather than ability.[6]

At the Chicago convention the regional disputes were most in evidence in the poor attendance at the convention. The 1971 Houston convention had drawn more than one thousand YAF activists, but in Chicago fewer than four hundred bothered to attend. Many chapters boycotted the convention in protest of the regional disparities on the board.[7] The election of Jeff Kane from Washington, sponsored by the national office, only confirmed to the disenchanted that a small coterie of YAF members controlled the organization. Though the disputes were quickly patched over after the convention, YAF was increasingly becoming a professional—and bureaucratic—organization based in the East with a declining number of chapters and little ability to build conservative cadres on campus.

These factional problems notwithstanding, throughout the remainder of 1975 and into 1976, YAF prepared for the upcoming political campaigns. Ronald Reagan was a nearly unanimous choice among most YAF members for president in 1976. YAF had backed away from supporting Gerald Ford, partially because of his continuing embrace of détente with the Soviet Union, but also because of his choice of Nelson Rockefeller for his vice president in 1974. Kane officially announced YAF's decision to switch their support to Reagan in the fall of 1975.[8]

Other motives underlay YAF's switch to Reagan. The conservative movement was confused about its continued support for the GOP. At the February 1975 meeting of the Conservative Political Action Conference (CPAC), sponsored in part by YAF, a third party was a major topic of conversation. Reagan spoke of the necessity of restoring conservative principle within the GOP and, tickling the fancy of many in attendance, suggested that "if there are those who cannot subscribe to those principles, let us go forward without them."[9] Other CPAC speakers echoed Reagan's call for principle but advocated forming a third party to challenge the liberalism still prevalent within the GOP. One result of such talk was the formation of an actual third-party vehicle, the Committee on Conservative Alternatives, including among its members Congressmen John Ashbrook (R-Ohio) and Robert Bauman (R-Md.), Senator Jesse Helms (R-N.C.), William Rusher, and Ron Docksai. The committee's purpose was "to provide a formal mechanism to review and assess the current political situation and to develop future opportunities" with respect to forming a conservative alternative to the two major parties.[10] This mechanism would be the basis for a conservative challenge to both parties, which would culminate, it was hoped in the optimistic mood following CPAC, in a conservative candidate (most likely Reagan) running to challenge both parties.[11]

William Rusher was one of the leading activists behind the third party idea. He published a book, *The Making of a New Majority Party,* in which he outlined the necessary conditions for third-party success existing in 1975. First, the old divisions between "haves and have nots," which increasingly had defined American electoral politics, were breaking down and being recast in terms of liberals versus conservatives. Liberals were defined by Rusher as those "obsessed with the need to rectify, by federal intervention, [historical] injustices"; conservatives as those who "oppose ever-expanding federal involvement in welfare" and the like.[12] Rusher also argued that the Democratic Party had its share of those troubled over "New Class" inroads, such as George Wallace, and that increasingly these Democrats (he pointed to the example of Strom Thurmond) switched parties out of allegiance to principle. Finally, Rusher argued that the development of a strong conservative movement outside the GOP and the concomitant domination of the GOP by liberal Rockefeller Republicans also prepared for a new majority to emerge.[13]

YAF members were intrigued by Rusher's proposals enough to warrant talk of a third-party candidate at their Chicago convention. Ron Docksai was quoted suggesting that "a third party candidacy is surely a possibility." But John Sears, the executive director of Citizens for Reagan, who spoke at the convention, stated that although Reagan had not yet made up his mind whether to run in 1976, "[he] had all but ruled out a third party candidacy."[14] YAF's subsequent endorsement of Reagan in a convention poll made it all but impossible for the organization to even suggest backing another candidate, especially one outside the GOP.[15]

Was a successful third political party even enough of a possibility to warrant serious consideration? Conservatives pointed to 1974 Gallup Polls suggesting that 38 percent of all respondents called themselves conservative in their political views. Further polls in New York showed a strengthened coalition of people supporting conservative positions on social issues, such as abortion, pornography, forced busing, and welfare. The post-Watergate disregard for politics also benefited conservative arguments for a third party, as did an emerging populist conservatism based in the South and the West.[16] These were necessary conditions for the existence of a third party, but they were not sufficient. The missing factor was leadership. With Reagan leaning toward challenging Ford in the Republican primaries, a third-party candidate of conservative principles would have a hard time defeating Reagan's combination of principle, experience, and charisma or Ford's control of the GOP apparatus. With George Wallace confined to a wheelchair and interested in making a run within the Democratic Party, what chance did third-party advocates have to challenge the national parties? Believing that principles matter more than leadership in democratic politics, third-party activists failed to motivate any significant national figure to run against the two parties. That left the American Independent Party (the party put together by Rusher and other conservative activists throughout 1976) to select delegates from a coterie of individuals fully disenchanted with the political process, including racists and extremists from whom conservatives had distanced their movement. One month after Ford narrowly defeated Reagan to determine the GOP candidacy, delegates to the 1976 American Independent Party convention chose the notorious racist Lester Maddox as their candidate, ending the drive for a third party, in William Rusher's phrase, "with a whimper."[17]

With YAF on board for Reagan, young people worked hard throughout the primary season to assure the Gipper's selection over Ford. Much as they had done in 1964, YAF provided young volunteers for the Reagan candidacy. However, recent changes in election laws prohibited YAF from recruiting their own members from the activists that worked on campaigns. The post-Watergate campaign reforms prohibited independent groups like YAF from setting up tables at campaign stops. Activities that had helped YAF recruit members during previous campaigns were now considered independent expenditures of the campaigns themselves, and most campaign managers, with monetary issues constantly on their mind, did not welcome such expenditures.[18] Thus, YAF efforts were confined to volunteer efforts such as canvassing, phone solicitation, and the like, which required committed supporters. Nonetheless, Frank Donatelli would boast a 25 percent increase in national membership following the 1976 campaign. Unlike the post-1964 membership boom, however, there is little evidence to support Donatelli's claims of significant membership expansion after the campaign.[19]

One significant change from 1964 was the number of YAF members and alumni serving as delegates to the national convention and playing a significant role within the Reagan campaign. Sixty-one YAF members served as delegates or alternates pledged to Reagan at the Kansas City convention, compared to just six in 1964. Charlie Black, a former YAF national staff member, served as Reagan's Midwest coordinator, and David Keene, former YAF national chairman, was his southern coordinator.[20] Other campaigns that autumn drew the support of YAF members, including James Buckley's unsuccessful reelection campaign against Daniel Patrick Moynihan and successful races such as those of Robert Dornan in California and Malcolm Wallop in Wyoming.[21] YAF activity on behalf of political candidates now represented a significant feature of activities within the organization.

Yet, other issues were important enough to build support for young conservatives. Détente was attacked with great relish because YAF members believed it contributed to a weakening of American resolve against the Soviet Union. This was confirmed for many in the 1979 Soviet invasion of Afghanistan. YAF also engaged in an effort to stop the SALT II treaty, which placed further limits on the mobilization of a powerful deterrent. Finally, YAF initiated Carter Watch, a program begun in December 1976 to monitor Carter's conduct in foreign and domestic policy. Carter Watch would become an accurate barometer of the organization's dismay at the state of America's economy and defense by the end of the 1970s.[22]

Organizationally, YAF remained in a rut. Part of the problem was the success conservatives were having in forming and funding organizations. YAF was not a tax-exempt organization and depended a great deal on a large number of small donations to keep it financially solvent. By the mid-1970s large donors were giving significant dollars to tax-exempt foundations, such as the Heritage Foundation or Young America's Foundation, a YAF offshoot started at Vanderbilt University in 1971. "YAF's tax status began to signify its doom to some extent," Ron Robinson related.[23] Also, the success of conservative politicians at the polls and the promulgation of numerous conservative publications and foundations drew young talent increasingly away from YAF. "Holding on to talented people for a long time," according to Robinson, "was difficult for YAF" when there were numerous competitors in town vying for talent. This would worsen during the 1980s with a conservative administration in office.[24]

Both Jeff Kane and Frank Donatelli presided over this difficult period in YAF's history. Still haunted politically by Nixon and smarting from the Reagan defeat in 1976, YAF was without adequate direction and its financial strength was declining. At the 1977 national convention, held in New York City, vice chairman John Buckley ran unopposed for the national chairman position vacated by Kane, who retired to private business in Maine.[25] Buckley had graduated from the University of Virginia and worked for several years on Capitol Hill before moving to Fund for a Conservative Majority. A libertarian on social issues, Buckley created havoc on the national board when he called for an end to YAF's opposition to legalized marijuana. The YAF platform was against legalization of drugs and Buckley thought it was time to revisit the issue. Buckley had failed to weigh the consequences of his position, which caused a tumult on the board, and he found that as the new national chairman he was left in the minority, with only eleven supporters.[26]

For one YAF member, James Lacy, Buckley's position was dangerous for YAF. Lacy had been a conservative activist in California since Reagan's gubernatorial victory in 1966. A descendant of a Russian soldier who served in the tsar's army and was stationed at the Winter Palace, Lacy grew up learning about Communism from his mother, who fled Russia during the Bolshevik revolution, eventually settling in southern California. His conservative anticommunism ingrained from birth, Lacy was active in the University of Southern California YAF chapter, leading a confrontation against Jane Fonda when she came to speak on campus in 1973.[27] Rising through the ranks of YAF, Lacy was proposed for a national board seat in 1975 (at the same time he was made state chairman of California YAF). Part of the activities in California involved fighting against the legalization of "victimless crimes" including drug use. Buckley's proposal to move YAF toward the libertarian position on drugs troubled him deeply.

At a November 1978 meeting of the national board, a confrontation between Buckley's faction and the majority group, led, ostensibly, by Frank Donatelli and Jeff Kane (both of whom retained their board seats as senior members after leaving their national offices in 1977), led to Buckley's resignation as national chairman, a first in the history of the organization. Perhaps out of frustration at his inability to prevail over the board regarding his libertarian philosophy, Buckley left the national chairman position vacant, as the board, somewhat stunned by the resignation, huddled to decide on a successor. After stating his interest in taking the position, James Lacy was nominated and unanimously elected to replace Buckley as the new national chairman.[28]

Lacy inherited an organization still incapable of expanding its membership roles or of delineating a common purpose on the nation's campuses, but one that was finally pulling out of its post–Watergate funk, both financially and programmatically. One reason for this renewal had to do with the conservative revival during the late 1970s. The desperate state of the nation's economy, signified by growing marginal tax rates, high inflation and interest rates (to produce a phenomenon known as stagflation), growing unemployment, and government regulation of business, helped conservatives foment a challenge to orthodox Keynesian economic thinking known as supply-side economics. Borrowing heavily from classical liberal economics, supply-siders theorized that cutting taxes, ending regulation, going back to the gold standard, and cutting government spending would provide the means for economic growth.[29] These initiatives were popularized by various politicians such as Republican Jack Kemp and Democrat Lloyd Bentsen, both of whom seized the supply-side message and attempted to enact laws designed to cut taxes and provide growth in the economy. The emphasis on growth, after years of stagnation, reinvigorated a coalition that included Wall Street, the middle class, and entrepreneurs, many of them in technological fields.

Further problems in American foreign policy contributed to a growing sense of crisis. YAF played a big role in criticizing the Carter administration for signing away the Panama Canal, for pushing for a quick ratification of the SALT II treaty, for its normalization of relations with the People's Republic of China, and for continuing détente with the Soviets when it seemed clear that the Soviets were expansionist. The December 1979 invasion of Afghanistan, coupled with the taking of American hostages in Iran, pointed most adequately to American weakness. While most pundits were content to write off America's tepid response to these crises as the continuing Vietnam malaise, conservatives were in the forefront of addressing the dangers to American interests stemming from Soviet expansion and revolutionary Iran.

The penultimate challenge to a decade of debate over the social issues was emerging from an unlikely source—evangelical Christians. The failure of Jimmy Carter, an announced born-again Christian, to further the pro-family and traditionalist values of the evangelical community led to the formation of mobilized and active grass roots opposition known as the religious Right. Jerry Falwell's emergence as the leader of a coalition of evangelical and fundamentalist Christians dedicated to fighting against the permissiveness and moral decay embodied in the abortion regime, gay rights issues, women's issues, and drugs fed into the growing unease many conservatives felt toward the Carter administration.[30]

Finally, a group of policy intellectuals who had once been Trotsykites and then liberals, many of whom were Jewish and well connected in intellectual circles in New York City, began to decry the excesses of post-1960s liberalism—its promotion of moral decay and of entitlement over opportunity and its tolerance of social decay through its embrace of personal politics. The neoconservatives, as they were derisively labeled, formed one of the most important blocs for the emerging Reagan coalition. A diverse lot, consisting of policy intellectuals such as Nathan Glazer and Irving Kristol, cultural aficionados such as Hilton Kramer and Gertrude

Himmelfarb, and anticommunists such as Norman Podhoretz and Jeanne Kirkpatrick, their arrival on the Right helped refocus the efforts of conservatives on policy positions and a restrengthened foreign policy that concentrated on a strong Western alliance and support for Israel.[31]

All of these groups helped push longtime conservatives in groups like YAF out of the limelight as they strove to gain influence within the Reagan campaign and the conservative movement. Yet, YAF still performed the part of the dutiful soldier. Under Lacy's leadership, YAF played an important role in the Reagan campaign in 1980, with many members serving as staff members for the campaign, including Lacy and Donatelli. YAF's new executive director, Robert Heckman, served as the head of the Fund for a Conservative Majority, a political action committee founded as the Young America's Campaign Committee in 1973 (a YAF offshoot), which sponsored conservative candidates with money and volunteers. The directors of the FCM were all YAF board members.[32] YAF members worked as volunteers in all the state primaries, many of them fully committed to the Reagan campaign.[33]

YAF's biggest effort in 1980 came from the Detroit '80 Youth Operation, a national project that sent some four hundred members to the GOP convention to work for Reagan.[34] YAF members distributed literature, marched in support of the candidate, attended rallies, and served as delegates to the convention itself. YAF veterans such as Robert Bauman commented on their presence at the Detroit convention, comparing it favorably to YAF's work for Goldwater in San Francisco in 1964.[35] Although YAF members were disappointed by Reagan's selection of George Bush as his running mate (Heckman booed when he was announced), they supported the platform of the GOP and relished the fact that longtime YAF supporter Ronald Reagan was now the presidential nominee of the Republican Party. After long years of effort, conservative activists had finally captured the GOP.

In the autumn YAF celebrated its twentieth anniversary with a dinner at Washington's Mayflower Hotel. More than seven hundred conservative activists, the majority YAF alumni, heard William F. Buckley and Congressman Robert Bauman speak on YAF's importance for the conservative movement. Ronald Reagan, on the campaign trail, sent taped remarks, and Nancy Reagan accepted a YAF award for her husband. The dinner was a huge success for YAF and seemed to point toward a bright future for the organization. As an essayist in the *New Guard* commented, "Though the tide has begun to turn—due in no small part to YAF's efforts—much work remains to put our country firmly in conservative hands."[36] The success of the Reagan campaign for YAF membership was showing as James Lacy claimed eighty thousand members (ten thousand of them activists) in the autumn of 1980.[37] Throughout the campaign, Students for Reagan, a program headed by the Fund for a Conservative Majority, mobilized a network of eight thousand college students to participate as organizers for Reagan on more than three hundred campuses.[38] After Reagan's victory, YAF members and alumni played significant roles in the transition effort, including Frank Donatelli, Carol Bauman, Don Devine, Jay Parker and Donald Lukens. The appointment of former YAF members such as Don Devine as head of the Office of Personnel Management and Richard Allen as National Security Advisor, along with the myriad YAF staffers interspersed throughout the bureaucracy of Washington, pointed out well YAF's significance during its twentieth year.[39]

During 1981 YAF kept its public profile. Reagan spoke at the YAF-sponsored CPAC meeting in March 1981, introduced to the crowd by national chairman James Lacy. Vice President George Bush, Paul Laxalt, and Budget Director David Stockman also spoke at the meeting.[40] Programmatically, YAF organized the Youth for the Reagan Agenda, dedicated to fighting for Reagan's economic program. James Lacy argued, "The project is focused on generating youth support for the President's economic program. . . . The only way to stop inflation and restore economic productivity is to scale back the size and scope of government." YAF members sent letters to congressional delegations and, in some cases, personally lobbied congressmen to pass Reagan's economic agenda of tax cuts and spending cuts.[41] Although YAF members did what they could to promote Reagan's economic agenda, just what effect they had on congressmen is unknown; nonetheless, during the spring and summer of 1981, with Reagan recovering from gunshot wounds he received during an assassination attempt in March, the economic program passed and Reagan gave YAF credit for helping push the program: "Cutting government spending and reducing taxation have always been YAF goals. Today, they're government policy. YAF's efforts to put these concepts in practice is most appreciated."[42]

In August 1981 YAF held its eleventh national convention in Boston. The convention, the first held since Reagan's election, featured speeches by the Gipper himself (taped), William F. Buckley, Reagan aide Lyn Nofziger, Labor Secretary Raymond Donovan, and controversial Interior Secretary James Watt. Watt's speech was picketed by eighty environmentalists, which prompted YAF members, many of them in suits, tuxedos, and formal dresses, to go out and shout down the protesters.[43] The most emotional part of the convention was a tribute to veterans of the Vietnam War. John McCain, now a senator from Arizona and a former POW, gave a stirring speech about his comrades, and Robert Heckman spoke on the fate of one MIA whose remains had been recently returned to the United States from Hanoi.[44] More than four hundred delegates participated at the Boston convention, which impressed Phil Donahue, the television talk show host who was staying in the same hotel. Donahue invited Lacy and Heckman to his show to talk about YAF. One month later the *Phil Donahue Show* devoted one hour to YAF and conservatism among the young.[45]

The Boston convention and the *Donahue Show* all positioned YAF to achieve what Lacy believed to be vital national publicity. The fact that YAF could command the attention of Cabinet members who would talk with young activists and gain national publicity to push its causes and defend Reagan's record strengthened the organization immensely throughout 1981. James Lacy argued that membership requests increased after the *Donahue* show and that fund-raising was going well. "We benefitted because if you were in YAF and wanted to go to a national YAF convention you had the chance to meet a truly national leader and to influence policy."[46] Yet, increasingly, the success that Lacy had in positioning YAF as the youth arm of the Reagan administration—a natural place for it to be—hurt its ability to fight for a conservative agenda for the campus. This, and increasingly bitter personal controversies on the national board—culminating in destructive and costly litigation—would destroy the organization within three years.

The main problem for YAF throughout 1982 was a lawsuit filed in Delaware Chancery Court contending that Lacy had misused his position as national chairman and should be removed from leadership of the organization. Though YAF always had its share of infighting, this sophomoric dispute—one that had more to do with personality conflicts than ideology or actual malfeasance—ended up seriously diminishing the organization's stature nationally and within the conservative movement.

The roots of the lawsuit date to the fall of 1981 when, because of a personality clash, Lacy fired Heckman from his position as executive director of the organization. He replaced him with New Jersey YAF member Sam Pimm. Heckman had spent more time with the FCM than he had on YAF matters and for some time had been a thorn in Lacy's side, "seeking to make policy for YAF . . . which was not the executive director's role as an employee of the organization." There was also conflict between Lacy and Heckman over where to hold the 1983 convention; Lacy wanted to hold the meeting in Los Angeles and Heckman in New York. At the August 1981 meeting of the national board, Lacy prevailed by one vote on this issue. The board was thoroughly divided between two factions. Lacy, because of the problems between the two men, asked Heckman to resign "and when he wouldn't we were forced to hold a meeting of the national board in November 1981 and we had a vote and I fired him and the board voted 13–12 to support his firing."[47]

Heckman returned to the Fund for a Conservative Majority, but his supporters on the board decided to challenge Lacy's YAF leadership through a lawsuit. Peter Flaherty, a Heckman supporter and a national board member, initiated the suit in 1982, supported by eleven others on the board.[48] Heckman was not a named plaintiff in the suit, but Lacy thought he was the Rasputin involved behind the scenes, determined to wreck YAF for firing him in 1981.[49]

What was the lawsuit about? In a letter to Lacy, sixteen YAF board members charged that Lacy had gone beyond his powers as national chairman. They charged that the "national office has ceased to function, New Guard has gone unpublished . . . and longtime vendors have gone unpaid." Lacy was also accused of "attempt[ing] to exercise control of YAF by personal fiat"; the suit charged that he had abused his expense privileges and called for an audit of the organization's finances, particularly Lacy's expense reports.[50] In a letter to Heckman supporter and FCM board member Mike Thompson, Suzanne Scholte outlined other serious accusations against Lacy, including the national office's interference with YAF regional meetings, the gerrymandering of regional offices, his abuse of the organization's by-laws, and the failure to publish the New Guard or Dialogue on Liberty.[51]

The real problem, aside from the personal charges of malfeasance made against Lacy's leadership, was power. Lacy controlled thirteen members of the twenty-five-member board. After Heckman's firing, a determined effort was made to challenge six directorships; the plaintiffs believed that those directors had been elected to office according to YAF's by-laws but were being prevented from taking their seats by Lacy. Instead, six members of Lacy's faction, holding their seats illegally, according to the plaintiffs, gave the national chairman illegal power on the board. The whole lawsuit boiled down to a dispute between the national office and a faction led by

Peter Flaherty and Kenneth Grasso over six board seats![52] An attempt by the plaintiffs to get a temporary restraining order to keep the nineteen disputed board members from meeting (in this case during August 1982) was denied by the Chancery Court.[53]

After a year of tumult, with Lacy defending the suit to the end—at a cost in attorney's fees of eighty-eight thousand dollars—the Delaware Chancery Court ruled in Lacy's favor on seven of eight issues.[54] The chancellor scolded the young people for bringing such a frivolous suit, stating, in a memorable rebuke, "I would feel less than candid if I did not point out at the outset of this decision that during the ten years of my progressively deteriorating career as a judge of the Court of Chancery this has to constitute the most sophomoric exercise that I have yet been compelled to endure in the name of disposing of legal issues."[55] The American Arbitration Society ruled on factual issues, deciding in favor of Lacy on all four matters brought to its attention.[56]

Although the lawsuit seriously diminished the organization's other efforts, Lacy has admitted that he had little choice but to defend the suit. Other conservative leaders were not so sure. A group of elders, led by Marvin Liebman, met to discuss YAF's future. In August the YAF convention was held in Los Angeles and Robert Dolan was elected national chairman to replace Lacy, who retired from the organization. In memoranda addressed to Dolan, Liebman and a group of veteran conservatives charged that "YAF has become irrelevant to the liberal establishment (as witnessed by the lack of media attention to the law suit) as well as to Republican and conservative establishments." Liebman also charged that "the great majority of board members are in their late twenties or thirties and are not students," that "the organization is currently $430,000 in debt . . . and is in desperate financial straits," and, perhaps most seriously, "YAF has lost all meaningful political clout. It is no longer a force in national politics, youth politics, or on campus." Liebman recommended closing down the organization and starting a new group he called United Students for America (USA), a "legitimate student organization" that would not be involved in Washington politics. YAF should be folded and new groups, made up of current YAF leaders and Young Republicans should take its place.[57] The next month Dolan was given an ultimatum by this distinguished group to either reform YAF or dissolve it. They gave him until June 1, 1984, to answer.[58]

James Lacy responded to Liebman's memo in a pointed letter to William Rusher. He blamed YAF's inadequacies during this period on the "Heckman-Flaherty-Fund for a Conservative Majority lawsuit" and argued that with the lawsuit settled, YAF could begin to address its debt and budget problems. He argued that YAF "retains substantial assets in the National headquarters building and grounds, and a strong active donor list" and that, though "projects were hampered by the lawsuit," YAF continued to publish the *New Guard,* to sponsor regional conferences, to cosponsor CPAC, and to hold a national convention. Lacy concluded that what YAF needed "is something people haven't been willing to give the organization for two years—a break. . . . I hope that you and your associates will continue to play an important role in nurturing, and not abandoning, YAF."[59]

Dolan decided not to abandon YAF but to revive it. In an interview with William Rusher published in the spring 1984 *New Guard,* Rusher admitted that although YAF had "a rather checkered and tortured recent past . . . it has the chance now to reinvigorate itself and make an important mark on the conservative youth movement."[60] For a while, anyway, Rusher's pronouncement seemed to be true. Robert Dolan, a longtime YAF leader from New York, had won election as national chairman. He had supported Lacy during the lawsuit and moved from New York to Washington to handle the workings of the suit. An outspoken and acerbic individual, Dolan was not one to mince words and spare feelings. With a severe financial crisis greeting him upon his assumption of power, Dolan set to work to raise money for the organization and restore its good name within the conservative movement.[61]

In the end, Dolan was successful. Believing, as a lesson learned in the lawsuit, that the old way of splitting the duties of YAF between the elected chairman and the executive director had failed, Dolan attempted to concentrate too much power in his own hands. Dolan possessed a sound understanding of the financial problems the organization faced and hoped to alleviate them once and for all. But, though he was successful in doing so, his management style was a bit too abrasive—"I had to be like the stereotypical New Yorker," he later stated—and Dolan made numerous enemies on the board who sought any excuse to get rid of him.[62]

Whatever his management style, Dolan had produced amazing results. He replaced Bruce Eberle and Associates, YAF's fund-raiser, with a new firm, Response Dynamics. He renegotiated the mortgage on YAF's headquarters in Sterling, Virginia, "on terms favorable to us." YAF sponsored two of the largest CPAC meetings to that time in 1984 and 1985 under his leadership, and some two hundred YAF members played a role at the 1984 Republican convention in Dallas, "on a limited budget."[63] Yet, his style antagonized others. He admitted to having no sponsor within the conservative movement, no Rusher, no Buckley, no congressman who would come to his rescue. Dolan angered Congressman Mickey Edwards when he resisted a funding arrangement that Edwards had installed during his handling of CPAC.[64] He angered board members, who accused him of misusing YAF funds. Several broke into the offices of executive director Richard Hahn in search of evidence against Dolan. Dolan contends they never found any, but as a result of the campaign of disinformation, which he believes was a continuing legacy of the Lacy-Flaherty lawsuit, a majority of the board forced Dolan to resign in March 1985.[65] After eighteen months under his guidance, YAF was in good financial health, with a surplus in the bank and a new contract with Response Dynamics. A year later, YAF, for all practical purposes, had ceased to exist.

Yet, YAF's collapse had little to do with internecine factionalism on the board. The main reason for YAF's collapse was its inability to rejuvenate a focus for mobilizing conservative students on campus. On campus, the Young Republicans were so conservative that the need for an independent group of conservative youth activists outside the GOP had evaporated. YAF's internal schisms and infighting had paralyzed the programmatic initiatives undertaken in the late 1970s and early 1980s. Unable to foment a new agenda for the organization—increasingly an appendage of a national conservative movement content with power inside the nation's capital— YAF as a grass roots organization intent on building conservative cadres withered beyond repair by the mid-1980s. Healthy finances and headquarters in the Washington suburbs could not overcome the fact that YAF was increasingly an anachronism.[66]

Terrell Cannon was the last national chairman of YAF. An attorney from Lincoln, Nebraska, Cannon did not possess the leadership ability needed to guide YAF through crisis. During 1985 he was convinced by some on the board intent on feathering their own nests that they could do a better job raising funds for the organization than Response Dynamics could, and so Cannon fired the direct mail firm and went in-house with Richard Delguadio, a New York YAF member instrumental in dumping Dolan, heading up fund-raising. He failed miserably. As Dolan reiterated, an organization used to taking in twenty thousand dollars a month was receiving less than two thousand dollars a month.[67] When YAF experienced another financial downturn because of the poor fund-raising efforts, Cannon overreacted by selling YAF's main asset as an organization—the Freedom Center in Sterling, Virginia. Although YAF was able to generate enough cash to pay off its debts through these actions, the organization now had no marketable assets and no direct mail contacts. Increasingly a laughingstock within the conservative movement, YAF, for all practical purposes, collapsed.

Yet, a YAF organization of a sort still exists on various campuses throughout the country. A national chairman is still elected, the Sharon Statement still serves as the organization's statement of principles (something the group calling itself YAF protects as its intellectual property), and YAF members are still active on various campuses (with chapters at Georgetown, the University of Virginia, and Boston College). These young people still fight the good fight for conservative principles and still seek to build support for conservative causes, but the effort at building cadres has now been taken up by a wide variety of conservative organizations dedicated to the cause of mobilizing young people on campus and possessing the resources and maturity to accomplish these ends.[68] What is remarkable, in the end, is not just that an organization like YAF existed, but that it existed and served the conservative political movement so long and so well. By creating cadres for conservatism, YAF helped the conservative movement achieve political power. Many more important organizations—both on the Right and on the Left—have achieved less.

Conclusion

I firmly believe that any man's finest hour—his greatest fulfillment to all he holds dear—is that moment when he has to work his heart out in a good cause and he's exhausted on the field of battle—victorious.

—Vince Lombardi

It may be a bit ironic, but in the 1980s, with a conservative president in the White House and conservative ideas under discussion in national political discourse, the oldest conservative student organization had effectively collapsed. After years of internal tumult, coupled with the success conservatives were having politically and institutionally, YAF experienced a period of "benign neglect" from which it never recovered. As the conservative movement grew in influence and power throughout the 1970s—and captured the Republican Party machinery—the necessity for an organization of young conservatives outside the GOP had evaporated.

Nonetheless, YAF had achieved what it set out to gain—political power for the conservative movement. Conservative activists, many of them YAF alumni, had helped build a conservative political movement capable of capturing a major party and helping reorient American politics toward the Right. Young conservatives gained vital political experience within YAF, which they then took with them into occupations in government, publishing, academia, and foundation work. They continue to practice their conservative activism in myriad ways, continued to gather yearly at CPAC conventions in Washington (a veritable Who's Who of YAF alumni), working to build a political majority, the one goal that has eluded their quest for transforming American politics.

YAF also helped keep anticommunist issues in vogue during a time when the fear of Communism was effectively muted by liberal politicians, radical intellectuals, and peace groups. In the immediate aftermath of the Vietnam War, YAF's staunch anticommunism and provictory strategy appeared ridiculous; in the long run, however, YAF's ability to sustain its anticommunism throughout the 1960s and 1970s, in the face of vociferous criticism of such views, paved the way for the return of an anticommunist Cold War mentality that contributed greatly to the collapse of Soviet Communism in Europe and the end of the Cold War. YAF members, by keeping their anticommunism alive through this period, helped build and restore this consensus in American politics during the 1980s.[1]

The development of conservative cadres allowed YAF alumni to play instrumental roles during the Reagan administration and after. More than their counterparts on the Left, YAF alumni were active figures in the nation's capital, helping create what liberal journalist Sidney Blumenthal has called, derisively but correctly, the counterestablishment.[2]

There are numerous examples from YAF's own leadership of continued service and dedication to the conservative cause. Robert Bauman was elected to Congress from Maryland's first congressional district in 1973. He quickly became one of the staunchest conservatives on Capitol Hill until a sex scandal involving his solicitation of an underage male prostitute became public in 1979, derailing a promising political career and his twenty-year marriage to Carol Dawson.[3] Carol Dawson parlayed her work in editing and politics into a tenure at the Consumer Products Safety Commission during the Reagan and Bush administrations.

Richard Viguerie, YAF's first executive director, established his own direct mail firm in the Washington area and was instrumental, along with YAF veteran Howard Phillips and conservative activist Paul Weyrich, in the formation of the New Right, an unformalized, populist-oriented conservative grass roots movement. He also founded the *Conservative Digest,* a short-lived but important New Right publication. After the failure of this enterprise in the mid-1980s, he returned to direct mail operations, which he currently conducts from the Washington area.[4]

Doug Caddy practiced law in Washington and was the first lawyer hired by Watergate burglars E. Howard Hunt and G. Gordon Liddy. He was forced by Judge John Sirica to testify against his clients during a grand jury hearing, and as a result Liddy and Hunt fired Caddy.[5] Subsequently, Caddy returned to Houston, where he continues to practice law. He is engaged in writing his memoirs.

Tom Charles Huston went on to work in the Nixon administration after a two-year stint in army intelligence. Huston wrote the infamous Huston Plan, which was designed to coordinate domestic intelligence operations and to coordinate the powers of separate intelligence agencies in the battle against the administration's domestic enemies. Although Nixon accepted the plan's recommendations, FBI director J. Edgar Hoover vetoed it and the plan never took effect.[6] Huston resigned from the administration in 1973 and returned to Indianapolis, where he practices law to this day.[7]

David Jones retired from YAF in 1967 and became director of the Charles Edison Youth Fund, an organization that granted money for conservative projects headed by young people. He currently serves as director of the Fund for American Studies, which replaced the Edison fund, headquartered in Washington.[8]

Alan MacKay retired as YAF's national chairman in 1969. He sought election to Congress from Massachusetts in 1971 (unsuccessfully). He currently works in corporate law in the Boston area and maintains some active interest in politics.[9]

David Keene became special assistant to Vice President Spiro Agnew in 1970 and served as Agnew's "conservative conscience" during the Nixon administration. After Agnew's resignation in 1973, Keene founded his own political consulting firm and became chairman of the American Conservative Union in 1980, a position he still holds. He served as an unofficial advisor for the 1996 Robert Dole presidential campaign and still appears regularly, in his capacity as a political consultant, on various television talk shows and current issues forums.[10]

Randall Teague was removed from YAF in 1971 and became an assistant to Congressman Jack Kemp until 1978. He practiced law in Boston and currently does so in Washington. He is no longer active politically but still meets regularly with YAF alumni in Washington.[11]

Ron Docksai left YAF in 1975 and received a Ph.D. in government while working as legislative director for the House Committee on Merchant Marines and Fisheries. He worked for Senator Orrin Hatch (R-Utah) for eight years and as special assistant to Office of Personnel Management director Don Devine. He was appointed by President Reagan as assistant director of Health and Human Services in 1985, a position he held until the end of the Reagan administration. He currently works in the private sector for Bayer Pharmaceuticals.[12]

Wayne Thorburn left YAF in 1974 and taught political science at Arkansas State University before moving on to become executive director of the Texas state Republican Party. He served in the Department of Education during the Reagan administration and with the Department of Housing and Urban Development under George Bush. He currently is a political consultant in Austin, Texas.[13]

Other prominent YAF leaders during the 1970s played active roles in the Reagan administration. Frank Donatelli served as regional director for the Reagan campaign in 1980 and later as director of political affairs in the Reagan White House.[14] James Lacy served as an assistant to Secretary of Commerce Malcolm Baldridge and worked for the Commerce Department before being elevated to general counsel of the Consumer Products Safety Commission in 1987. He returned to Commerce during the Bush administration, then left in 1991 to practice law in California with his wife.[15]

Two national board members received major political appointments within the Reagan administration. Richard Allen, a YAF alumnus from Indiana, served as Reagan's first national security advisor, a position he held until 1982. He gained his position through his work as a national security aide to Richard Nixon and his work on behalf of the Committee on the Present Danger.[16] Donald Devine, who served briefly on YAF's national board, was appointed head of the Office of Personnel Management. Before that he was professor of political science at the University of Maryland and had served as a campaign manager for Reagan's 1976 presidential campaign.[17] He currently works as a political consultant in Washington.

Other YAF alumni currently hold office in Congress, including James Kolbe (R-Ariz.) and Dana Rohrabacher (R-Calif.). Several serve as federal court judges, including Daniel Manion, and Diarmuid O'Scannlain. Tommy Thompson, the current governor of Wisconsin, was a YAF "fellow traveler" at the University of Wisconsin, where he was active in Youth for Goldwater.

Others continue to do important work outside of politics. Lee Edwards teaches politics at the Catholic University in Washington and heads his own public relations firm. He has authored numerous books on conservative topics, including biographies of Goldwater and Reagan.[18] Don Feder, who headed Massachusetts YAF, is a syndicated conservative newspaper columnist in Boston. David Brudnoy is a radio talk-show host in Boston on one of the more popular shows in the area. His very public airing of his gay lifestyle, which came about after his contraction of the AIDS virus, combined with his conservative political views, makes him a very controversial public figure. It even landed him on the *Oprah Winfrey* show in 1996.[19] Jameson Campaigne heads his own publishing firm, Green Hill Publishers and Jameson Books, in Ottawa, Illinois. He publishes on a variety of topics, including conservative ones, and remains very active in conservative politics.[20] R. Emmett Tyrrell turned the Indiana University conservative magazine the *Alternative* into the *American Spectator,* moved it from Bloomington to Washington, and during the Clinton administration has made it into a veritable Menckenesque forum for attacks on the Clintons themselves and their "New Left heritage."[21]

Although YAF succeeded in creating a viable network of political activists, certainly a necessity during the 1960s and 1970s when conservatives in Washington could be counted on one hand, their success at doing so may endanger the very health of their movement. With the conservative movement established in power in Washington, younger conservatives were captured by the glamour and opportunities of political life in the nation's capital, abandoning the cultural and academic life to radicals and liberals. As R. Emmett Tyrrell has so ably argued, conservatives have been unable, or unwilling, to create a viable political culture to function alongside their policy ideas. "[Liberals] understood that politics is more than a set of policies. In democracy it is the promotion of culture, a web of principles, sympathies, manners, all the fruits of the intellect. . . . Conservatives are not anti-intellectual. They were conservative policy intellectuals, people who bring high intellect to bear on one or two areas of policy, after which the mind wanders."[22] What conservatism needs most, according to Tyrrell, is to create a viable counterculture. Failing this, the political revolution is doomed.

Lee Edwards also recognized this as one of the conservative movement's major problems: "We need more conservatives in the academy and in the arts. We need conservative poets and dramatists as much as we need senators and mayors. . . . There are just too many conservatives in Washington."[23] Jameson Campaigne argued that though it would be nice to have more conservatives enter the academy and the arts, the real fact is that many conservatives are not interested in that lifestyle because of its promotion of relativism in morals. There are conservative sanctuaries within academia—at Hillsdale College, the economics department of the University of Chicago, and the Hoover Institution at Stanford—but "the rise of talk radio," according to Campaigne, has diminished "a lot of the influence of the academy, which is a good thing."[24]

While YAF alumni have been caught up in Washington politics, other conservatives have been critical of the conservative movement's emphasis on national politics because of their contempt for the corruption they see emanating from "inside the beltway" politics. They believe that both the conservative movement and liberal politicians have supported the growing power of the federal government in the postwar world, and they see very little difference between having one in power and having the other in power. Consisting mainly of descendants of an Old Right—which formed in reaction to the New Deal—this strand of conservatism is gaining renewed strength with the end of the Cold War and is proving to be an important part of the new conservative movement now in the process of emerging. The considerable popularity and success of, populist candidates such as Pat Buchanan and Howard Phillips demonstrates this most aptly.[25]

Conservatives, therefore, are finding it difficult to create a working majority. Factions within the conservative movement continue to ask important questions of it: how important is politics anyway? Would conservatism be better off as an ideology without a focus on politics? Would it be better to return to the halcyon days of Albert Jay Nock's remnant, before Buckley, before Goldwater, before YAF, before power? The questions are important ones for any movement, and how they are addressed will be significant for the future strength and success of a conservatism now dependent on the political process for its future strength and no longer on committed grass roots activism.

But regardless of the fractures within contemporary conservatism, the story of YAF represents the crux of the history of the past quarter century— the seeming exhaustion of liberalism, the victory of freedom over totalitarianism in the Cold War, the return to prominence of free market economics, and the battleground over culture. In every one of these cases, cadres of YAF activists played some small role. They may not be well known for what they did, having been forgotten or ignored in the historical *zeitgeist* as extremist oddities, but what they helped bring about was nothing short of revolutionary. The transformation of American politics in the past twenty-five years owes much to a generation of young activists—and the thousands of their peers influenced by this activism—who stood firm against the radical and liberal tide and contributed to the contemporary conservative renascence in America.

Appendixes

Appendix A

The Sharon Statement
Drafted at Sharon, Connecticut, September 11, 1960

In this time of moral and political crisis, it is the responsibility of the youth of America to affirm certain eternal truths.

We, as young conservatives, believe:

That foremost among the transcendent values is the individual's use of his God-given free will, whence derives his right to be free from the restrictions of arbitrary force;

That liberty is indivisible, and that political freedom cannot long exist without economic freedom;

That the purposes of government are to protect those freedoms through the preservation of internal order, the provision of national defense, and the administration of justice;

That when government ventures beyond these rightful functions, it accumulates power which tends to diminish order and liberty;

That the Constitution of the United States is the best arrangement yet devised for empowering government to fulfill its proper role, while restraining it from concentration of power;

That the genius of the Constitution—the division of powers—is summed up in the clause which reserves primacy to the several states, or to the people, in those spheres not specifically delegated to the Federal government;

That the market economy, allocating resources by the free play of supply and demand, is the single economic system compatible with the requirements of personal freedom and constitutional government, and that it is at the same time the most productive supplier of human needs;

That when government interferes with the work of the market economy, it tends to reduce the moral and physical strength of the nation; that when it takes from one man to bestow on another, it diminishes the incentive of the first, the integrity of the second, and the moral autonomy of both;

That we will be free only so long as the national sovereignty of the United States is secure; that history shows that periods of freedom are rare, and can only exist when free citizens defend their rights against all enemies;

That the forces of international Communism are, at present, the greatest single threat to these liberties;

That the United States should stress victory over, rather than coexistence with, this menace; and

That American foreign policy must be judged by this criterion: does it serve the just interests of the United States?

Appendix B

YAF National Board Members, 1960–1974[*]

James Abstine
Richard Allen

Carol (Dawson)
  Bauman
Robert Bauman
Charles Black
William Boerum
Lynn Bouchey
Allen Brandstadter
Gary J. Brown

Douglas Caddy
Jameson Campaigne, Jr.
Dan Carmen
Fred Coldren
Tom Colvin
Michael R. Connelly
Lammot Copeland, Jr.
Richard Cowan
Robert F. Croll

Mary K. Davis
Ronald Dear
Neil Dentzer

Richard Derham
Donald Devine
William Dobson
Ronald Docksai
Frank Donatelli
Patrick Dowd
James Dullenty

Bruce Eberle
Lee Edwards
Bradley Evans

James Farley
Donald Feder
Mary Fisk
Albert O. Forrester
David Franke

George Gaines
Robert A. Gaston
Antoni Gollan
Alan Gottlieb
Jack Gullahorn

James C. Hager
Robert Harley

J. Harold Herring, Jr.
James E. Hinish, Jr.
Tom Charles Huston

Craig Ihde

David Jones
Daniel Joy

David Keene
Herbert Kohler
James Kolbe
Kay Kolbe
Roger Koopman

Charles Leftwich, Jr.
Joseph Leo
Fulton Lewis III
James Linen IV
Stephen Loewy

Alan MacKay
William Madden
Daniel Manion
Marilyn (Manion)
  Thies

[*] An accurate list of national board members after 1974 could not be obtained.

Stephen Mayerhofer
George McDonnell
Rosemary McGrath
Charles McIlwaine
Carl McIntire, Jr.
John Meyer
James Minarik
Robert Moffit
Jack Molesworth
Maureen Butler
 Moore

Richard Noble
Patrick Nolan
Jerry Norton

Michael O'Connor
Diarmuid O'Scannlain
William Overmoe

Jay Parker
Ted Parkhurst, Jr.
Donald Pemberton
Fred Peterson
Howard Phillips
Thomas L. Phillips
Gerald O. Plas
Richard F. Plechner
Louisa Porter

Daniel Rea, Jr.
Robert Richards
Ron Robinson

John J. Sainsbury
William Saracino
Robert Schuchman
William Schulz
Louisa Sciubba

Ray T. Semmons
Donald Shafto
Scott Stanley, Jr.
Herbert Stupp

Randall C. Teague
Kenneth Thompson
Michael Thompson
Wayne Thorburn

David K. Walter
Donald Walker
A. M. "Bud"
 Wandling
Mark Watson
John Weicher
Richard Wilson
David Wood

Edmund Zanini

Appendix C

YAF Officers, 1960–86

National Chairmen

Robert Schuchman, 1960–63
Robert Bauman, 1963–65
Tom Charles Huston, 1965–67
J. Alan MacKay, 1967–69
David Keene, 1969–71
Ronald Docksai, 1971–75
Jeffrey Kane, 1975–77
John Buckley, 1977–78
James V. Lacy, 1978–83
Robert Dolan, 1983–85
Terrell Cannon, 1985–86

Executive Directors and Executive Secretaries

Douglas Caddy, 1960–62
Richard Viguerie, 1961–65
David Jones, 1963–69
Randall Teague, 1969–71

Wayne Thorburn, 1971–73
Frank Donatelli, 1973–77
Ron Robinson, 1977–79
Robert Heckman, 1979–81
Sam Pimm, 1981–83
Richard Hahn, 1983–85

New Guard *Editors (Partial List)*

Lee Edwards, 1961–63
Carol Bauman, 1963–65
David Franke, 1965–67
Arnie Steinberg, 1967–69
Kenneth Grubbs, 1969–70
Daniel Joy, 1970–71
Jerry Norton, 1971–73
Mary Fisk, 1973–76
David Boaz, 1976–78
Richard LaMountain, 1978–82
Susan Juroe, 1982–84
R. Cort Kirkwood, 1984–85

Notes

NOTES TO INTRODUCTION

1. John A. Andrew, III, *The Other Side of the Sixties: Young Americans for Freedom and the Rise of Conservative Politics* (New Brunswick, N.J.: Rutgers University Press, 1997).

2. For the quote, see William Martin, *With God on Our Side: The Rise of the Religious Right in America* (New York: Broadway Books, 1996), 87–88; author conversation with Morton Blackwell, April 24, 1997.

NOTES TO CHAPTER I

1. George H. Nash, *The Conservative Intellectual Movement in America: Since 1945*, rev. ed. (Wilmington, Del.: Intercollegiate Studies Institute, 1996), 11.

2. Ibid., 11–14; Godfrey Hodgson, *The World Turned Right Side Up: A History of the Conservative Ascendancy in America* (New York: Houghton Mifflin, 1996), 25–29; Albert Jay Nock, *Our Enemy, the State* (New York: William Morrow, 1935); and Nock, *Memoirs of a Superfluous Man* (New York: Harper and Brothers, 1943). *The Freeman* would be resurrected in the 1930s by a Nockian disciple, Frank Chodorov. Henry Regnery, *A Few Reasonable Words: Selected Writings* (Wilmington, Del.: Intercollegiate Studies Institute, 1996), 32–51 provides a good summary of Nock's life and influence, as does Charles H. Hamilton in his introduction to Nock, *The State of the Union: Essays in Social Criticism* (Indianapolis: Liberty Fund, 1991), xi–xxiv.

3. For both perspectives, see Nash, *Conservative Intellectual Movement*, 11–14; Russell Kirk, *The Sword of Imagination: Memoirs of a Half-Century of Literary Conflict* (Grand Rapids, Mich.: Eerdmans, 1995), 168–69; and John B. Judis, *William F. Buckley, Jr.: Patron Saint of the Conservatives* (New York: Touchstone, 1988), 44–46.

4. F. A. Hayek, *The Road to Serfdom* (Chicago: University of Chicago Press, 1994), 4.

5. Ibid., 261.

6. Richard Weaver, *Ideas Have Consequences* (Chicago: University of Chicago Press, 1948), 4.

7. Ibid.

8. Nash, *Conservative Intellectual Movement,* 33–35.

9. For a sound discussion of Strauss's and Voegelin's ideas, see Ted V. McAllister, *Revolt against Modernity: Leo Strauss, Eric Voegelin, and the Search for a Postliberal Order* (Lawrence: University Press of Kansas, 1996); for a critique of Strauss and other "antimodernists," see Stephen Holmes, *The Anatomy of Antiliberalism* (Cambridge, Mass.: Harvard University Press, 1993). Holmes neglects the influence of Voegelin's thought in his book.

10. Kirk, *Sword of Imagination,* 67; Nash, *Conservative Intellectual Movement,* 61–68.

11. Russell Kirk, *The Conservative Mind: From Burke to Eliot,* 3rd rev. ed. (Chicago: Henry Regnery, 1960), 7–8.

12. Russell Kirk, *The Politics of Prudence* (Bryn Mawr, Pa.: Intercollegiate Studies Institute, 1993), 287.

13. The finest history of the ADA is Steven M. Gillon, *Politics and Vision: The ADA and American Liberalism, 1947–1985* (New York: Oxford University Press, 1987); Alonzo Hamby, *Beyond the New Deal: Harry S. Truman and American Liberalism* (New York: Columbia University Press, 1972) is very useful on liberal battles during this period, as is John Ehrman, *The Rise of Neoconservatism: Intellectuals and Foreign Affairs, 1945–1994* (New Haven: Yale University Press, 1995). See also, for the definitive contemporary statement, Arthur M. Schlesinger, Jr., *The Vital Center: The Politics of Freedom* (New York: Houghton Mifflin, 1949).

14. Eugene Lyons, *The Red Decade: The Stalinist Penetration of America* (Indianapolis: Bobbs-Merrill, 1941). See Richard Gid Powers, *Not without Honor: The History of American Anticommunism* (New York: Free Press, 1996), 117–154, for an analysis of anticommunism during the 1930s.

15. For the Hiss-Chambers case, see Whittaker Chambers, *Witness* (New York: Random House, 1952); Allen Weinstein, *Perjury: The Hiss-Chambers Case,* rev. ed. (New York: Knopf, 1997); and Sam Tanenhaus, *Whittaker Chambers: A Biography* (New York: Random House, 1997).

16. See Tanenhaus, *Whittaker Chambers,* for the portrayal of Chambers as a despairing and pessimistic intellectual. For further evidence, see William F. Buckley, Jr., ed., *Odyssey of a Friend: Whittaker Chambers's Letters to William F. Buckley, Jr., 1954–1961* (New York: G.P. Putnam's, 1961). For confirmations of Hiss's guilt, which still is disputed by Hiss partisans, see Weinstein, *Perjury;* Tanenhaus, *Whittaker Chambers;* and Harvey Klehr, John Earl Haynes, and Frederikh Igorevich Firsov, *The Secret World of American Communism* (New Haven: Yale University Press, 1996), 81–82, 117–118.

17. Nash, *Conservative Intellectual Movement,* 89–90.

18. For Burnham's intellectual development, see John Patrick Diggins, *Up from Communism: Conservative Odysseys in American Intellectual Development* (New York: Columbia University Press, 1994), 160–98, 303–37.

19. Burnham became, in essence, the first neoconservative. For this view, see

Gary Dorrien, *The Neoconservative Mind: Politics, Culture, and the War of Ideology* (Philadelphia: Temple University Press, 1993); for a different view, which puts emphasis on Burnham's ideas about social class, see Samuel Francis, *Power and History: The Political Thought of James Burnham* (Lanham, Md.: University Press of America, 1984).

20. James Burnham, *The Struggle for the World* (New York: John Day, 1947), 248. For the influence of Mackinder on Burnham, see Dorrien, *Neoconservative Mind*, 44–50; and Nash, *Conservative Intellectual Movement*, 82–83.

21. For Burnham, see his *The Coming Defeat of Communism* (New York: John Day, 1950); for Kennan, see Mr. X, "The Sources of Soviet Conduct," *Foreign Affairs* 25 (July 1947): 566–82.

22. James Burnham, *Containment or Liberation?* (New York: John Day, 1953); and Ehrman, *Rise of Neoconservatism*. Burnham backed away from the liberation strategy after Stalin's death in 1953, but ironically it continued to be the rhetorical strategy employed by the Eisenhower administration until the Hungary crisis in 1956. See Stephen F. Ambrose, *Eisenhower*, vol. 2, *The President* (New York: Simon and Schuster, 1984).

23. For a discussion of this labeling, see Kirk, *Sword of Imagination*, 140–46; and McAllister, *Revolt*, 262–271.

24. Powers, *Not without Honor*, gives the best recent overview of the diversity in anticommunist thought. See, for specific elaborations of this diversity, Patrick Allitt, *Catholic Intellectuals and Conservative Politics in America, 1950–1985* (Ithaca: Cornell University Press, 1993); Fred Schwarz, *Beating the Unbeatable Foe* (Washington, D.C.: Regnery Press, 1996); Marvin Liebman, *Coming Out Conservative: An Autobiography* (San Francisco: Chronicle Books, 1992); and the dated but still useful Seymour Martin Lipset and Earl Raab, *The Politics of Unreason: Right-Wing Extremism in America, 1790–1977*, 2d ed. (Chicago: University of Chicago Press, 1978).

25. Nash, *Conservative Intellectual Movement*, 118–71, provides the most thorough scholarly treatment of this development. For the definitive contemporary statement, see Frank S. Meyer, *In Defense of Freedom and Related Essays* (Indianapolis: Liberty Fund, 1996), 33–151.

26. Judis, *Buckley*, 20–22.

27. Ibid., 29–34.

28. Ibid., 40–50.

29. Ibid., 44–50.

30. William F. Buckley, Jr., *God and Man at Yale* (Chicago: Henry Regnery, 1951), foreword (unpaginated).

31. McGeorge Bundy, "The Attack on Yale," *Atlantic Monthly,* November 1951, 50–52; William F. Buckley, Jr., "The Changes at Yale," *Atlantic Monthly,* December 1951, 78, 80, 82. William A. Rusher, *The Rise of the Right* (New York: William Morrow, 1984), 38–43, claims that Bundy's review served as the unofficial Yale position on the book. See Judis, *Buckley*, 92–98; and Nash, *Conservative*

Intellectual Movement, 140–41, for other reviews of the book. Henry Regnery, the book's publisher, wrote elegantly of the book's importance for conservatism and its reception in the press, in *Memoirs of a Dissident Publisher* (Chicago: Regnery Books, 1985), 167–173. Regnery's importance as a publisher of conservative writing cannot be underestimated in the development of a conservative movement in the postwar period. See "Henry Regnery: A Tribute," *Modern Age,* fall 1996, 312–20.

32. Both are described in Liebman, *Coming Out,* 92–104, 105–11. See also Stanley Bachrack, *The Committee of One Million: "China Lobby" Politics, 1953–1971* (New York: Columbia University Press, 1976).

33. Rusher, *Rise of the Right,* 15–20.

34. Interview with William Rusher, September 18, 1994.

35. Rusher, *Rise of the Right,* 67–70; F. Clifton White, with Jerome Tuccille, *Politics as a Noble Calling: The Memoirs of F. Clifton White* (Ottawa, Ill.: Jameson Books, 1995).

36. Interview with Tom Charles Huston, January 17, 1995.

37. M. Stanton Evans, *Revolt on the Campus* (Chicago: Henry Regnery, 1961), 64; David Franke, "To Develop Leaders," *New Guard,* October 1961, 13.

38. See "The Campus Conservative Clubs," an ISI advertisement that put forth the organization's mission to "spread conservative ideas, with full confidence that these ideas will in due course have beneficial consequences." *National Review,* June 6, 1959, 127.

39. Evans, *Revolt,* 66.

40. Several of these clubs thrived during the late 1950s and received attention in the pages of *National Review.* See Russell Kirk, "Why Not Try Businessmen?" *National Review,* February 13, 1960, 107; and Kirk, "They Are Stirring in the Colleges," *National Review,* March 12, 1960, 171.

41. Interview with M. Stanton Evans, February 24, 1995; Evans, *Revolt,* 5–9; Carol D. Bauman, "Mercury of the Midwest (Profiles in Conservatism)," *New Guard,* April 1961, 7. The *Indianapolis News* was one of several papers owned by Eugene Pulliam, a conservative publisher who was instrumental in the early career of Arizona senator Barry Goldwater. Pulliam owned the *Arizona Republican,* a paper that supported Goldwater. See Robert Alan Goldberg, *Barry Goldwater* (New Haven: Yale University Press, 1995), 78–79. Pulliam was also the grandfather of future vice president Dan Quayle.

42. Evans, *Revolt,* 6; interview with Evans.

43. Jameson Campaigne, Sr., to Eugene Pulliam, March 28, 1962, Jameson Campaigne, Sr., Papers, box 6 (March 1–31, 1962), Hoover Institution, Stanford, Calif.; interview with Jameson Campaigne, Jr., March 8, 1995.

44. Nash, *Conservative Intellectual Movement,* 27–28.

45. The *American Mercury* was taken over in 1949 by businessman Russell Maguire, a conspiracy theorist and vehement anti-Semite. The *Mercury's* descent into populist racism began earlier, however, as Elizabeth Dilling, a profascist and

anti-Semitic propagandist, published in the magazine regularly. See Glen Jean-somme, *Women of the Far Right: The Mothers' Movement and World War II* (Chicago: University of Chicago Press, 1996), 10–28.

46. Memorandum to Editors of *National Review* from Frank Meyer, May 10, 1960, box 10, Inter-Office Memos, William F. Buckley, Jr., Papers, Yale University, Sterling Library, New Haven, Conn. (hereafter WFB MSS).

47. Powers, *Not without Honor,* 272.

48. Buckley's and Bozell's defense of the Wisconsin senator, *McCarthy and His Enemies* (Chicago: Henry Regnery, 1956), was a popular feature on ISI book lists.

49. This is a point made in most studies of the reawakening of radical student activism during the early 1960s. See Tom Hayden, *Reunion: A Memoir* (New York: Collier Books, 1988); Todd Gitlin, *The Sixties: Years of Hope, Days of Rage* (New York: Bantam Books, 1987); Terry Anderson, *The Movement and the Sixties: Protest in America from Greensboro to Wounded Knee* (New York: Oxford University Press, 1995); and David Horowitz, *Radical Son: A Generational Odyssey* (New York: Free Press, 1997).

50. Interview with Lee Edwards, February 22, 1995; for the significance of Edwards's father's relationship with McCarthy, see Richard Norton Smith, *The Colonel: The Life and Legend of Robert M. McCormick, 1880–1955* (New York: Houghton Mifflin, 1997), 498–99, 500.

51. Interview with Douglas Caddy, March 18, 1997; Douglas Caddy, "Birth of the Conservative Movement," unpublished manuscript, Private Papers of Douglas Caddy (copy in Schneider's possession).

52. According to studies by sociologists Margaret and Richard Braungart, family and religious motivations were more important influences than the demagoguery of McCarthy himself. See "The Life-Course Development of Left- and Right-Wing Youth Activist Leaders from the 1960s," *Political Psychology* 11 (1990): 243–82.

53. Ambrose, *Eisenhower,* 355.

54. "The Hungary Pledge" stipulated that the assignees "affirm that a total quarantine . . . of the Soviet Union . . . be maintained at least until all Soviet forces are withdrawn from Hungary." *National Review,* December 8, 1956, 5.

55. Both incidents are described in Liebman, *Coming Out,* 113–16. The Army of Liberation story may be apocryphal; I have been unable to find further corroboration. The event involving Massey was covered, according to Liebman, by the *New York Daily News* but the *New York Times* did not cover this particular protest. Illona Massey did participate in picket lines in Washington, D.C., on October 27, a full week before the Soviet crackdown. See *New York Times,* October 28, 1956, 34.

56. The oath read as follows: "I, _____, do solemnly swear (or affirm) that I will bear true faith and allegiance to the United States of America and will support

and defend the Constitution and laws of the United States of America against all its enemies, foreign and domestic."

The affidavit read: "I, _____, do solemnly swear (or affirm) that I do not believe in, and am not a member of and do not support any organization that believes in or teaches the overthrow of the United States government by force or violence or by any illegal or unconstitutional methods." See Evans, *Revolt,* 75.

57. A. W. Griswold, "Loyalty: An Issue of Academic Freedom," *New York Times Magazine,* December 20, 1959, 18–20.

58. Kennedy offered his justification for rescission in "Let's Get Rid of Loyalty Oaths," *Coronet,* April 1960, 88–94.

59. Evans, *Revolt,* 75–76; Kevin Sullivan, "Oathism on the Campus," *Nation,* December 5, 1959, 416–19; "Fuss over Loyalty Oaths—Will It Stop Loans to Students?" *U.S. News and World Report,* December 7, 1959, 58–60.

60. The committee's founding was announced in *National Review,* January 16, 1960, 28; and by Gerald W. Johnson, "An Outburst of Servility," *New Republic,* February 8, 1960, 11.

61. Interview with David Franke, May 15, 1995.

62. Interview with Caddy.

63. Evans, *Revolt,* 77–80. Franke admitted that it was difficult to call the loyalty oath groups chapters. Most likely, they were individual students that both Caddy and Franke were in contact with at different colleges. Interview with Franke.

64. Interview with Carol Dawson, September 4, 1994.

65. Styles Bridges to Douglas Caddy and David Franke, January 18, 1960, Private Papers of Douglas Caddy; Senate, Styles Bridges, Remarks in the Senate on Student Committee for the Loyalty Oath, February 15, 1960, 86th Cong., 2d sess., *Cong. Rec.* (February 18, 1960) 106: 2607–9.

66. Evans, *Revolt,* 82.

67. Only nineteen colleges withdrew from the act as of March 1960. Senate, Bridges, 2608.

68. Evans, *Revolt,* 84; *National Review,* January 30, 1960, 61; and "For or against the Loyalty Oath?" *National Review,* February 27, 1960, 126–27.

69. Interview with Edwards.

70. There are three recent biographies and several older, but still quite useful, political biographies of Goldwater. For a better example of the latter, see Edwin McDowell, *Portrait of an Arizonan: Barry Goldwater* (Chicago: Henry Regnery, 1964), chaps. 1–5; also see Goldwater's two memoirs: Barry Goldwater, *With No Apologies* (New York: William Morrow, 1979); and Goldwater, with Jack Casserly, *Goldwater* (New York: Doubleday, 1988); the recent biographies are Lee Edwards, *Goldwater: The Man Who Made a Revolution* (Washington, D.C.: Regnery, 1995); Goldberg, *Goldwater;* and Peter Iverson, *Barry Goldwater: Native Arizonan* (Norman: University of Oklahoma Press, 1997).

71. Goldwater, *With No Apologies,* 91; Goldberg, *Goldwater,* 108–10; Edwards, *Goldwater,* 132–33.

72. Goldwater, *With No Apologies,* 93–94.

73. Ibid., 94.

74. Edwards, *Goldwater,* 100; Goldberg, *Goldwater,* 135; Goldwater, *With No Apologies,* 70.

75. Rusher, *Rise of the Right,* 67; interview with Rusher.

76. For a fine history of this development, see Mary C. Brennan, *Turning Right in the Sixties: The Conservative Capture of the GOP* (Chapel Hill: University of North Carolina Press, 1995).

77. Robert Welch, *The Politician* (Belmont, Mass.: Belmont, 1963), 278.

78. For Manion's firing, see David W. Reinhard, *The Republican Right since 1945* (Lexington: University Press of Kentucky, 1983), 117; *New York Times,* February 16, 1954, 1; and Robert J, Donovan, *Eisenhower: The Inside Story* (New York: Doubleday, 1956), 105.

79. Clarence Manion to William E. Jenner, April 11, 1957, box 3, folder 10, Clarence Manion Papers, Chicago Historical Society. Chicago, Ill.

80. Goldwater, *With No Apologies,* 95.

81. Manion to William F. Buckley, Jr., September 28, 1959, box 68, folder 4, Manion MSS.

82. Ibid.

83. Goldwater, *With No Apologies,* 96–99; Reinhard, *Republican Right,* 150–55.

84. See *National Review,* May 21, 1960, 316; Press Release, Youth for Goldwater for Vice President, May 12, 1960, Private Papers of Douglas Caddy; interview with Caddy; and Andrew, *Other Side,* 27–28.

85. Evans, *Revolt,* 88–89. Harley was president of the Washington, D.C., College YR, Richard Noble was treasurer of the California YR, and John Weicher was a student at the University of Chicago and a former staff member at *Human Events.*

86. Press Release, Private Papers of Douglas Caddy; Andrew, *Other Side,* 27–28; Evans, *Revolt,* 92; and Liebman, *Coming Out,* 146.

87. Again, the announcement of forty-five chapters, as David Franke told me, probably represented forty-five supporters on forty-five campuses, not fully staffed chapters with active members. Interview with Franke; interview with Caddy.

88. Barry M. Goldwater, *The Conscience of a Conservative* (Shepherdsville, Ky.: Victor Publishing, 1960), 13.

89. Memo from Frank Meyer to Editors, May 10, 1960, box 10, Inter-Office Memos, WFB MSS.

90. Interview with Franke; interview with Campaigne. Douglas Caddy discounts the eastern-midwestern alliance thesis, believing instead that the Washington-headquartered Youth for Goldwater for Vice President committee did the most to bring this about. Interview with Caddy.

91. Goldwater, *With No Apologies,* 105–14; Rusher, *Rise of the Right,* 87–89; and Reinhard, *Republican Right,* 153–55. The young people in the Youth for Goldwater drive, if they were aware of the Fifth Avenue meeting, did not let it deter their efforts on behalf of Goldwater. Lee Edwards related, "We were young people, and young people always believe they are going to win." Interview with Edwards.

92. Liebman, *Coming Out,* 147; interview with Marvin Liebman, September 1, 1994. The two committees, Goldwater for Vice President and Judd for Vice President, were so interconnected that they shared the same suite in Chicago's Pick-Congress Hotel. Liebman worked for both Judd and Goldwater at the convention. Interview with Caddy.

93. The excitement was palpable and noticed in the press. *New York Times,* July 23, 1960, 1.

94. Evans, *Revolt,* 101.

95. Interview with Franke.

96. Interview with Caddy.

97. Brennan, *Turning Right,* 36–37.

98. *National Review,* August 13, 1960, 9, recognized the influence of young people at the 1960 convention. "Youth was everywhere at the Republican convention. . . . But those who were serious, the ones who will be working hardest to guide the Republican Party in the future, were conservatives: and most of them Goldwater fans. . . . What's more, they are going to be around a long time to come, which is something the Republican leadership should take note of." See also Brennan, *Turning Right,* 39–81.

99. The number of people gathered at the luncheon is open to question. Liebman, in *Coming Out,* 150, claimed six or seven people present. Douglas Caddy claimed that the meeting was open to anyone who wanted to come and that Goldwater was present. Interview with Caddy.

100. Liebman, *Coming Out,* 150; interview with Liebman; Evans, *Revolt,* 108–9.

NOTES TO CHAPTER 2

1. Judis, *Buckley,* 29–33.

2. Ibid., 29–30.

3. Liebman, *Coming Out,* 151. Doug Caddy claims the house was already volunteered by Buckley at the Republican convention. Interview with Caddy.

4. See E. J. Dionne, Jr., *Why Americans Hate Politics* (New York: Simon and Schuster, 1991), 35–37; and Andrew, *Other Side,* 54–56, 146–50.

5. William F. Buckley, "Young Americans for Freedom," *National Review,* September 24, 1960, 161.

6. The source for the number of students is a list in box 12, YAF, September

10, 1960, WFB MSS. The list has ninety-eight names of those in attendance but it is difficult to ascertain its accuracy. For example, Jameson Campaigne informed me he was at the Sharon meeting, yet his name does not appear on the list. Whether the names on the list represented a confirmation of those who would be attending, or an actual list of those present, remains a mystery. Judis claims that only eighty people attended the conference, whereas William Rusher suggests ninety were present. See Judis, *Buckley*, 188; and Rusher, *Rise of the Right*, 89; interview with Campaigne. For a solid overview of the conference itself, see Andrew, *Other Side*, 53–74.

7. Interview with Franke; interview with Caddy.

8. The Canadian, Brian Whalen, attended Loyola University in Chicago. In October 1962 Henry Regnery received notice of the establishment of a Young Canadians for Freedom. It is unclear whether Whalen had anything to do with the founding of the "Canadian YAF." See letter to Regnery, October 7, 1962, box 81 (Correspondence), folder 1, Henry Regnery Papers, Hoover Institution.

9. David L. Westby and Richard G. Braungart, "Class and Politics in the Family Backgrounds of Student Political Activism," *American Sociological Review* 31 (October 1966): 690–92.

10. Ibid.

11. Margaret and Richard Braungart have engaged in some of the major work in this field, exploring the social status of both conservative and leftist student groups in the 1960s. See, e.g., "Life-Course Development," 254–269; Richard Braungart, "SDS and YAF: A Comparison of Two Student Radical Groups in the Mid-1960s," *Youth and Society* 2 (June 1971): 441–57; and Richard Braungart, with David L. Westby, "The Alienation of Generations and Status Politics: Alternative Explanations of Student Political Activism," in Roberta Sigel, ed., *Learning about Politics: A Reader in Political Socialization* (New York: Random House, 1970), 476–89.

12. See Westby and Braungart, "Class and Politics." Also see Laurence F. Schiff, "The Obedient Rebels: A Study of College Conversions to Conservatism," *Journal of Social Issues* 20 (October 1964): 74–95; Schiff, "Dynamic Young Fogies— Rebels on the Right," *Trans-Action* 4 (November 1966): 31–36; and Edward Cain, *They'd Rather Be Right: Youth and the Conservative Movement* (New York: Macmillan, 1963).

13. Interview with Caddy. For McIntire's father's role on the anticommunist Right, see Martin, *God On Our Side*, 35–40; also see Harry Overstreet and Bonaro Overstreet, *The Strange Tactics of Extremism* (New York: Norton, 1964), 143–56.

14. Allitt, *Catholic Intellectuals*, 89–101.

15. Interview with Dawson; interview with Caddy; interview with Howard Phillips, March 28, 1997.

16. Andrew, *Other Side*, 56–60; Evans, *Revolt*; interview with Dawson; interview with Evans.

17. For the complete text of the Sharon Statement, see Appendix A.

18. Interview with Edwards.

19. Interview with Campaigne.

20. Edward C. Facey, "Conservatives or Individualists: Which Are We?" and John Weicher, "Mr. Facey's Article: A Comment," in *New Individualist Review,* summer 1961, 24–27.

21. Interview with Evans.

22. The fusionist conception in American conservative thought was derived by Frank Meyer in several essays in *National Review* and later in a book entitled *What Is Conservatism?* as a way of conjoining libertarian views regarding limited state interference with traditional views regarding the maintenance of social order. Meyer believed that it was quite natural, within America's constitutional order, that liberty (the pursuit of happiness) could be reconciled with social order (primarily religious in nature). For a good survey of fusionist thought, a term Meyer was never very happy with, see Nash, *Conservative Intellectual Movement,* chap. 5; and Paul Gottfried and Thomas Fleming, *The Conservative Movement* (Boston: Twayne, 1988), 18–19.

23. Gerhart Niemeyer to Buckley, with attachment, "Letter to Young Conservatives," September 22, 1960, box 11, Niemeyer, WFB MSS. See also Niemeyer to James Burnham, box 10, folder 7 (Subject File, U.S. Politics, 1960–1970), James Burnham Papers, Hoover Institution.

24. M. Stanton Evans, *The Theme Is Freedom: Religion, Politics, and the American Tradition* (Washington, D.C.: Regnery, 1994), 38.

25. Interview with Rusher.

26. Compare this with the debate at Port Huron between elder radicals such as Michael Harrington, upset at the soft tone that the Port Huron Statement took toward the Soviet Union, and younger New Leftists such as Tom Hayden. The breach between the adult radicals like Harrington (who was involved with SDS's parent organization, the League for Industrial Democracy) and the younger New Leftists would never heal. See Hayden, *Reunion,* 87, 89–93; James Miller, *Democracy Is in the Streets* (New York: Simon and Schuster, 1987); and Gitlin, *The Sixties,* 115–20.

27. The term conservative in the late 1950s referred not to the anticommunist, libertarian, pro–free market ideology with which it would come to be associated, but rather to a traditionalist typology implying, pejoratively, a return to the premodern conception of prescriptive tradition and the worship of the divine. For a fuller discussion of the meanings associated with *conservative,* see McAllister, *Revolt,* 8–13, 262–70; and Regnery, *Few Reasonable Words.*

28. Interview with Edwards.

29. Interview with Franke. Franke did become the organization's first treasurer.

30. Franke seems to believe that this is part of the reason Schuchman was picked. Interview with Franke. Caddy confirmed the Ivy League rationale but

stated that Schuchman's religion had nothing to do with his selection. Interview with Caddy.

31. Andrew, *Other Side,* 71, 72, 74.

32. After working several years as an attorney, Schuchman grew tired of law and returned to graduate school in law and economics at the University of Chicago, where he worked under Milton Friedman. He died of a brain embolism in 1966.

33. Evans, *Revolt,* 110.

34. Interview with Dawson; Lee Edwards, "Why . . ." *New Guard,* March 1961, 3.

35. Interview with Franke.

36. Rusher, *Rise of the Right,* 114.

37. Ibid., 115. Liebman never denied this accusation. Interview with Liebman.

38. Liebman, *Coming Out,* 152–53; interview with Liebman; interview with William F. Buckley, August 16, 1994. Caddy claims he does not remember such extravagance on the part of his former boss. Interview with Caddy.

39. Interview with Rusher.

40. Memorandum from Liebman to YAF Officers and Directors, March 23, 1961, box 17, YAF, WFB MSS. In the memo Liebman claims that within the year he had been working for YAF, gratis, forty-five thousand dollars had been raised for the organization.

41. Buckley to Joe Topalian, March 20, 1961, box 17, YAF, WFB MSS; interview with Buckley.

42. David Franke, "Tower's Victory in Texas," *National Review,* January 10, 1961, 16, 30.

43. Franke, "Breaking the Liberal Barrier," *New Guard,* April 1961, 10; interview with Franke; interview with Liebman. Liebman's influence here as a former Communist agitator was crucial.

44. "We'll Take Manhattan, the Bronx and . . ." *New Guard,* March 1961, 4; *New York Times,* March 4, 1961, 1; Buckley, "YAF Night at Manhattan Center," *National Review,* March 25, 1961, 187.

45. Interview with Liebman.

46. Ibid.

47. Caddy claims that a *Newsweek* reporter doing a story on conservative students pressed him for the organization's membership. When he dutifully reported the lower number, the reporter stated that he couldn't print that because there would be no story, so Caddy went along with having a higher figure substituted, a figure that became twenty-five thousand. Interview with Caddy.

48. The problem of actual membership *versus* claimed membership would plague executive directors throughout YAF's history. Interview with Liebman; interview with Rusher; interview with Dawson; interview with Randall Cornell Teague, September 22, 1994; and interview with Franke.

49. Randall Teague, who would assume the duties of executive director in

1969, related that YAF's ratio of claimed to actual membership could reliably be placed at 3:1 during his tenure. Interview with Teague. Teague's successors, Wayne Thorburn and Ron Robinson, confirmed the reliability of Teague's assertion. Interview with Thorburn, July 24, 1997; interview with Robinson, July 29, 1997.

50. Interview with Caddy.

51. Several people who knew Caddy well attest to this. Interview with Franke; interview with Buckley; interview with Rusher. Caddy discounts the claim, believing that others, such as William Rusher, were greater behind-the-scenes operatives than he. Interview with Caddy.

52. Interview with Franke. The Policy Committee was made up of the organization's national chairman, national director, treasurer, and secretary. It had little effect on controlling chapters but some effect on setting an agenda for future YAF activities.

53. Telegram from Buckley, Evans, Liebman, and Rusher to Caddy, Franke, Bauman, and Schuchman, May 19, 1961, box 17, YAF, WFB MSS.

54. Letter and Memo from Liebman to Bauman, Caddy, Franke, and Schuchman, May 24, 1961, box 17, YAF, WFB MSS.

55. Rusher memo to Buckley, Liebman, and Frank Meyer, September 5, 1961, box 17, YAF, WFB MSS; Rusher, *Rise of the Right,* 115.

56. Interview with Caddy; interview with William Cotter, May 1, 1997.

57. Interview with Cotter. Cotter claimed that Rusher attempted to get him to vote his way at a board meeting and remove Caddy as national director while he was in the army. When Cotter refused, an effort to paint him as a subversive influence (along with Caddy, Howard Phillips, and Scott Stanley) ensued.

58. Interview with Cotter.

59. Rusher, *Rise of the Right,* 115; interview with Rusher; interview with Liebman. Cotter claimed that Liebman was a pushover in disputes, which was why he needed Rusher, a tougher infighter, to help him through this. Interview with Cotter.

60. The aforementioned Carol Dawson. She married Robert Bauman in November 1960.

61. Interview with Franke.

62. Interview with Richard Viguerie, March 26, 1997.

63. Memorandum to YAF Board of Directors from Bauman, Croll, Edwards, Franke, Kolbe, Madden, and Schulz, August 12, 1961, box 17, YAF, WFB MSS.

64. Cotter did take his position as YAF organizational secretary quite seriously: his office released a twenty-page college and community organizing manual in 1961 that offered constructive tips on how to form YAF chapters and how to organize for action. YAF College and Community Organizational Manual, Campus ADA File, box 32, folder 223 (NSA Working Papers, 1961–1962), Americans for Democratic Action Papers, State Historical Society of Wisconsin, Madison, Wis. (hereafter ADA MSS).

65. Interview with Caddy; interview with Cotter; interview with Viguerie.

66. Interview with Phillips; interview with Cotter.

67. Interview with Cotter.

68. Interview with Cotter; interview with Phillips; interview with Scott Stanley, May 15, 1997.

69. Interview with Phillips.

70. Richard Viguerie, *The New Right: We're Ready to Lead* (Falls Church, Va.: Viguerie Co., 1981), 27–31; interview with Viguerie.

71. Rusher to L. Brent Bozell, September 28, 1961, box 17, YAF, WFB MSS; Rusher, *Rise of the Right,* 114–16; interview with Rusher; interview with Liebman; interview with Dawson.

72. Interview with Caddy. The September 2 meeting caused bad blood between Liebman and Caddy, with Liebman suggesting that Caddy find employment elsewhere when he ended his military service. Liebman to Caddy, October 23, 1961, Private Papers of Douglas Caddy. Caddy has subsequently claimed that in his only meeting with Liebman since the 1961 meeting, Liebman told him of Rusher's and Liebman's alliance and of feigned threats that Liebman would resign if the Caddy faction did not back down. Caddy letter to author, June 27, 1997, in author's possession.

73. Interview with Phillips.

74. Interview with Rusher.

75. Memo to Liebman, Buckley, and Meyer from Rusher, September 5, 1961, box 17, YAF, WFB MSS.

76. Interview with Cotter; interview with Phillips; interview with Caddy.

77. Rusher, *Rise of the Right,* 114–16; Liebman, *Coming Out,* 153–56.

78. Interview with Cotter.

79. William Rusher to L. Brent Bozell, September 28, 1961, box 17, YAF, WFB MSS.

80. Ibid.; interview with Rusher; Rusher, *Rise of the Right,* 114–16.

81. Caddy to Liebman, January 21, 1962, box 21, Liebman, WFB MSS.

82. Interview with Caddy; interview with Cotter.

83. Interview with Cotter. There is no evidence to support their assertions.

84. A proposed YAF budget listed expenses through June 30, 1961, as $69,173 and contributions as the same. The estimated total budget for one-half year (April–December 1961) was $86,000, one-third of which went for administrative expenses. The only salary paid by YAF was to William Cotter, who made $15,000 per year (which also paid traveling expenses). Cotter claimed his salary was only $500 per month. See YAF Estimated Budget, box 141, folder 3 (YAF, 1960–1978), A. C. Wedemeyer Papers, Hoover Institution; interview with Cotter. Gen. Albert C. Wedemeyer served on YAF's national advisory board.

85. For the Nash candidacy, see *New York Times,* September 6, 1961, 28; and "Next Time," *National Review,* September 21, 1961, 184; Marvin Kitman, "New

Wave from the Right," *New Leader,* September 18, 1961, 12. Nash was a twenty-nine-year-old advertising man and a "dedicated young conservative in the Goldwater tradition."

86. On the Nash campaign and splits between Caddy and Franke at this time: interview with Franke; interview with Caddy; see Nash to *Human Events,* May 22, 1962, and Caddy to Buckley, May 28, 1962, box 19, Caddy, WFB MSS. In the letter to Buckley, Caddy stated: "The letter from Ed Nash speaks for itself. Since Bill Rusher is given as a reference to the libelous charges made in the letter, I thought it would be of interest to you as the type of viciousness which has brought YAF to its current internal impotence."

87. Interview with Caddy.

88. Interview with Franke.

89. Interview with Caddy.

90. Ibid.; interview with Phillips; interview with Cotter.

91. Rusher, *Rise of the Right,* 115.

92. He did this in a privately circulated book, not published until 1963, titled *The Politician* (Belmont, Mass.: Belmont, 1963). Prominent conservatives and friends of Welch received copies, but it was unavailable to the grass roots members of the John Birch Society until 1963. Therefore, it can be argued that many members of the JBS were unaware, but later may have agreed with, many of Welch's more extreme pronouncements on the Communist conspiracy. See William B. Hixson, Jr., *Search for the American Right Wing: An Analysis of the Social Science Record, 1955–1987* (Princeton, N.J.: Princeton University Press, 1992); Reinhard, *Republican Right,* 174; Rusher, *Rise of the Right,* 114, 115; and Lipset and Raab, *Politics of Unreason,* 248–87.

93. "Questions and Answers," *National Review,* April 22, 1961, 241–43; Judis, *Buckley,* 194–97, contains the best summary of the growing disenchantment between Buckley and the Birch Society.

94. Judis, *Buckley,* 193–200; Rusher, *Rise of the Right,* 189–90; and "The Question of Robert Welch," *National Review,* February 13, 1962, 83–88.

95. Stanley denies that he was a member of the Birch Society at that time. After he took over the editorial duties of Welch's publications, he was made an honorary member, but that was in 1964 at the earliest. Interview with Stanley.

96. I have been unable to find a record of the NAM meeting. The source is twofold: Rusher to William Madden, July 17, 1962, box 99, National Review, Marvin Liebman Papers, Hoover Institution; and The Rockwell Report, "Jew-Led Kosher Conservatives" (February 15, 1962), box 37, YAF—Misc., Liebman MSS. The *Rockwell Report* was the publication of the American Nazi Party and its leader George Lincoln Rockwell.

97. Interview with Stanley.

98. Ibid.

99. Judis, *Buckley,* 199.

100. Memorandum to Board of Directors from Liebman, January 17, 1962, box 23, YAF, WFB MSS. Caddy replied to Liebman's memo with glee, stating that he was glad "to get your memorandum this week resigning as the $3,580 a month public relations consultant to YAF." The letter was sent to Buckley with Liebman's note in the margins about his desire "to extricate myself from YAF." See Caddy to Liebman, January 21, 1962, box 21, Liebman, WFB MSS.

101. Liebman, *Coming Out,* 154.

102. A copy of the *Rockwell Report* can be found in both the Liebman papers, box 37, YAF—Misc. and in box 23, YAF, WFB MSS. The cover is also described in Liebman, *Coming Out,* 156.

103. The only source for the allegation is Liebman, *Coming Out,* 154. Caddy and Stanley vehemently denied any involvement with such an effort. Interview with Caddy; interview with Stanley.

104. Interview with Caddy.

105. Ibid.; interview with Phillips; interview with Stanley; interview with Cotter.

106. Interview with Stanley. Stanley argued that one of the more impressive things about Robert Welch was his tolerance toward people of different beliefs and faiths (Communists excepted). "There were many disagreements on the part of Birch Society members," Stanley argued, "much more so than what was allowed in the conservative movement at that time."

107. Memorandum to All Concerned from Marvin Liebman, January 17, 1962, box 99, National Review, Liebman MSS.

108. Memorandum from Liebman to Rusher, March 5, 1962, box 21, Liebman, WFB MSS. Liebman argued "that it is time for *National Review* to take up a cudgel or two in my behalf. These rumors and gossip are getting out of hand. Not only do they affect me personally; they also considerably damage my potential usefullness [*sic*] to the Conservative movement."

109. Confidential Memorandum to Board of Directors from Liebman, February 16, 1962, box 23, YAF, WFB MSS.

110. Caddy to Charles Edison, February 25, 1962, box 21, Liebman, WFB MSS. Caddy vehemently denied any involvement in anti-Semitic smears against Liebman, as did William Cotter. Interview with Caddy; interview with Cotter.

111. Liebman, *Coming Out,* 153.

112. Hoover, who did not attend the rally, received a report from his former aide, Frank Mason. Mason's information was received secondhand via Henry Regnery. Mason to Herbert Hoover, March 8, 1962, Herbert Hoover Post-Presidential Papers, HH PPI (Post-Presidential Index), Correspondence File (Mason), Herbert Hoover Presidential Library, West Branch, Iowa.

113. See special rally coverage, including the reprinted speeches, in *New Guard,* March 1962, and April 1962, for photo coverage and highlights.

114. "18,000 Rightists Rally at Garden," *New York Times,* March 8, 1962, 1,

21; Noel Parmental, Jr., "Gnostics at the Garden," *Commonweal,* March 30, 1962; Stephen V. Roberts, "Image on the Right," *Nation,* May 19, 1962; and "Notes from the YAF Rally," *National Review,* March 27, 1962, 37.

115. *Time,* March 16, 1962, 31; *Newsweek,* March 19, 1962, 37.

116. Minutes of the Meeting of the National Board of Directors, YAF, Shelburne Hotel, New York, March 8, 1962, box 23, YAF, WFB MSS. The votes lined up according to factions, with Caddy, Phillips, Cotter, and Stanley voting against the motion or abstaining. Stanley did not run for reelection to the board at the YAF convention in September 1962; he quietly left the organization at that time. Cotter left after the March 8 meeting to work for the National Association of Manufacturers and later on Wall Street. He served in two different capacities in the Nixon administration. Phillips also left YAF that year, returning to Boston to build up the regular Republican Party there. He later headed the Office of Economic Opportunity during the Nixon administration before founding the Conservative Caucus, an organization dedicated to building conservative support at the grass roots. In 1996 he ran for president as the candidate of the U.S. Taxpayer's Party. Interview with Cotter; interview with Stanley; interview with Phillips.

117. Bauman was the "prosecutor" against Stanley at the meeting. Interview with Stanley; interview with Robert Bauman, July 25, 1995.

118. Interview with Bauman; Robert E. Bauman, *The Gentleman from Maryland: The Conscience of a Gay Conservative* (New York: Arbor House, 1986).

119. Buckley to Goldwater, July 12, 1962, and Telegram, Buckley to Goldwater, July 11, 1962, box 23, YAF, WFB MSS. Buckley suggested that Stan Evans take over the organization and straighten out the mess, but Evans by this time had removed himself from an active role in YAF. Interview with Evans.

120. Robert Bauman reported Caddy's disruptive actions in removing files from the office to Caddy's employer, the U.S. Chamber of Commerce, and Caddy was summarily dismissed. Rusher to Madden, July 17, 1962, box 99, National Review, Liebman MSS.

121. Ibid.

122. Ibid.

123. Gary Russell, "YAF Charts Far-Reaching Program," *New Guard,* November 1962, 8–9.

NOTES TO CHAPTER 3

1. Interview with Campaigne; interview with Don Devine, August 28, 1996.

2. Lee Edwards, "Bread and Circuses," *New Guard,* July 1961, 2.

3. "What Can I Do?" *New Guard,* July 1961, 3.

4. Edwards, "Taking a Covered Wagon to the New Frontier," *New Guard,* March 1961, 2; "Let Him Begin," *New Guard,* August 1961, 2; see also Andrew, *Other Side,* 32–52.

5. Brennan, *Turning Right,* 44–46.

6. Hayden, *Reunion,* 32, 35, 58; for a more radical view of Kennedy, see Horowitz, *Radical Son,* 105–6.

7. Miller, *Democracy,* 16, argues compellingly that the civic republican vision in the Port Huron Statement was crucial in defining SDS as an organization in the early 1960s.

8. See Phyllis Schlafly, *A Choice, Not an Echo* (Alton, Ill.: Pere Marquette Press, 1964), for the most important conservative case against liberal Republicanism. For further splits within the party, see Brennan, *Turning Right,* 44–50; and Andrew, *Other Side,* 32–52.

9. Antoni Gollan, "At the CORE of Racial Tension," *New Guard,* August 1961, 13–14, 17.

10. Powers, *Not without Honor,* 281.

11. Interview with David Jones, October 10, 1994; interview with Teague.

12. "Meredith at Mississippi," *New Guard,* November 1962, 4.

13. Ibid. Lee Edwards argued in the editorial: "As conservatives we understand and support the theory of states' rights but as conservatives concerned about freedom and respectful of order, we cannot endorse lawlessness, insurrection or racism. If [James] Meredith is a "tool" of the NAACP he is a charlatan of the worst stripe. But if he is a young man with a family interested in the best possible education, we wish him well as he pursues his course of studies." Also see Goldwater, *Conscience of a Conservative,* 31–37.

14. "Goldwater's Speech on Civil Rights," June 18, 1964, reprinted in F. Clifton White, *Suite 3505: The Story of the Draft Goldwater Movement* (New Rochelle, N.Y.: Arlington House, 1967), 429–31.

15. Antoni Gollan, "Negroes Have Been Failed," *New Guard,* October 1963, 6; Edwards, *Goldwater,* 234–41. One black YAF member explained his support for Barry Goldwater this way: [Goldwater] "is a constitutional integrationist [who] has fought to protect the rights of the Negro, the Indian and the white man without infringing upon the rights of all men." James A. Parker, "Why I'm Backing Barry Goldwater," *New Guard,* November 1964, 11–12.

16. Gollan, "Negroes," 6. Gollan also talked about two Southern conservative campus groups (without identifying them by name) that listed stores in the community that segregated Negroes so that "those offended could take their business elsewhere."

17. See William H. Chafe, *Never Stop Running: Allard Lowenstein and the Struggle to Save American Liberalism* (New York: Basic Books, 1993), 92–100.

18. Interview with Dawson; Carol Dawson, "Preliminary Report on the 13th Annual Congress of the National Student Association, Minneapolis, Mn., August 17–September 1, 1960," box 12, YAF, WFB MSS.

19. Howard Phillips, "Inside NSA," *New Guard,* April 1961, 12.

20. Ibid.

21. Press Release, CRNSO, n.d., Legislative File, box 50, folder 257 (Right-Wing Student Organizations, 1961–1962), ADA MSS.

22. Howard Phillips, "The Isolated Elite of NSA," *New Guard,* August 1961, 11–12; Tom Huston, "The Rise and Fall of NSA," *New Guard,* April 1964, 8–10; Andrew, *Other Side,* 93.

23. Al Haber quoted in Huston, "Rise and Fall," 9.

24. Huston, "Rise and Fall."

25. Interview with Phillips; "NSA: The Opposition," *New Guard,* October 1961, 3.

26. *New York Times,* August 29, 1961, 12.

27. Letters to various media outlets from Howard Wachtel, July 28–August 4, 1961; Wachtel to Prof. Carl Auerbach, June 23, 1961, box 31, folder 221; ADA Press Release, n.d. (summer 1961), Campus ADA File, box 17, folder 174 (NSA Correspondence, Jan. 1954–Jan. 1964), all in ADA MSS.

28. Memorandum on NSA Congress from Al Haber, June 8, 1961, box 2, folder 6, series I (NSA: Liberal Study Group, 1961, June 8–August 22), Students for a Democratic Society Papers, State Historical Society of Wisconsin (hereafter SDS MSS).

29. *Nation,* September 16, 1961, 4.

30. Tom Charles Huston, "Revolt Ahead in NSA?" *New Guard,* August 1962, 9, 12. An NSA report seemed to indicate the effect that YAF and other right-wing groups were having on the retention of student council membership in the organization. See Memorandum to Organizational Representative from Ed Garvey, n.d., Legislative File, box 50, folder 257 (Right-Wing Student Organizations, 1961–1962), ADA MSS.

31. Interview with Huston.

32. Huston, "Student Leaders Form New Alliance," *New Guard,* June 1964, 10–12.

33. Interview with Phillips. The main reason for the vitriol, according to Phillips, was that the dean of the college at Harvard was on the advisory board of the NSA.

34. Phillips, "Inside NSA," 12.

35. The *New Guard* publicized the story in March and April 1967. Flippantly, David Jones suggested that YAF apply for a CIA subsidy and "if necessary in order to qualify, we would be willing to increase our opposition to the policies of the present Administration . . . and would increase our opposition to the government's no-win policy in Vietnam." *New Guard,* March 1967, 3–7; April 1967, 3–5. See also Alan W. Bock, "NSA's 20th Annual Farce," *New Guard,* October 1967, 6–9; and "NSA Exodus Continues," *New Guard,* December 1967, 3–4.

36. Sol Stern, "A Short Account of International Student Politics and the Cold War," *Ramparts,* March 1967. As David Horowitz, then editor of *Ramparts,* stated in *Radical Son,* 159–60, "a further link . . . between the campus and the war . . .

was established when a student came to *Ramparts* with information that the CIA was funneling secret funds into the National Student Association. . . . In the hands of *Rampart's* editors, a moral equivalence between Russia's police state and America's democracy, was established . . . that seemed to confirm the New Left's view of the world."

37. After the CIA revelations, David Friedman, economist Milton Friedman's son, a YAF member and a Ph.D. candidate in Physics at the University of Chicago, coined a poetic tribute to NSA worth quoting in full:

I Once Went to NSA

I once went to NSA, early in my life
I spent two weeks of sleepless nights, supporting student strife
We castigated governments, at home and far away
Now *Ramparts* says that I was just, a spy for the CIA
We told the farthest sultan, just how to mend his ways
All left-wing students got, our left-wing student praise
We fought against the fascists, to save the world from YAF
Why didn't Dulles tell them, that he had bought the staff?
All anti-yanqui rebel youths, we fought so hard to save;
We used to think we were the spray, upon the future's wave.
We worked through the nights for civil rights, in the rooms of the
    LSG (Liberal Study Group)
We knew we ran the congress, with our brave minority
In certain years we had our fears, when the rightists raised a fuss
But we always ran the congress; I wonder who ran us
For two long weeks we filled the air, with flying wheat and chaff
Then all unsettled questions were decided by the staff.
For two long weeks we filled the halls, with our righteous Liberal
    rages;
The rest of the year was run by the staff, and the men who paid their
    wages.
I've lost my faith forever more, let *Ramparts* fold, I pray
Before they learn the FBI is running ADA.
(New Guard, Summer 1967, 17)

38. The course, created by high school teacher and (after 1961), Florida state YAF chairman David Jones, was adopted as part of the curriculum by the Florida legislature. Jones would be elected to YAF's national board in 1962 and would be appointed executive director of YAF in 1963, a position he held until 1969. Interview with Jones.

39. "Resolution on Cuba," *New Guard*, November 1962, 9.

40. Historian Phillip Nash, who has studied the trade of American Jupiter

missiles in Italy and Turkey for the removal of Soviet missiles in Cuba, quotes one YAF member who approved of the deal, which would help end the conflict. See *The Other Missiles of October: Eisenhower, Kennedy and the Jupiters, 1957–1963* (Chapel Hill: University of North Carolina Press, 1997), 117.

41. M. Stanton Evans, *The Politics of Surrender* (New York: Devin-Adair, 1966), 430–31; Richard Reeves, *President Kennedy: Profile of Power* (New York: Simon and Schuster, 1993), 140, 167.

42. The main reason for U.S. support for the Congo was the desire to prevail over the Soviet Union for the loyalty of independent African regimes. See Thomas J. Noer, *Cold War and Black Liberation: The U.S. and White Rule in Africa, 1948–1968* (Columbia: University of Missouri Press, 1985); Henry F. Jackson, *From the Congo to Soweto: U.S. Foreign Policy toward Africa since 1945* (New York: William Morrow, 1982), 21–52; and Evans, *Politics of Surrender*, 432–45.

43. Part of the problem the United Nations had with Katangese secession was due to the Katangese Army, made up of 80 percent Belgian army troops and paid white mercenaries. See Ernest W. Lefever, *Crisis in the Congo: A United Nations Force in Action* (Washington, D.C.: Brookings Institution, 1965), 73, 75.

44. Telegram from U.S. Embassy, Paris, to Department of State, December 5, 1961, and memorandum from Dean Rusk to JFK, February 1, 1961, both in *Foreign Relations of the United States: The Congo Crisis, 1961–1963* (Washington, D.C.: GPO, 1994), 287–88, 40–45.

45. Memo from Assistant Secretary of State for African Affairs, G. Mennen Williams to Under Secretary of State George Ball, February 7, 1962, *Foreign Relations*, 380–81.

46. Tshombe was later called back to govern the Congo in 1964 but was overthrown in a coup d'état in 1968. He died in 1969 under mysterious circumstances after being kidnapped and held captive in Algeria amid rumors of an attempt to restore him to power.

47. For a defense of atmospheric testing, see Lewis L. Strauss, *Men and Decisions* (Garden City, N.Y.: Doubleday, 1962), 404–27. Strauss was Eisenhower's head of the Atomic Energy Commission and a YAF national advisory board member.

48. For a summary of the testing issues in the late 1950s, see McGeorge Bundy, *Danger and Survival: Choices about the Bomb in the First Fifty Years* (New York: Random House, 1988), 333–34; Spencer R. Weart, *Nuclear Fear: A History of Images* (Cambridge, Mass.: Harvard University Press, 1988), 199–212; Glenn T. Seaborg, *Kennedy, Khrushchev, and the Test Ban* (Berkeley: University of California Press, 1981); Howard Ball, *Justice Downwind: America's Atomic Testing Program in the 1950s* (New York: Oxford University Press, 1986); Earl H. Voss, *Nuclear Ambush: The Test-Ban Trap* (Chicago: Henry Regnery, 1963); and Robert A. Divine, *Blowing in the Wind: The Nuclear Test Ban Debate, 1954–1960* (New York: Oxford University Press, 1978).

49. Reeves, *President Kennedy*, 311. Kennedy, Reeves wrote, "was haunted by

the fear of [nuclear proliferation] and . . . the single most compelling reason for a test ban was to prevent Communist China from developing a bomb." Also see Seaborg, *Kennedy, Khrushchev, and the Test Ban,* 172–86.

50. Reeves, *President Kennedy,* 476, 553.

51. Testimony is reprinted in Seaborg, *Kennedy, Khrushchev, and the Test Ban,* 271–272.

52. "Why We Oppose Test Ban Treaty II," *New Guard,* August 1963, 3–5.

53. Ibid., 5.

54. *New Guard,* September 1963, 5.

55. Interview with Bauman; Testimony of Robert E. Bauman, National Chairman, YAF, Senate Foreign Relations Committee, *Hearings on Nuclear Test Ban Treaty,* 88th Cong., 1st sess., 1963, 712–21.

56. "Thurmond Praises YAF in Senate," *New Guard,* October 1963, 8; *Cong. Rec.* 88th Cong., 1st Sess., 1963, 109, pt. 12: 17642.

57. Powers, *Not without Honor,* 308–11, although not concerned with the test ban debate, makes a similar point about the Kennedy administration's approach to anticommunist issues, including Vietnam.

58. Détente was heralded by Soviet leader Nikita Khrushchev as well, since he believed it would buy the Soviets time to consolidate socialism. See Vladislav Zubok and Constantine Pleshakov, *Inside the Kremlin's Cold War: From Stalin to Khrushchev* (Cambridge, Mass.: Harvard University Press, 1996), 270–74. Despite conservative hyperbole, the test ban treaty codified rules under which nuclear expansion could be conducted. See, for this point, John Lewis Gaddis, *We Now Know: Rethinking Cold War History* (Oxford: Clarendon Press, 1997), 280.

59. John Lewis Gaddis, "The Unexpected Ronald Reagan," in Gaddis, *The United States and the End of the Cold War: Implications, Reconsiderations, Provocations* (New York: Oxford University Press, 1992), 119–32; and Strobe Talbott, *The Master of the Game: Paul Nitze and the Nuclear Peace* (New York: Knopf, 1988).

60. Interview with J. Alan MacKay, September 26, 1996.

61. Interview with Campaigne.

62. Ibid.

63. Donald J. Lambro, "Who Is Lee Harvey Oswald?" *New Guard,* November–December 1963, 9–10.

NOTES TO CHAPTER 4

1. The historiography on this topic is enormous. For a fair sampling, see Kevin Phillips, *The Emerging Republican Majority* (New Rochelle, N.Y.: Arlington House, 1969); Dionne, *Why Americans Hate Politics;* Brennan, *Turning Right;* Ronald Radosh, *Divided They Fell: The Demise of the Democratic Party, 1964–1996* (New York: Free Press, 1996); Martin P. Wattenberg, *The Decline of American Political Parties, 1952–1984* (Cambridge, Mass.: Harvard University Press, 1986); Walter Dean Burn-

ham, *Critical Elections and the Mainsprings of American Politics* (New York: Norton, 1970); James Sundquist, *Dynamics of the Party System: Alignment and Realignment of Political Parties in the United States,* rev. ed. (Washington, D.C.: The Brookings Institution, 1983); and Steve Fraser and Gary Gerstle, eds., *The Rise and Fall of the New Deal Order, 1930–1980* (Princeton, N.J.: Princeton University Press, 1989).

2. A process best described in Brennan, *Turning Right,* 60–66; Andrew, *Other Side,* 187–204; Hodgson, *World Turned Right Side Up,* 92–98; Rusher, *Rise of the Right,* 98–112; and White, *Suite 3505.*

3. Brennan, *Turning Right,* 36–38; Andrew, *Other Side,* 32–52; Rusher, *Rise of the Right,* 88–90.

4. Andrew, *Other Side,* 48–52; Brennan, *Turning Right,* 29–38; Edwards, *Goldwater,* 82–102; and Goldberg, *Goldwater,* 118–48.

5. Goldberg, *Goldwater,* 149–51; and Edwards, *Goldwater,* 144–45.

6. Edwards, *Goldwater,* 144–45.

7. Rusher, *Rise of the Right,* 129–59; White, *Suite 3505;* Edwards, *Goldwater,* 144–91; Goldberg, *Goldwater,* 149–80; Brennan, *Turning Right,* 60–81; White, *Politics as a Noble Calling;* and Karl Hess, *In a Cause That Will Triumph: The Goldwater Campaign and the Future of Conservatism* (Garden City, N.Y.: Doubleday, 1967).

8. Only Andrew, *Other Side,* 175–84, 187–95, has fully explored this in any detail.

9. "Can Goldwater Win?" *New Guard,* December 1962–January 1963, 4–5. Other editorials plugging the candidacy appeared in the succeeding months. See "Goldwater in '63 and '64," *New Guard,* February 1963, 4; and "We Like Barry," *New Guard,* April 1963, 4–5.

10. "3000 Cheer Goldwater," *New Guard,* May 1963, 12.

11. "Youth for Goldwater," *New Guard,* October 1963, 9; Andrew, *Other Side,* 171–72; Edwards, *Goldwater,* 158–59.

12. Andrew, *Other Side,* 268.

13. Edwards, *Goldwater,* 350–57. Tommy Thompson, the current governor of Wisconsin, was active in Youth for Goldwater at the University of Wisconsin in 1964. See his *Power to the People: An American State at Work* (New York: Harper Collins, 1996), 64. Hillary Rodham Clinton actively supported Goldwater at her Park Ridge, Illinois, high school. See David Brock, *The Seduction of Hillary Rodham Clinton* (New York: Free Press, 1996). For other examples of young people mobilized politically by the Goldwater campaign, see Samuel G. Freedman, *The Inheritance: How Three Families and America Moved from Roosevelt to Reagan and Beyond* (New York: Simon and Schuster, 1996), 238–40, 254–55.

14. "YAF Converges upon Washington, D.C. for Political Action, D.C. Rally," *New Guard,* August 1963, 13; "Fans Give Goldwater Boost at Rally Here," *Washington Post,* July 5, 1963, 1, 6; "Washington Rally Opens Campaign to Draft Senator Goldwater for G.O.P.," *New York Times,* July 5, 1963, 11; interview with Dawson.

15. Edwards, *Goldwater*, 170–80; White, *Suite 3505*, 181–89; and White, *Politics as a Noble Calling*, 153.

16. M. Stanton Evans, "Goldwater, Rockefeller and the Young Republicans," *National Review*, August 13, 1963, 97.

17. Rusher, *Rise of the Right*, 98.

18. White, *Suite 3505*, 166–74; Andrew, *Other Side*, 175–76.

19. White, *Suite 3505*, 173; Evans, "Goldwater and the YR's," 97–100.

20. Andrew, *Other Side*, 176–77; Remarks of Congressman John Ashbrook, *Cong. Rec.*, 88th Cong., 1st sess., August 23, 1963, vol. 109, 12: 15691–701.

21. Goldwater, *Goldwater*, 144–48; Edwards, *Goldwater*, 177–79; and Goldberg, *Goldwater*, 190.

22. "YAF's 3rd Annual National Awards Rally," *New Guard*, November–December 1963, 14–15.

23. Andrew, *Other Side*, 188–89.

24. Interview with Huston; *New Guard*, July 1963, 15.

25. Interview with Jones; interview with Teague.

26. Marilyn Manion, "What You Can Do in 1964," *New Guard*, February 1964, 13, 15.

27. *New Guard*, January 1964, 16–19.

28. *New Guard*, May 1964, 14–19, back cover.

29. One poll at the University of Mississippi showed Goldwater with a commanding lead over any other candidate, signifying, perhaps, growing conservative Republican strength in the South. See "Way Down South in the Land of Barry," *New Guard*, April 1964, 16–17.

30. *New Guard*, March 1964, 17–23.

31. Richard Taylor, "And Now, Presenting . . . The Goldwaters!" *New Guard*, March 1964, 14. An album advertisement, with song titles such as "Cuba," "Pinkos," "Welfare State," and "The Other Bobby," can be found in the same issue on page 20.

32. *New Guard*, August 1963, 12.

33. One YAF member, Tony Dolan, became a conservative folksinger during the 1960s and later a speechwriter for President Reagan.

34. Lee Edwards, "Watch This Man!" *New Guard*, March 1964, 13; see "YAF around the Nation," in the same issue.

35. "YAF at San Francisco: A Generation Arrives," *New Guard*, August 1964, 13.

36. Ibid., 3 (emphasis in original).

37. D. E. "Buz" Lukens, "The 1964 Republican Platform," *New Guard*, July 1964, 6–8, 11; Andrew, *Other Side*, 39, 40.

38. Edwards, *Goldwater*, 256–58; White, *Suite 3505*, 389–91.

39. Edwards, *Goldwater*, 257.

40. White, *Suite 3505*, 434–36, contains the full text of the letter.

41. *New Guard,* August 1964, 14.

42. Interview with Campaigne.

43. Interview with Franke.

44. *New Guard,* August 1964, 16.

45. Ibid., 17.

46. Edwards, *Goldwater,* 264–67.

47. Interview with Campaigne. Campaigne claims the incident may have had more to do with Mailer's attraction to Campaigne's girlfriend, who was attending the convention as an alternate delegate. For Mailer's account, see "In the Red Light: A History of the Republican Convention in 1964," *Esquire,* November 1964, 83–89, 167–79.

48. Interview with Bauman.

49. Interview with Campaigne.

50. See Edwards, *Goldwater,* 267–80; White, *Suite 3505,* 11–18; and Theodore H. White, *The Making of the President, 1964* (New York: Atheneum, 1965), 217–20.

51. Edwards, *Goldwater,* 272–73.

52. Ibid., 299–302.

53. "Voices of Moderation," *National Review,* August 11, 1964, 675–677.

54. William F. Buckley, Jr., "The Vile Campaign," *National Review,* October 6, 1964, 858.

55. Edwards, *Goldwater,* 318, 320–22, 341–43.

56. Richard Viguerie parlayed his experience in fund-raising for YAF into a direct mail career during he campaign. While working for the Goldwater for President Committee, Viguerie realized that most financial contributions were small (ten dollars or twenty dollars at most). By getting the names of the contributors on lists and then selling the lists to conservative organizations for a percentage of the take, Viguerie could make thousands of dollars as a list broker. In March 1965 YAF's national board, unhappy with the prospect of their house list being sold to other organizations, asked for Viguerie's resignation. David Jones, as executive director, would take over key fund-raising responsibilities. Interview with Jones; interview with Rusher; interview with Liebman; Minutes of the Meeting of the National Board of Directors, YAF, March 7, 1965, Washington, D.C., Private Papers of Jameson Campaigne, Jr. (hereafter PPJC).

57. Carol Bauman to William F. Buckley, Jr., August 18, 1964, box 29, Bauman, WFB MSS.

58. Interview with Bauman; interview with Buckley.

59. Interview with Rusher.

60. Ibid.

61. William F. Buckley, Jr., "We, Too, Will Continue," *New Guard,* December 1964, 11.

62. Interview with Bauman. Although Bauman possessed enough political savvy

to realize that Goldwater would not win, Buckley's speech made him rethink his own future involvement in the conservative movement.

63. "Growth in Chapters Marks Post-Election Period: YAF-Sponsored Publications Proliferate in All Regions," *New Guard,* December 1964, 20.

64. "National YAF Board Meets in Washington: Adopts Ten-Point Program for 1965," *New Guard,* January 1965, 25.

65. Interview with Jones.

66. "The American Conservative Union" (Background of ACU: meetings of 12/1 and 12/19/64), box 57, Liebman MSS.

67. Ibid.

68. Rusher, *Rise of the Right,* 182.

NOTES TO CHAPTER 5

1. *Public Papers of the Presidents: Ronald Reagan: 1988* (Washington, D.C.: GPO, 1991), 1495–96.

2. For this argument, see Norman Podhoretz, *Why We Were in Vietnam* (New York: Simon and Schuster, 1982); Adam Garfinkle, *Telltale Hearts: The Origins and Impact of the Vietnam Antiwar Movement* (New York: St. Martin's Griffin, 1997); Guenter Lewy, *America in Vietnam* (New York: Oxford University Press, 1977); and Thomas W. Pauken, *The Thirty Years War: the Politics of the Sixties Generation* (Ottawa Ill.: Jameson Books, 1995).

3. Interview with David Keene, September 28, 1994.

4. Powers, *Not Without Honor,* 317–28, argues that Kennedy and his advisors never framed American justification for Vietnam in terms of anticommunism. Rather, as "moderate" Cold Warriors, they attempted to rationalize the war on the basis of nation-building, counterinsurgency, and other policies.

5. Goldwater, *Conscience of a Conservative,* 122.

6. This is not too inconsistent a position. South Korea, which the Americans had defended from Communist invasion between 1950 and 1953, was not a democracy, and American policymakers and journalists were not interested that it become one *during the war.* In South Vietnam, however, American policy was intertwined with efforts to build democracy during wartime, a difficult if not impossible task. See Garfinkle, *Telltale Hearts,* 2.

7. "International Anti-Communist Youth Group Born," *New Guard,* December 1961, 19.

8. Robert G. Harley, "South Viet Nam: Asian Battleground," *New Guard,* January 1962, 14–15.

9. "It's Now or Never," *New Guard,* April 1962, 4–5.

10. For Diem, see "Another China?" *New Guard,* October 1963, 3; also see Mark Stewart, "That War in Vietnam," *New Guard,* January 1964, 7.

11. Richard Derham, "Should Freedom Take the Offensive?" *New Guard,* December 1964, 13–14, 18.

12. See Powers, *Not without Honor,* 395–96, 411–15.

13. "YAF Pickets Support LBJ on Vietnam," *New Guard,* March 1965, 22–23.

14. "President Receives Strong YAF Support on Vietnam, Dominican Republic Intervention," *New Guard,* June 1965, 20.

15. "Feast versus Fast," *New Guard,* September 1965, 25.

16. "YAF Chapters Support U.S., Vietnam," *New Guard,* December 1965, 21.

17. "Let It Bring Hope . . . ," *New Guard,* February 1966, 22–24.

18. Huston was thought by elder YAF leaders to harbor sympathy with the John Birch Society. Alan MacKay, who had attended the Sharon Conference and was twenty-nine years old in 1965, was made vice chairman primarily to ensure some maturity in YAF leadership. Although Huston was an intelligent and passionate YAF leader, many thought him immature and too far right politically. Ironically, he would later serve in the Nixon administration, which conservatives believed too liberal. Interview with MacKay.

19. Tom Charles Huston, *Building a Free Society,* YAF pamphlet, PPJC. Huston said that after giving the speech, which upset many in the audience, he was chased out of the hotel by angry YAF members. "I thought they were going to lynch me," he recalled. Interview with Huston; interview with Bauman. The speech is interesting when weighed against Huston's later views during the Nixon administration.

20. "YAF Members Receive Asian Fellowships," *New Guard,* September 1965, 26.

21. Liebman, *Coming Out,* 119.

22. Minutes of the Meeting of the National Board of Directors, YAF, March 19–20, 1966, PPJC.

23. Memorandum to All Concerned from Prof. David Rowe, May 16, 1966, box 108, folder 572, Liebman MSS.

24. "Interim Report on the Activities of the International Freedom Corps Volunteers," July 29, 1966, box 108, folder 581, Liebman MSS.

25. Interview with Keene.

26. "Interim Report," Liebman MSS.

27. SCFC Press Release, October 13, 1966, box 108, folder 60, Liebman MSS.

28. Interview with Keene.

29. Ibid.; interview with Huston.

30. R. J. Bocklet, "East-West Trade: Coup for the East, Danger to the West," *New Guard,* February 1965, 12–14, 22.

31. "YAF Chapters Support Goodyear, Picket Firestone," *New Guard,* May 1965, 21; Evans, *Politics of Surrender,* 84–85.

32. "Firestone Calls Off Deal with Reds," *New Guard,* 5 June 1965, 21.

33. "Slashed Tires," *Washington Post,* May 12, 1965, 16.

34. Quoted in "Firestone Calls Off Deal with Reds," *New Guard,* June 1965, 21.

35. *Cong. Rec.,* 89th Cong., 1st sess., 1966, 111, pt. 13: 18226–34, 18256.

36. "A Statement of Policy: Trading with the Enemy," *New Guard,* August 1965, 5.

37. Ibid.

38. Terry Anderson, "The New American Revolution: The Movement and Business," in David Farber, ed., *The Sixties: From Memory to History* (Chapel Hill: University of North Carolina Press, 1994), 175–205.

39. Liebman, *Coming Out,* 264–65.

40. Interview with Evans.

41. Anderson, "New American Revolution," 181.

42. The violence was located at the University of Wisconsin campus at Madison, where, in the spring of 1968, the Dow Days protests led to confrontation between students and the Madison police department. See Tom Bates, *Rads: The 1970 Bombing of the Army Math Research Center at the University of Wisconsin and Its Aftermath* (New York: Harper Collins, 1992), esp. chap. 2; and David A. Keene, "Freedom, Force, and the University," *New Guard,* March 1968, 10–12.

43. Alan MacKay, YAF's vice chairman at the time, recognized that some young people were zealots concerning any foreign trade with Eastern European nations. He saw himself as more pragmatic, insisting that some trade with the Eastern bloc was beneficial if it was not used for a military or secret police purpose. "There were board members who wanted to 'mau-mau' any company who did business in Eastern Europe. I thought our approach should be more sensitive and selective than that." MacKay's work as house counsel for the Cabot Corporation, which traded carbon black, a form of soot used in the production of automobile tires, may have had something to do with his pragmatism on this question. Interview with MacKay.

44. *Chicago Tribune,* November 27, 1966, sec. 4, 10.

45. "YAF Exposes, Halts Company's Efforts to Trade with the Enemy," *New Guard,* January 1967, 4–5; "Conservative Group to Fight Car Trade Deal with Soviets," *New York Times,* January 5, 1967, 6.

46. "California YAF vs. IBM," *New Guard,* September 1967, 20–21.

47. Minutes of the Meeting of the National Board of Directors, YAF, Hotel America, Washington, D.C., February 9–11, 1968, PPJC.

48. An outline of the various activities in the Stop-IBM campaign may be found in Arnold Steinberg to William F. Buckley, Jr., February 7, 1968, box 57, YAF, WFB MSS. Also see "YAF Campaign against IBM Communist Trade Continues," *New Guard,* April 1968, 3–5, 27; and "East-West Trade," *New Guard,* March 1969, 16.

49. Arthur Nielsen, Jr., to A. K. Watson, April 11, 1968, box 57, YAF, WFB MSS.

50. Memo to Buckley from Steinberg, April 17, 1968, box 57, YAF, WFB MSS.

51. Alan MacKay was elected YAF's national chairman at a March 1967 board meeting held to replace Huston, who had left for service in the Army. He won election outright at YAF's national convention in Pittsburgh in September 1967 and held the chairmanship until August 1969.

52. H.G. Torbert, Jr., to William Proxmire; Proxmire to MacKay, both April 19, 1968, box 57, YAF, WFB MSS.

53. Steinberg to Buckley, April 29, 1968, box 57, YAF, WFB MSS; interview with MacKay.

54. Interview with MacKay.

55. Ronald Docksai to William F. Buckley, Jr., with enclosure, "The Western View," June 30, 1968, box 57, YAF, WFB MSS.

56. Albert Watson to Ronald Docksai, June 28, 1968, box 57, YAF, WFB MSS.

57. Transcript, *Manion Forum,* August 4, 1968, "The View from the Right Side of the Campus," PPJC; interview with MacKay.

58. Memorandum to David Jones and All Concerned from Lee Edwards, December 22, 1967, box 43, Edwards, WFB MSS.

59. Memorandum re: International Communism on Trial from David Jones to YAF Advisory Board, March 5, 1968, box 51 (YAF, 1960–1968), General Accessions, Kenneth Colegrove Papers, Herbert Hoover Presidential Library, West Branch, Iowa.

60. Ibid.; interview with Edwards.

61. *Washington Post* coverage of the four-day trial was sporadic and buried in the Metro section of the paper. Coverage also focused on the "stacked deck" against the defense. See *Washington Post,* February 20, 1968, sec. II, 6; February 21, 1968, sec. III, 12.

NOTES TO CHAPTER 6

1. Except for evidence of interaction between YAF and SDS chapters gleaned from Kenneth Heineman's fine study *Campus Wars: The Peace Movement at American State Universities in the Vietnam Era* (New York: New York University Press, 1993), 148, 152–53, 206–7, there was little concern in the YAF national office or, it appears, in SDS's either, with what the opposition was doing.

2. Tom Hayden, *Youth and Conservatism,* pamphlet, box 1, ser. I, folder 3, SDS MSS. Hayden saw YAF focused "not on ideas but on their implementation. It wanted action, it wanted influence, and it wanted power." Hayden and Todd Gitlin, both early leaders of SDS, recount only three incidents each of conflict with YAF. See Hayden, *Reunion,* 38, 51, 445, 478; and Gitlin, *The Sixties,* 89, 99, 413. From YAF's perspective, SDS did not merit much attention until it became active

in the antiwar movement in 1965. From that time forward, the *New Guard* editors were concerned about activities on the Left, culminating with a regularly featured "Report on the Left" beginning in the February 1966 issue.

3. See David Lance Goines, *The Free Speech Movement: Coming of Age in the 1960s* (Berkeley: Ten Speed Press, 1993), 492–93. The YAF member, Dan Rosenthal, allegedly disrupted organizational meetings of the free speech coalition during the fall semester but carried a sign reading "Fuck Communism" during the next spring's "filthy speech movement," apparently with little sense of the irony in hindering free speech while supporting profanity.

4. For evidence concerning the negative view YAF members shared regarding the goals of the Free Speech Movement (FSM), see Allan Brownfield, "Student Rebels," *New Guard,* March 1965, 17–18; Richard S. Wheeler and M. M. Morton, "Rebellion at Berkeley," *New Guard,* September 1965, 6–10, 30; and Tom Charles Huston, "Life in the Multiversity," *New Guard,* November 1966, 8–12, 20; for local chapter views see David Levy, "Freedom and FSM," *Man and State* 3 (December 1964, 2, reprint in box 2, folder 4 (Publications and Clippings, 1964–1965), Free Speech Movement Papers, State Historical Society of Wisconsin. Levy stated: "The goal of FSM, free speech on campus, is beyond criticism. The tactics of FSM . . . are another matter. . . . The great evil of the tactics of FSM is to establish the precedent that decisions . . . are to be made with threats of force. . . . When FSM conducts its dialogue with the administration with mass rallies, marches, and sit-ins, there is no end to the irrelevant emotionality which can be used to cloud the issues."

5. David Franke, "The National Teach-In," *New Guard,* June 1965, 5–6.

6. "Aid and Comfort to the Enemy," *New Guard,* October 1965, 6.

7. For SDS's problems, see Gitlin, *The Sixties,* 319–61; Hayden, *Reunion,* 291–326; and Miller, *Democracy.* For the Black Panthers, see Hugh Pearson, *The Shadow of the Panther: Huey Newton and the Price of Black Power in America* Reading, Mass.: Addison Wesley, 1994); and Peter Collier and David Horowitz, *Destructive Generation: Second Thoughts about the Sixties* (New York: Free Press, 1996), 141–65.

8. Thomas Watson, Jr., to Arnold Steinberg, September 19, 1968, box 57, YAF, WFB MSS.

9. In early 1968 one chapter at Marquette University, in reaction to continued protest against Dow Chemical Company, greeted Dow recruiters on campus with a "wild and wooly reception" supportive of their right to interview prospective employees. *New Guard,* February 1968, 24.

10. Minutes of the Meeting of the National Board of Directors, YAF, Windsor Park Hotel, Washington, D.C., April 20–21, 1968, PPJC; interview with Campaigne.

11. John Meyer, "What Happened at Columbia (and Why)," *New Guard,* September 1968, 14–17.

12. Ibid.; Hayden, *Reunion,* 272–84; and Anderson, *Movement and the Sixties,*

194–200. These events are also described in James Simon Kunen, *The Strawberry Statement: Notes of a College Revolutionary* (New York: Random House, 1969), 20, 23–40.

13. Kunen, *Strawberry Statement,* 20, describes the anti-SDS resistance as people "who couldn't get their shit together" and who were "totally disorganized" and made up of "jocks."

14. Meyer, "What Happened at Columbia," 16.

15. Anderson, *Movement and the Sixties,* 198–99; and Meyer, "What Happened at Columbia," 16–17.

16. Confidential Memorandum to David Jones from William Steel, May 22, 1968, PPJC.

17. Ibid.

18. Manuscript by R. Emmett Tyrrell, Jr., "The Demise of the Politics of Emptiness," PPJC; also, see *New Guard,* September 1968, 18–19.

19. R. Emmett Tyrrell, Jr., *The Conservative Crack-Up* (New York: Simon and Schuster, 1992), 43–47; interview with Tyrrell, January 8, 1995.

20. Tyrrell, *Conservative Crack-Up,* 48.

21. *The Alternative* was renamed the *American Spectator* in 1976 and was moved from Bloomington, Indiana, to Washington, D.C., during the 1980s. The first issue of the *Alternative* depicted a popular young conservative portrait during the 1960s: a B-52 bomber in the shape of a peace sign with the words "drop it" on either side of the plane's wings.

22. See Gareth Davies, *From Opportunity to Entitlement: The Transformation and Decline of Great Society Liberalism* (Lawrence: University Press of Kansas, 1996), for the historical developments in 1960s liberalism; and Ehrman, *Rise of Neoconservatism,* for the intellectual heritage.

23. This point is made by J. David Hoeveler, *Watch on the Right: Conservative Intellectuals in the Reagan Era* (Madison: University of Wisconsin Press, 1991), 207–32.

24. "New York YAF Liberates Student Mobilization Headquarters," *New Guard,* October 1968, 22.

25. Docksai absconded with a SDS mailing list from the office (not exactly demonstrating a healthy conservative respect for property rights) and wrote *New Guard* editor Arnie Steinberg to "see what Marvin Liebman might recommend" doing with it. Docksai to Steinberg, November 6, 1968, box 37 (YAF—Miscellaneous), Liebman MSS; "New York YAF Liberates SDS Office," *New Guard,* December 1968, 25.

26. "Massachusetts YAF Liberates Resistance Office," *New Guard,* January 1969, 22.

27. Ibid.

28. "Purdue YAF Counters Left," *New Guard,* December 1968, 24.

29. Phillip Abbott Luce, "Against the Wall," *New Guard,* March 1969, 30.

30. "Blue Buttons: From California to East Coast," *New Guard,* summer 1969, 26; YAF blue button pamphlet, PPJC.

31. Interestingly, Hayakawa's semantics studies were criticized by traditional conservatives during the early 1950s for their relativism. See Nash, *Conservative Intellectual Movement,* 44. Hayakawa would parlay his notoriety for resisting radicals on campus into a Republican U.S. Senate seat from California in 1976. See Hayden, *Reunion,* 474–76, for that particular campaign.

32. Anderson, *Movement and the Sixties,* 297–99.

33. "UC-Berkeley YAF's Non-Negotiable Demands," *New Guard,* Summer 1969, 32.

34. Phillip Abbott Luce, "Against the Wall," *New Guard,* March 1969, 30–31.

35. Ibid.; Harvey Hukari, Jr., "How to Combat Campus Radicals," *Human Events,* November 15, 1969, 11–12, 14.

36. Phillip Abbott Luce to California YAF, February 24, 1969, box 1, Subject File (YAF—Memoranda and Circulars), Patrick Dowd Papers, Hoover Institution, Stanford, California.

37. Testimony of Patrick Dowd before the California Assembly Sub-Committee on Educational Environment, March 3, 1969, box 1, Subject File (YAF—Memoranda and Circulars), Dowd MSS.

38. "Disorder at PSA? YAF Will Sue," *New Guard,* December 1968, 26.

39. "The YAF Story—1969," *New Guard,* January 1970, 20–21; Minutes of the Meeting of the National Board of Directors, YAF, The Wigwam, Columbus, Ohio, June 19–21, 1969, PPJC.

40. Interview with Campaigne.

41. Jameson Campaigne, Jr., "Proposal, Re: YAF Policy," addendum to Minutes of National Board, June 19–21, 1969, PPJC.

42. Minutes of the Meeting of the National Board of Directors, YAF, Arlington, Va., November 8–9, 1968, PPJC.

43. See funding letter from Max Rafferty to William F. Buckley, Jr., plus enclosures, re: Young America's Freedom Offensive, February 24, 1969, box 67, YAF, WFB MSS.

44. David Jones to William F. Buckley, Jr., October 2, 1968, box 57, YAF, WFB MSS.

45. Tom Wells, *The War Within: America's Battle over Vietnam* (Berkeley: University of California Press, 1994), 342–43; interview with Huston. Huston did not believe that YAF could effectively coordinate antiradical activity without support from moderate students.

46. Wells, *War Within,* 410.

47. James Farley to Randall Teague, May 1, 1969, Box 1 (Correspondence—Letters Received, 1969–1969), Dowd MSS.

48. "Farley Says 'No' to Left," *New Guard,* summer 1969, 26.

49. There were also prowar parades and anti–New Left groups active outside of YAF. See Freedman, *Inheritance,* 267–72.

50. Confidential Memorandum from Ron Dear to YAF State Chairmen and National Board, November 13, 1969, PPJC.

51. Lee Edwards, "The Other Sixties: A Flag Waver's Memoir," *Policy Review* (fall 1988): 64; interview with Edwards; "Counterattack on Dissent," *Time,* November 21, 1969, 23–26. Tom Wells estimated the crowd at forty-five hundred. Wells, *War Within,* 387.

52. "YAF Counters November Moratorium," *New Guard,* January 1970, 4–5.

53. The Boston march was held on December 7. *Boston Globe,* December 8, 1969, enclosure in 91st Cong., box 83, folder 10, Barry Goldwater Papers, Arizona Historical Foundation, Tempe, Arizona. The October 15 Mobe rally on Boston Commons, in comparison, drew more than one hundred thousand people. Wells, *War Within,* 372.

54. Randall Teague to Goldwater, March 6, 1970, 91: 83/10, Goldwater MSS.

55. As far as can be ascertained, "Tell It to Hanoi" activities were held on at least thirty-two separate campuses. See "Partial Listing of YAF Counter-Moratorium Activities," n.d., PPJC.

56. Minutes of the Meeting of the National Board of Directors, YAF, Columbus, Ohio, June 18–20, 1969, PPJC; Ron Dear, "Young America's Freedom Offensive: A 1969 Report," *New Guard,* January 1970, 12–15.

57. Probably this was mostly the result of the sheer numbers and growing anger of student protest after Kent State. Kenneth Heineman states that there were 1,350 campus protests involving more than 4.5 million participants in the wake of the Cambodia incursion and the Kent State (and Jackson State) shootings. Heineman, *Campus Wars,* 249.

58. "YAF's Legal Attack," *New Guard,* Summer 1970, 30–33; interview with Keene; interview with Teague.

59. YAF Pamphlet, *The Open University,* PPJC. Jameson Campaigne wrote the pamphlet. Interview with Campaigne.

60. Kirk, *Sword of Imagination,* 414 (for the quote), 414–17 for a discussion of campus disturbances in the 1960s.

61. Ibid. The quote is Bruno Bettelheim's.

62. Testimony of David A. Keene, National Chairman, YAF, before the President's Commission on Campus Unrest, July 24, 1970, PPJC.

63. Bates, *Rads.*

64. "Making Sense of the Sixties," part 1, "Seeds of the Sixties," WETA television production; Keene was on friendly terms with one of the bombers, David Fine, who worked for the college newspaper, had written a favorable article about Keene entitled, "A Portrait of the Conservative as a Young Man." Keene's relationship with other Madison radicals was less than friendly, however. During a

debate, a black city councilman told Keene after one comment that "when the revolution comes, people like you will be shot." Interview with Keene; David Broder, *Changing of the Guard: Power and Leadership in America* (New York: Simon and Schuster, 1980), 176.

65. "University Research Committee: A Faculty-Student Inquiry into the Cause of Campus Disorders and a Rebuttal of the Scranton Commission Report Sponsored by YAF," n.d [fall 1970], PPJC.

66. *Public Papers of the President: Richard Nixon: 1970* (Washington, D.C.: GPO, 1971), 759. Nixon had ordered Scranton not to "let higher education off with a pat on the ass." Scranton's commission seemed to do just that. Wells, *War Within*, 448 (for the Nixon quote).

NOTES TO CHAPTER 7

1. "Goldwater's Ghost Now Haunts New Left," *New York Post,* January 8, 1969, 8; "Goldwater Aide Now a Radical: Adopts Anarchism Philosophy," *New York Times,* September 29, 1969, 62.

2. Karl Hess to Buckley, January 18, 1969, Box 61, Hess, WFB MSS.

3. Nash, *Conservative Intellectual Movement,* 171–85.

4. Interview with Evans.

5. For the presence of such views on the Right, see Leo Ribuffo, *The Old Christian Right: The Protestant Far Right from the Great Depression to the Cold War* (Philadelphia: Temple University Press, 1983); Hixson, *Search for the American Right Wing*; and Michael Kazin, *The Populist Persuasion: An American History* (New York: Basic Books, 1994).

6. For Wallace, see Ron Docksai, "A Conservative's Guide to George Corley Wallace," September 6, 1968, box 57, YAF, WFB MSS; and Dennis McMahon to YAF Leaders, August 23, 1969, PPJC. For the Catholic ultratraditionalists, see Allitt, *Catholic Intellectuals,* 141–60; Bradley Warren Evans, "The Young Conservatives: Coming Unglued?" *Triumph,* November 1970, 11–15. For a defense of the "rat finks," see "Rat Finks and Fink-Baiters," *New Guard,* September 1966, 13–16; for a critical view, see "California Libertarian Report no. 1," edited by William Steel and Ron Kimberling, box 2, Subject File (YAF—National Board), Dowd MSS. The New Jersey YAF, which had a large libertarian contingent who were purged after the 1969 convention, was accused of harboring "rat finks" from the 1966 YR controversy in that state.

7. Allitt, *Catholic Intellectuals,* 157. The anecdote may be apocryphal, but YAF never was an organization attuned to traditionalist religious movements.

8. See Jerome Tuccille, *Radical Libertarianism: A Right-Wing Alternative* (Indianapolis: Bobbs-Merrill, 1970); Tuccille, *It Usually Begins with Ayn Rand* (New York: Stein and Day, 1971); and Murray Rothbard, *For a New Liberty* (New York: Macmillan, 1973).

9. Frank S. Meyer, "The Twisted Tree of Liberty," *New Guard,* January 1968, 9–10; originally published in *National Review,* January 16, 1962.

10. He even attempted to convince Buckley of this opinion. See Hess to Buckley, January 18, 1969, box 61, Hess, WFB MSS; Tuccille, *It Usually Begins with Ayn Rand,* 75–80. Rothbard rejected the "moral hang-ups" and the "suicidal crusade for global nuclear war against the communists" that he associated with the "Buckleyite" right wing. See Rothbard to Felix Morley, December 7, 1964, box 23 (Murray Rothbard, 1964–1996), Correspondence and Subject File, Felix Morley Papers, Herbert Hoover Presidential Library, West Branch, Iowa.

11. Rothbard, *For a New Liberty;* Rothbard, "Life in the Old Right," *Chronicles,* August 1994, 15–19.

12. Jerome Tuccille, "The False Libertarians," *New Guard,* April 1969, 14–15.

13. Karl Hess, "In Defense of Hess," *New Guard,* April 1969, 15–16.

14. Luce testified before HUAC two times, in 1964 when he called the committee "the scum of Congress" and in 1966 as a paid informer for the committee against the Progressive Labor Party. See Walter Goodman, *The Committee: The Extraordinary Career of the House Committee on Un-American Activities* (New York: Farrar, Straus, and Giroux, 1968), 446–47, 474–75, 480.

15. YAF Pamphlet, *Phillip Abbott Luce,* box 1, Subject File (YAF—California State Chapter, Advisory Board Meetings), Dowd MSS.

16. Luce, "Against the Wall," *New Guard,* September 1968, 6–7.

17. Luce to California YAF, February 24, 1969, box 1, Subject File (YAF—Memoranda and Circulars), Dowd MSS.

18. Arnie Steinberg to William F. Buckley, Jr., May 21, 1969, box 67, YAF, WFB MSS.

19. Tuccille, *It Usually Begins with Ayn Rand,* 84–91.

20. Libertarian Caucus, Memo no. 3, June 19, 1969, PPJC.

21. Libertarian Caucus, Memo no. 4, June 26, 1969, PPJC. (emphasis in the original).

22. Ralph Fucetola to Jay Parker, June 30, 1969, PPJC.

23. Don Feder to Libertarian Caucus (Steel, Dowd, Ernsberger, Fucetola), July 17, 1969, box 1 (Correspondence—Letters Received, 1966–1969), Dowd MSS.

24. Phillip Abbott Luce to William Steel, July 25, 1969, box 1 (Correspondence—Letters Received, 1966–1969), Dowd MSS; the letter is also in PPJC.

25. Tuccille, *It Usually Begins with Ayn Rand,* 102.

26. Murray Rothbard, "Listen, YAF," *Libertarian Forum,* August 15, 1969, 1–2.

27. "The Tranquil Statement," adopted August 12, 1969, aboard the *Tranquil* for presentation to the 1969 National YAF Convention by the Anarchist Caucus, PPJC; see also Letter to Members and Delegates of YAF from Anarcho-Libertarian Alliance, n.d., PPJC.

28. Memo to California and National YAF Leaders from Randall Cornell

Teague, August 20, 1969, PPJC; interview with Teague. The decision to remove Dowd and Brandstadter seems to have been inspired partly by a desire to restore balance to Cal-YAF, a decision based more on politics than on substantiated charges of bad conduct.

29. There were two slated candidacies. One was the conservative caucus, made up of Keene for national chairman, Mike Thompson for vice chairman, Ron Docksai for national secretary, and Dan Manion for treasurer. The libertarian caucus slated William Steel, Dana Rohrabacher, William Chaisson of New Jersey, and four others. Harvey Hukari, Jr., of Stanford, ran as an independent candidate for national chairman in protest of the slated candidacies. See memorandum from David Keene to YAF Leaders, summer 1969; Conservative Caucus flyers; Libertarian Caucus flyers, all in PPJC.

30. Tuccille, *It Usually Begins with Ayn Rand*, 101.

31. Ibid.

32. William F. Buckley, Jr., Address to YAF National Convention, St. Louis, 1969, box 65, Speeches—YAF, WFB MSS. Tuccille claimed that Buckley adjusted his remarks in order to attack Rothbard and Hess, but in his prepared speech for the convention, remarks attacking Rothbard and Hess were already included in the address. It seems clear that Buckley had some foreknowledge of what to expect at St. Louis and prepared his address accordingly. Tuccille, *Radical Libertarianism*, 101; interview with Buckley.

33. Tuccille, *Radical Libertarianism*, 96–97.

34. One example of this organization was the publication of a daily conservative caucus newsletter at the convention, which appealed to "positive and constructive alternative[s] to the negative-collectivist forces attempting to take over YAF." The caucus had a suite from which it passed out a "survival kit" to help delegates survive their "encounters with 'CRAZIES' (persons who took a trip and blew their own minds)." See "Combined Issue 1 and 2 of Conservative Caucus," PPJC.

35. Tuccille, *Radical Libertarianism*, 103–5.

36. The only person with significant "radical-libertarian" credentials remaining on the board was Patrick Dowd.

37. A majority plank calling for resisting the draft through legal channels, as well as YAF's call for a voluntary military, was passed.

38. Tuccille, *Radical Libertarianism*, 106–7; Rothbard, *For a New Liberty*, 6–7; "Young Conservatives Vow Militancy against Left," *New York Times*, August 31, 1969, 34.

39. Milton Friedman, "The Case for a Voluntary Army," *New Guard*, May 1967, 12–16.

40. Russell Kirk, "Our Archaic Draft," *New Guard*, May 1967, 11.

41. A symposium on the draft was printed in the pages of the *New Individualist Review*, the publication of the campus chapter of the ISI at the University of

Chicago. It included essays by YAF member David Friedman and sociologist and SDS founder Richard Flacks. See "Symposium on Conscription," *New Individualist Review,* Spring 1967, 3–59.

42. John A. Andrew III, "Pro-War and Anti-Draft: Young Americans for Freedom and the War in Viet Nam," unpublished paper used with author's permission (copy in Schneider's possession).

43. Tuccille, *Radical Libertarianism,* 101; Rothbard, *For a New Liberty,* 6–7.

44. SIL claimed to have more than three thousand members by the end of the year.

45. Minutes of the Meeting of the National Board of Directors, YAF, Stouffer's Riverfront Inn, St. Louis, Mo., August 31, 1969, box 2, Subject File (YAF National Board), Dowd MSS. Keene never fulfilled his promise to go to California.

46. California Libertarian Report—Post-Convention Issue no. 1, box 2, Subject File (YAF National Board), Dowd MSS.

47. See "Young Authoritarians for Freedom," n.d., box 2, Subject File (YAF—National Board Memos and Circulars), Dowd MSS; for YAF's draft position see Randall Teague, "Statement on the Draft," September 29, 1969, box 2, Subject File (National Board Minutes—1970), Dowd MSS.

48. Ron Dear to YAF Members, September 17, 1969, PPJC.

49. Interview with Keene.

50. See William F. Buckley, Jr., to Ronald Reagan, September 30, 1969; Reagan to Buckley, October 7, 1969; Reagan to Keene, October 8, 1969; and Buckley to Reagan, October 16, 1969, all in box 64, Reagan, WFB MSS.

51. Memo to Chapter Chairmen from Luce, September 26, 1969, PPJC.

52. Ronald Dear to Buckley, with enclosures, October 10, 1969, box 67, YAF, WFB MSS. These issues were discussed at the October national board meeting. Minutes of the Meeting of the National Board of Directors, YAF, Franklin Room, Sheraton-Park Hotel, Washington, D.C., October 3–5, 1969, PPJC.

53. This view was shared by William Rusher, who worried that YAF might follow SDS's model of self-destruction. Interview with Rusher; also see Bill Steel to Rusher, box 284, folder 2487, WFB MSS. Forwarding the letter to Buckley, Rusher wrote in the margin: "a letter from Bill Steel—a good man gone wrong. Shows how 'libertarianism' is ruining some ex-YAF leaders."

54. Keene was busy with his won campaign for the Wisconsin State Senate throughout the fall. Instead of going to California himself, he sent Washington state attorney and YAF board member Richard Derham to investigate the situation there. Cal-YAF libertarians claimed that Derham only gave cursory attention to matters before making his recommendations to Keene. See William Steel to Keene, November 12, 1969,; David Friedman to Frank Meyer, December 1, 1969, both in box 284, folder 2487, WFB MSS.

55. See Confidential Memo to National YAF Leadership from David Keene, January 16, 1970, box 2, Subject File (YAF—National Board Memoranda), Dowd

MSS. Also see Harvey Hukari, Jr., "How to Combat Campus Radicals," *Human Events,* November 15, 1969, 11–12, 14. The reaction to Saracino's appointment and Hukari's departure was fiery. See Patrick Dowd to YAF Members, n.d., box 1, Subject File (YAF—Memos and Circulars); Bradley Warren Evans to Steel, December 9, 1969, box 2, Subject File (YAF—National Board); and Dowd to Jim Minarik, December 21, 1969, box 2, Subject File (Letters Sent, 1969–1970), all in Dowd MSS; Steel to Keene, November 12, 1969, box 284, folder 2487; David Friedman to Frank Meyer, December 1, 1969, box 67, YAF; and Teague to Buckley, with enclosures, December 22, 1969, box 274, folder 2487, all in WFB MSS; and Steel to Dan Manion, n.d.; and press statement by Patrick Dowd, re: Cal-YAF situation, November 21, 1969, both in PPJC.

56. Press Statement by Patrick Dowd, PPJC. Keene harshly refuted the claims made by libertarians. Keene to Dowd, December 3, 1969, box 2, Subject File (National Board—Minutes, 1970); and Dowd to Keene, December 6, 1969, box 1, Correspondence File (Letters Sent, 1969–1970), Dowd MSS.

57. Dowd to Keene, December 6, 1969, Dowd MSS.

58. Rothbard, *For a New Liberty,* 7. Ernsberger was the former leader of the Penn State University YAF chapter. Heineman, *Campus Wars,* 206.

59. See William F. Buckley, Jr., to Ronald Reagan, September 30, 1969; Reagan to Buckley, October 7, 1969; Reagan to David Keene, October 8, 1969; Buckley to Reagan, October 16, 1969; and Keene to Reagan, October 30, 1969, all in box 64, Reagan, WFB MSS.

60. See Minutes of the Meeting of the National Board of Directors, YAF, Sheraton-Park Hotel, Washington, D.C., October 3–5, 1969, PPJC.

61. William Rusher noticed the "top down" leadership style of the board in January 1970 after attending one board meeting. "Quite possibly the national board has gotten a little lazy in recent years, preferring to solve personality conflicts by charter withdrawals and individual expulsions . . . but I am reasonably confident that they have now seen the error of their ways, and are making a sincere effort to meet their critics half-way." Memo to Buckley from Rusher, January 7, 1970, box 284, folder 2488, WFB MSS.

62. Memorandum to National Board from Randall Teague, November 24, 1969, box 1, Subject File (YAF—Memos and Circulars), Dowd MSS.

63. YAF budgets for years prior to 1968 have been difficult to obtain. A budget for the fiscal year 1969–1970 shows that YAF was budgeting close to $375,000 for its office expenses and activities, one-third of which (approximately $130,000) went to salaries. Memo to YAF Board of Directors from Randall Teague, June 26, 1969. Fiscal Year 1969–1970 Budget, box 2, Subject File (YAF—National Board); a financial statement for the five months preceding December 1969 shows YAF with assets of $219,000, an income of $535,000, and expenses of $414,000. YAF Financial Statement, December 1969, box 2, Subject File (YAF—National Board Memoranda); also see Memo to National Board from Randall Teague, re: Financial

Situation, December 17, 1969, box 1, Subject File (YAF—National Board Memoranda); for membership numbers and increases see Confidential Memo to National Board from Teague, November 24, 1969, box 1, Subject File (YAF—Memos and Circulars), all in Dowd MSS.

NOTES TO CHAPTER 8

1. Ron Docksai to National Board, January 29, 1971, box 3, Subject File (YAF National Board Memoranda), Dowd MSS.

2. Minutes of the Meeting of the National Board of Directors, YAF, Washington, D.C., February 5–7, 1971, box 3, Subject File (YAF National Board Memoranda), Dowd MSS.

3. Theodore H. White, *The Making of the President, 1968* (New York: Atheneum, 1969), 179–80. Reagan won 182 votes at the convention, with 86 coming from California, which voted for him as a favorite son candidate.

4. See summer 1966 poll in *New Guard*, September 1966, 6. Fifty-three percent of the YAF members polled liked Reagan, but only 8 percent thought him likely to be the 1968 GOP nominee. Meanwhile, 15 percent liked Nixon, but 74 percent thought him likely to win the nomination.

5. Rusher, *Rise of the Right*, 195–202; interview with Rusher; interview with Keene; and David A. Keene, "The Conservative Case for Richard Nixon," *New Guard*, summer 1968, 10–11.

6. Rusher, *Rise of the Right*, 209–17; and Brennan, *Turning Right*, 121–28.

7. For the view that conservative influence at the 1968 convention was strong, see Brennan, *Turning Right*, 126–127.

8. The *New Guard* spelled out some of this disenchantment in an editorial, "Should Conservatives Support Richard Nixon?" in which, lacking any alternative, the editors enjoined YAF members to work on behalf of Nixon, however imperfect a candidate he was. A far weightier critique of Nixon, "What Nixon Should Be Doing in 1972," appeared in May. See *New Guard*, January–February 1971, 5–8; and May 1971, 5–9.

9. *New Guard*, January–February 1971, 6; Joan Hoff, *Nixon Reconsidered* (New York: Basic Books, 1994), has discussed, favorably, Nixon's domestic policy. Bradley Warren Evans, "Welfare, Workfare, and Eyewash," *New Guard*, February 1970, 17–18.

10. See Robert M. Collins, "Growth Liberalism in the Sixties: Great Societies at Home and Grand Designs Abroad," in Farber, ed., *The Sixties*, 11–44.

11. Conservative critiques of Nixon's domestic policies can be found in Brennan, *Turning Right*, 135–37.

12. For recommendations of how he could, see *New Guard*, April 1970, 9–19, a series of articles on environmental pollution and the free market.

13. "Nixonomics," *New Guard*, November 1971, 12–14; Gaines Smith, "How

We Lost the War on Poverty," *New Guard,* June 1973, 4–7; Mary Fisk, "An Interview with Howard Phillips," *New Guard,* December 1973, 12–15.

14. See Judis, *Buckley,* 328–29; Kirk, *Sword of Imagination,* 328–36; and Patrick J. Buchanan, *Right from the Beginning* (Boston: Little, Brown, 1988). New evidence reflecting what Nixon thought of YAF members such as Tom Huston is seen in Stanley I. Kutler, ed., *Abuse of Power: The New Nixon Tapes* (New York: Free Press, 1997), 5, 7, 8, 10, 12–16, 36, 37.

15. Watergate represented nothing more than a brief setback for conservatives, not a disaster. In the wake of Watergate, conservative grassroots activities continued unabated and led to the formation of the New Right in the early 1970s and the religious Right by the end of the decade. That these grassroots activities were not necessarily tied up with Republican Party candidates gave this new "populist conservatism" an independent base outside the two major parties. See Broder, *Changing of the Guard,* 160–88; Rusher, *Rise of the Right,* 263–310; Dionne, *Why Americans Hate Politics,* 203–5; and Samuel T. Francis, "Message From MARS: The Social Politics of the New Right," in Robert W. Whitaker, ed., *The New Right Papers* (New York: St. Martin's Press, 1982), 65–83.

16. Memo to Buckley, Stan Evans, Tom Winter, and Docksai from Teague, Rusher, John Jones, and Allan Ryskind, April 16, 1971, box 284, folder 2492, WFB MSS; interview with Teague.

17. Wayne Thorburn, "Agenda for the New Politics," *New Guard,* October 1971, 13; Rusher, *Rise of the Right,* 239–241; "A Declaration," *National Review,* August 10, 1971.

18. For YAF and Ashbrook, see Jerry Norton, "The Ashbrook Campaign: The Making of a Conservative Candidate," *New Guard,* March 1972, 5–9; for a reply to Norton, supportive of Nixon, see Larry Mongillo, "Conservatives and 1972: A Rebuttal," *New Guard,* March 1972, 9–10.

19. The first CPAC, held in January 1973, was cosponsored by YAF, ACU, and *Human Events.* The conference still meets annually in Washington although YAF no longer exists to sponsor it.

20. Memorandum to Randall Teague from Jerry Norton, n.d. [fall 1970], box 3, Subject File (YAF—National Board Memoranda), Dowd MSS.

21. Ron Docksai to Jerry Norton, October 22, 1970, box 3, Subject File (YAF—National Board Memoranda).

22. Memo to Harry Cashen, David Keene, Warren Parker, et al. from Teague, March 15, 1971, PPJC.

23. Ibid.

24. Ron Robinson to Teague, April 5, 1971, PPJC (emphasis in original).

25. Interview with Keene.

26. Interview with Huston. Huston still believes that "if it hadn't been for Watergate, South Vietnam would not have fallen."

27. Wells, *War Within,* 319–20.

28. Memorandum to National Board from Ron Docksai, April 7, 1971, PPJC.

29. Docksai, "YAF: This Year and Beyond," address to 1971 regional conferences, box 284, folder 2492, WFB MSS.

30. Teague to Buckley, July 16, 1971, box 284, folder 2493, WFB MSS.

31. Docksai responded: "I cannot promise you we will be supporters of the President in the future, but I do pledge that future actions we take will be exercised only after the greatest deliberation and consultation with the most responsible parties." Goldwater to Docksai, August 30, 1971, 92: 72/10; Docksai to Goldwater, September 14, 1971, 92: 72/12, both in Goldwater MSS.

32. Confidential Memorandum to National Board from Docksai, August 17, 1971, PPJC.

33. Agnew, Reagan, and James Buckley were suggested as nominees, with Reagan's name withdrawn before the presidential balloting. After Reagan's withdrawal, "a massive shift in support to Agnew was readily apparent." Agnew received 976 votes, Reagan 204, and Congressman Phil Crane, 105. "Houston: Making It Perfectly Clear," *New Guard,* November 1971, 2–3.

34. Ibid.

35. "Inaugural Remarks of Ronald F. Docksai," September 5, 1971, YAF Convention, Houston, Texas, PPJC.

36. "Houston: Making It Perfectly Clear," 3.

37. Thorburn, "Agenda for the New Politics," *New Guard,* October 1971, 12–13.

38. Wayne Thorburn contends that there was a place for activist "bombthrowers" within YAF. Not everyone could be a philosopher-king. Interview with Thorburn.

39. Membership numbers are estimates at best. Randall Teague claimed that membership levels were inflated by a 3:1 ratio throughout the 1960s. Individuals who joined the national organization were always fewer than those on the local level. For example, YAF claimed to have more than fifty thousand members in 1969, but only about eighteen thousand of that number would have been official national members. A better handle on membership estimates can be acquired by examining the organization's claims of active chapters. Throughout 1970 and 1971, the national office claimed more than five hundred chapters. See Jerry Norton and J. A. Parker, "On the Chapters Moving towards 600," *New Guard,* January–February 1971, 24–26. In January 1972 Charlie Black, later head of the Republican National Committee during the Bush Administration, claimed three hundred new chapters *since* Norton's and Parker's 1971 article. This would have meant the total was close to nine hundred chapters. See "A Presence in History," *New Guard,* January–February 1971, 18–20. One way to estimate membership is to examine the publication filings of the *New Guard* with the U.S. Postal Service, appearing in every December issue after 1970. In 1970 *New Guard* subscriptions were 16,839; in

1971, 13,500; by 1973, 12,000; and in 1974, 6,000. These declining numbers may reveal the real nature of YAF membership during the early 1970s.

40. Teague to Buckley, January 27, 1971, box 284, folder 2492, WFB MSS; and appendix B, "Cutbacks in YAF Spending," Minutes of the Meeting of the National Board of Directors, YAF, Sheraton-Park Hotel, Washington, D.C., February 5–7, 1971, box 3, Subject File (YAF—National Board Memoranda), Dowd MSS.

41. Docksai and Teague commented on the bleak financial situation (a first in the organization's history) in *New Guard,* May 1971, 31.

42. Docksai and Teague attempted to get Goldwater to solicit funds but without success. Teague and Docksai to Goldwater, March 16, 1971, 92: 72/10, Goldwater MSS.

43. Memo to Frances Bronson (Buckley's assistant) from Rusher, March 23, 1971, box 284, folder 2492, WFB MSS. Even though the financial situation seemed to be settled in March, Thomas Sefton, president of the San Diego Trust and Savings Bank and a personal friend of Goldwater's, wrote the senator about financial problems he had heard about as late as April. Goldwater reassured Sefton that things were under control. Sefton to Goldwater, April 19, 1971; Goldwater to Sefton, May 4, 1971, 92: 72/10, both in Goldwater MSS.

44. Minutes of the Meeting of the National Board of Directors, YAF, Columbus, Ohio, May 28–30, 1971, PPJC. The bonus was $5,000 appended to Teague's $19,500 annual salary. For the decision to fire Teague, see Minutes of the Meeting of the National Board of Directors, YAF, Sheraton-Park Hilton, Washington, D.C., October 30–November 1, 1971, PPJC. Thorburn was a longtime YAF member who founded a YAF chapter at Tufts University in 1961. He remained active in the organization while pursuing graduate studies at Penn State and at the University of Maryland. He served on various staff positions in Washington for YAF until taking over as executive director after Teague's dismissal. Interview with Thorburn.

45. Interview with Teague.

46. Interview with Keene.

47. Teague claimed that a faction made up of Keene, Huston, and Campaigne decided to get rid of "Dave Jone's legacy" on the board. Interview with Teague. Several YAF board members (wishing to remain anonymous) said Teague was removed for cause, primarily financial irregularities, including misusing YAF funds for personal expenditures, as well as the need to reduce the power of the executive director over the board. For evidence of the second financial downturn, see Memorandum to Board from Thorburn, May 22, 1972, PPJC.

48. Docksai to Rusher, December 4, 1971, PPJC. Nixon never thought much of an Ashbrook threat, believing the congressman to be somewhat lazy. Kutler, *Abuse of Power,* 19–21.

49. Theodore H. White, *The Making of the President, 1972* (New York: Atheneum, 1973), 86. Still, Ashbrook did better in the New Hampshire primaries than Pete McCloskey, who ran from the liberal wing of the party.

50. See Minutes of the Meeting of the National Board of Directors, YAF, Washington, D.C., February 4–6, 1972, PPJC; Ron Docksai to Lylian Herzer, April 6, 1972, box 127, folder 653, WFB MSS; and Memorandum to National Board from Docksai, April 25, 1972, PPJC.

51. Docksai to National Board, April 25, 1972, PPJC. See a summary of YAF participation in Youth against McGovern activities in *New Guard,* January–February 1973, 31. The YAM effort gained little national media attention.

52. *New Guard,* January–February 1973, 31.

53. "The Elections," *New Guard,* January–February 1973, 2–3.

54. Jim Minarik to Ron Docksai, June 2, 1972, PPJC. Minarik contributed to the factionalism he complained of, since he had supported Teague and the next year fought for the removal of Thorburn from the executive director's office. Interview with Thorburn.

55. Wayne Thorburn to National Board, May 22, 1972, PPJC. A 1973 financial audit confirmed YAF's financial woes. See YAF Comparative Balance Sheet, n.d. [1973], PPJC. The organization experienced a twenty-one thousand dollar loss for the fiscal year ending July 31, 1973.

56. Confidential Memorandum to National Board from Docksai, August 1, 1972, PPJC. The infighting was a holdover from the removal of Teague from office the previous year. Richard Derham, as treasurer of YAF, seeking to investigate whether Thorburn had misused funds, "spent his entire week's vacation" going over YAF's books, but he found no malfeasance he could lay at Thorburn's feet. Interview with Thorburn; interview with Ron Robinson, July 29, 1997.

57. For a description of the project, see Robert Moffit, "Introduction to MQE," *New Guard,* May 1973, 13–14.

58. For the resolution, see Minutes of the Meeting of the National Board of Directors, YAF, The Summit Hotel, New York, February 23–25, 1973, PPJC; *New Guard,* June 1973, 20–21.

59. For discussions of the amnesty issue, see *New Guard,* July–August 1973, 25–26; *New Guard,* September 1973, 20; and October 1973, 22–23. The issue itself did not disappear, and several YAF members continued to fight against amnesty.

60. For YAF's abortion position, see National Board Minutes, February 23–25, 1973, PPJC; for the ERA, see Phyllis Schlafly, "Let's Stop ERA," *New Guard,* September 1973, 4–6; for the social issues and their effect on conservatism, see Samuel Francis, "Message from MARS, " in Whitaker, *New Right Papers,* 65–83; and Hodgson, *World Turned Right Side Up,* 158–85.

61. David Brudnoy, *Life Is Not a Rehearsal: A Memoir* (New York: Doubleday, 1997), 129–42.

62. A movie or a book review by Brudnoy appeared in every issue of the *New*

Guard between January 1970 and December 1973. In addition, he published prolifically in *National Review, The Alternative,* and numerous other publications. For his individualist views, see "Decriminalizing Crimes without Victims: The Time Is Now," *New Guard,* April 1973, 4–8.

63. "YAF Defense Project Outlined," *New Guard,* March 1973, 22.

64. John L. Jones to Frank Donatelli, January 11, 1974, PPJC.

65. *New Guard,* December 1973, 33.

66. John Meyer to National Board and Staff, n.d. [February 1974], PPJC.

67. Ron Robinson to National Board, n.d. [February 1974], PPJC.

68. Ron Robinson to National Board, February 15, 1974, PPJC.

69. Ibid. New York had the highest membership (with over 1,300 in both months).

70. *Washington Post,* January 26, 1974, 1; Memorandum to National Board from Docksai, January 28, 1974, PPJC.

71. Memo to National Board from Docksai, January 28, 1974, PPJC.

72. Memorandum to National Board from Bill Saracino, February 10, 1974, PPJC (emphasis in original).

73. Although minutes of this meeting have not been found, it seems clear from postmeeting correspondence that the board could not decide with any assurance what YAF's policy should be regarding Watergate.

74. Docksai to Jim Norton, March 21, 1974, PPJC.

75. Goldberg, *Goldwater,* 273–83.

76. See, as an example of the bitterness, the harsh exchange from Docksai to Campaigne, July 7, 1974, and Campaigne to Docksai, July 10, 1974, both in PPJC.

NOTES TO CHAPTER 9

1. Interview with Robinson; interview with Thorburn; interview with Frank Donatelli, August 14, 1997.

2. Interview with Robinson. Robinson would be appointed executive director (succeeding Donatelli) in 1977. Robert Heckman, also from New York, would succeed Robinson in 1979. Sam Pimm, a member from New Jersey, would take over for Heckman in 1981. Robert Dolan, also from New York, was elected national chairman in 1983.

3. Interview with Robinson; interview with Thorburn; interview with Donatelli; *New Guard,* March 1974, 31.

4. "Convention Raises Kane," *New Guard,* October 1975, 30–31.

5. The convention did not merit any coverage in the *Chicago Tribune.*

6. Jameson Campaigne to Ron Docksai, July 10, 1974, and Docksai to Campaigne, July 14, 1974, PPJC.

7. Interview with Donatelli.

8. *Washington Post,* October 4, 1975, 2.

9. Ronald Reagan, ". . . Let Us Go Forward without Them," *New Guard,* April 1975, 30–33.

10. Ibid., 18–19. Other board members were M. Stanton Evans (ACU), Eli Howell (an advisor to George Wallace), Cyril Joly, James Lyon, J. Daniel Mahoney (New York Conservative Party), Phyllis Schlafly, Robert Walker (a former aide to Reagan), and Thomas Winter (editor of *Human Events*).

11. Rusher, *Rise of the Right,* 271–73.

12. William A. Rusher, *The Making of a New Majority Party* (Ottawa, Ill.: Green Hill Publishers, 1975), 80–81.

13. Ibid., 82–84; Rusher, *Rise of the Right,* 263–69.

14. Rusher, *Rise of the Right,* 273, related that Reagan had done so in March 1975, only a month after his CPAC address.

15. *Washington Post,* August 18, 1975, 3.

16. *The New Guard* published several views on the necessity of a third party. See Jesse Helms, "American Parties: A Time for Choosing;" Lee Edwards, "A Conservative Party: Has Its Time Come?" and Ron Docksai, "Lessons From History," *New Guard,* December 1974, 6–14.

17. Rusher, *Rise of the Right,* 288–90.

18. Interview with Robinson.

19. Frank Donatelli, "Developing the Cadre," *New Guard,* January–February 1977, 15. The post office circulation filings of the *New Guard* confirm this. Subscriptions remained at sixty-five hundred in 1979, the same as the 1974 number. Donatelli insisted that membership increased after the 1976 campaign, but he did relate that his claim of a 25 percent increase may have been too high. Interview with Donatelli.

20. Jeff Kane, "The Liberation of the Conservative Movement," *New Guard,* January–February 1977, 14.

21. Donatelli, "Developing the Cadre," *New Guard,* January–February 1977, 15.

22. "YAF Begins 'Carter Watch,'" *Dialogue on Liberty,* December 1976, 1. *Dialogue on Liberty* was a YAF newsletter published quarterly in addition to the monthly *New Guard.*

23. Interview with Robinson.

24. Ibid.

25. Kane heads one of the largest Budweiser beer distributorships on the East Coast.

26. Interview with Robinson; interview with James V. Lacy, July 29, 1997. The board had twenty-five members.

27. "Jane Fonda Burned in Effigy at Her U.S.C. Talk," *Los Angeles Times,* April 24, 1973, 24; interview with Lacy.

28. Interview with Lacy; interview with Robinson.

29. Paul Craig Roberts, *The Supply Side Revolution: An Insider's Account of*

Policymaking in Washington (Cambridge, Mass.: Harvard University Press, 1984), 7–34; Robert L. Bartley, *The Seven Fat Years: And How To Do It Again* (New York: Free Press, 1995), 25–42.

30. Hodgson, *World Turned Right Side Up,* 158–84.

31. Ehrman, *Rise of Neoconservatism;* Dorrien, *Neoconservative Mind;* and Hodgson, *World Turned Right Side Up,* 128–57.

32. *The New Guard* 20, April 1980, 6. In 1980 the *New Guard* switched to a quarterly, with eight-page newsletters bearing the name *New Guard* distributed monthly. As James Lacy stated later, "the decision was based on the expense of the publication." Interview with Lacy. It also pointed to a problem with membership numbers, which Lacy discounts. Both the quarterly magazine and monthly newsletters were named *New Guard.*

33. *Dialogue on Liberty,* winter 1980, 7; *The New Guard* 20, Jan. 1980 1: 1, 4–5.

34. The count of 400 YAF members in Detroit is in the *Washington Post,* July 21, 1980, 2; *New Guard,* fall 1980, 39, claimed only 125 YAF members present in Detroit.

35. "Reagan's Triumph Parallels YAF's Resurgence," *Washington Post,* July 21, 1980, 2; "YAF's Detroit '80 Youth Operation," *Human Events,* August 2, 1980, 694; *Dialogue on Liberty,* summer 1980, 1, 4–6; and *The New Guard* 20, May 1980, 1, 4–6.

36. "YAF and the Future," *New Guard,* fall 1980, 40; M. Stanton Evans, "The Conservative Mainstream: YAF at Twenty," *National Review,* October 31, 1980, 1326.

37. Lacy admitted that the membership claim was "a combination of active student members and contributors." Interview with Lacy. Post office filings reveal a different membership story after 1980: subscriptions to YAF's magazine never exceeded sixty-five hundred for this period.

38. *Dialogue on Liberty,* fall-winter 1980, 2.

39. "YAF Members and Alumni Head Reagan Transition Efforts," *New Guard* 20, November 1980, 1–2.

40. "CPAC '81 Demonstrates Conservative Strength," *New Guard* 21, February 1981, 1–3; David Stockman, interestingly, was not a YAF member during his college days at Michigan State University. Instead he was active in SDS and other campus radical groups. See *The Triumph of Politics: The Inside Story of the Reagan Revolution* (New York: Avon Books, 1987), 24–26.

41. *Dialogue on Liberty,* spring 1981, 6.

42. "Youth for Reagan Agenda Celebrates Passage of Economic Recovery Program," *New Guard* 21, May 1981, 1.

43. *New York Times,* August 22, 1981, 7.

44. David Pietrusza, "Coming of Age: YAF at 21," *National Review,* September 18, 1981, 1081.

45. Interview with Lacy; the *Phil Donahue Show,* n.d. [September 1981].

46. Interview with Lacy.

47. Ibid.

48. Supporters of the suit formed the Committee to Save YAF. Members were: Suzanne Scholte (Virginia), Kenneth Grasso (New York), Richard Abell (Washington), John Abernathy (New York), Kenneth Boehm (Virginia), Douglas Brusa (Mid-Atlantic director), Michael Cassa, Lloyd Daugherty (Southern Director), William Hawkins (Virginia), Larry Hunter (South Carolina), Mark Judd (Michigan), Douglas Kagan (Plains Director), Gerard Kassar (New York), Edmund Lesley (Midwest Director), Barry Paul, and Paul Prince (Ohio).

49. Interview with Lacy. Robert Dolan, Lacy's vice chairman at this time, confirmed Lacy's account. Interview with Robert Dolan, September 9, 1997.

50. Kenneth Grasso to James Lacy, May 26, 1982, with enclosure, box 141, folder 4 (YAF, 1982–1984), Re: Lacy Mess, A. C. Wedemeyer MSS. Lacy claims that the idea that sixteen board members were aligned against him was nothing more than misinformation on the part of the plaintiffs. "Otherwise they would have been the majority and I wouldn't have been national chairman." Interview with Lacy.

51. Suzanne Scholte to Mike Thompson, March 23, 1982, box 141, folder 4, A. C. Wedemeyer MSS. There was no interruption in the publication of either magazine during this period.

52. *Flaherty v. Lacy,* Plaintiff's Supplemental Answers to Interrogatories, March 3, 1982, Delaware Chancery Court, Private Papers of James Lacy (hereafter, PPJL).

53. *Flaherty v. Lacy,* 1982 West Law 17858 (Del. Ch.), August 27, 1982. After the court's decision in May 1983, another restraining order was sought by the plaintiffs to keep the board from meeting and voting on seven new directors. It was again denied. Grover Brown, Chancellor, to Vernon Proctor, Esq., and Stephen Herrmann, Esq., May 23, 1983, PPJL.

54. Interview with Lacy.

55. *Flaherty v. Lacy,* 1983 West Law 18000 (Del. Ch.), May 23, 1983.

56. Interview with Lacy.

57. Memorandum to William F. Buckley, et al. from Marvin Liebman, September 13, 1983, box 8 (YAF—1983), 1985 Jan. Addition, WFB MSS.

58. Draft Letter, Buckley to Robert Dolan, October 5, 1983, box 8, WFB MSS.

59. Lacy to Rusher, September 26, 1983, PPJL; interview with Lacy. Lacy reiterated that many of the matters discussed in Liebman's memo were wrong. The $430,000 debt he mentioned was natural, owed to Bruce Eberle and Associates (YAF's fund-raisers) in lieu of a new direct mail campaign.

60. "New Guard Interview: Bill Rusher," *New Guard,* spring 1984, 28–31, 41.

61. Interview with Dolan.

62. Ibid.; interview with Lacy.

63. Interview with Dolan.

64. Edwards was, during 1984 and 1985, head of the American Conservative Union, a group that cosponsored CPAC with YAF. He had paid a professional consultant (the wife of a conservative activist) a percentage of the gross receipts from CPAC (amounting to some thirty thousand dollars) for her handling of the convention. When Dolan objected and threatened to remove YAF's funds, Edwards called him and chewed him out. Dolan refused to back down, arguing that the arrangement, which would have left YAF in debt, was not fair. Interview with Dolan.

65. *New York Times,* March 10, 1985, 25.

66. Richard Hahn, YAF's executive director, was still claiming eighty thousand members and supporters in late 1984. *New Guard,* winter 1984–1985, 4.

67. Interview with Dolan.

68. Young America's Foundation is the premier organization for mobilizing young conservatives for political action on campus. Young America's Foundation is headed by Ron Robinson, formerly executive director of the Young Americans for Freedom. Interview with Robinson.

NOTES TO THE CONCLUSION

1. Powers, *Not without Honor,* 365–90.

2. Sidney Blumenthal, *The Rise of the Counter-Establishment: From Conservative Ideology to Political Power* (New York: Harper and Row, 1986).

3. Bauman, *Gentleman from Maryland*; interview with Bauman. Bauman currently lives an openly gay lifestyle and works for various libertarian causes.

4. Viguerie, *The New Right*; interview with Viguerie.

5. Douglas Caddy, "Did Judge Sirica Cause the Watergate Cover-Up?" 1997, unpublished manuscript in Schneider's possession; interview with Caddy; also Kutler, *Abuse of Power,* 54, 93–94.

6. Discussion of the Huston Plan by Nixon and his aides can be found in Kutler, *Abuse of Power,* 507–520.

7. Interview with Huston.

8. Interview with Jones.

9. Interview with MacKay.

10. Interview with Keene.

11. Interview with Teague.

12. Letter to author from Ron Docksai, February 27, 1997.

13. Interview with Thorburn.

14. Interview with Donatelli.

15. Interview with Lacy.

16. Andrew, *Other Side,* 218–19.

17. Ronald Brownstein and Nina Easton, eds., *Reagan's Ruling Class: Portraits of the President's Top One-Hundred Officials* (New York: Pantheon, 1983), 707–14.

18. Interview with Edwards.

19. Brudnoy, *Life Is Not a Rehearsal*.

20. Interview with Campaigne.

21. Tyrrell, *Conservative Crack-Up*; and R. Emmett Tyrrell, Jr., *Boy Clinton: The Political Biography* (Washington, D.C.: Regnery, 1996); interview with Tyrrell.

22. Tyrrell, *Conservative Crack-Up*, 207.

23. Edwards, "The Other Sixties," 65.

24. Interview with Campaigne.

25. For a critical analysis of this trend from a neoconservative perspective, see David Frum, *Dead Right* (New York: Basic Books, 1994), 99–143; for a positive assessment, see Gottfried and Fleming, *Conservative Movement,* 96–111.

Bibliography

MANUSCRIPT SOURCES CONSULTED

Arizona Historical Foundation, Tempe, Arizona
    Paul Fannin Papers
    Barry Goldwater Papers
    John Rhodes Papers
Chicago Historical Society, Chicago, Illinois
    Clarence Manion Papers
    Sterling Morton Papers
Herbert Hoover Presidential Library, West Branch, Iowa
    Kenneth Colegrove Papers
    Bourke Hickenlooper Papers
    Herbert Hoover Post-Presidential Papers
    Neil MacNeil Papers
    Felix Morley Papers
    Westbrook Pegler Papers
    Lewis Strauss Papers
    Walter Trohan Papers
Hoover Institution on War, Revolution and Peace, Stanford, California
    James Burnham Papers
    Jameson G. Campaigne, Sr., Papers
    John Chamberlain Papers
    College Republicans—National Committee Records
    Ralph de Toledano Papers
    Patrick Dowd Papers
    Donald Dozer Papers
    Joseph Dumbacher (SDS Member) Papers
    John Erlichman Papers
    Free Society Association Records
    Jeffrey Hart Papers
    Sidney Hook Papers
    Stanley Hornbeck Papers
    Walter Judd Papers

Denison Kitchel Papers
Alfred Kohlberg Papers
Thomas Lane Papers
Marvin Liebman Papers
New Left Collection
Radical Right Collection
Henry Regnery Papers
Edward Teller Papers
A. C. Wedemeyer Papers
Karl Wittfogel Papers
John F. Kennedy Presidential Library, Boston, Massachusetts
Democratic National Committee Papers
Robert F. Kennedy Papers, Attorney General Series
President's Central Files
Arthur Schlesinger, Jr., Papers
White House Name File
Lee White Papers
Library of Congress, Washington, D.C.
William Rusher Papers
Private Papers of Douglas Caddy (in Schneider's possession)
Private Papers of Jameson Campaigne, Jr., Ottawa, Ill.
Private Papers of James Lacy (in Schneider's possession)
Southwestern University, Georgetown, Texas
John Tower Papers
State Historical Society of Wisconsin, Madison, Wisconsin
Americans for Democratic Action Papers
Free Speech Movement Papers
Social Action Collection
Students for a Democratic Society Papers
Sterling Library, Yale University, New Haven, Connecticut
William F. Buckley, Jr. Papers

INTERVIEWS (CONDUCTED VIA TELEPHONE
UNLESS OTHERWISE NOTED)

Robert Bauman, July 25, 1995
William F. Buckley, Jr., August 16, 1994
Douglas Caddy, March 18, 1997
Jameson Campaigne, Jr., March 8, 1995, Ottawa, Ill. (interviewed in person)
Randall Cornell Teague, September 22, 1994
William Cotter, May 1, 1997

Carol Dawson, September 4, 1994
Donald Devine, August 28, 1996
Robert Dolan, September 9, 1997
Frank Donatelli, August 14, 1997
Lee Edwards, February 22, 1995
M. Stanton Evans, February 24, 1995
David Franke, May 15, 1995
Tom Charles Huston, January 17, 1995
David Jones, October 10, 1994
David Keene, September 28, 1994
James V. Lacy, July 29, 1997
Marvin Liebman, September 1, 1994
J. Alan MacKay, September 26, 1996
Howard Phillips, March 28, 1997
Ron Robinson, July 29, 1997
William A. Rusher, September 18, 1994, Chicago, Ill. (interviewed in person)
Scott Stanley, Jr., May 15, 1997
Wayne Thorburn, July 24, 1997
R. Emmett Tyrrell, Jr., January 8, 1995
Richard Vigeurie, March 26, 1997

PUBLISHED GOVERNMENT DOCUMENTS

Foreign Relations of the United States: The Congo Crisis, 1961–1963. Washington, D.C.:
GPO, 1994.
Public Papers of the Presidents: Ronald Reagan, 1988. Washington, D.C.: GPO,
1991.
Public Papers of the Presidents: Richard Nixon, 1970. Washington, D.C.: GPO, 1971.
Senate Foreign Relations Committee. *Hearings on Nuclear Test Ban Treaty.* 88th
Cong. 1st sess. 1963.

NEWSPAPERS/MAGAZINES

American Opinion
Atlantic Monthly
Chicago Tribune
Freeman
Human Events
Modern Age
National Review

New Guard
New Individualist Review
New Republic
New York Times
Newsweek
The Nation
Time
Triumph
U.S. News and World Report
Washington Post

ARTICLES

Braungart, Margaret M., and Richard G. Braungart. "The Effects of the 1960's Political Generation on Former Left- and Right-Wing Youth Activist Leaders." *Social Problems* 38 (3) (August 1991): 297–315.

———. "The Life-Course Development of Left- and Right-Wing Youth Activist Leaders from the 1960's." *Political Psychology* 11 (1990): 243–82.

Braungart, Richard. "SDS and YAF: A Comparison of Two Student Radical Groups in the Mid-1960's." *Youth and Society* 2 (June 1971): 441–57.

Braungart, Richard, with David L. Westby. "The Alienation of Generations and Status Politics: Alternative Explanations of Student Political Activism." In Roberta Sigel, ed., *Learning About Politics: A Reader in Political Socialization,* 476–89. New York: Random House, 1970.

Brinkley, Alan. "The Problem of American Conservatism." *American Historical Review* 99 (April 1994): 409–29.

Edwards, Lee. "The Other Sixties: A Flag Waver's Memoir." *Policy Review* (fall 1988): 58–65.

Farber, David. "The 60's: Myth and Reality." *Chronicle of Higher Education,* December 7, 1994, sec. 2, 1–2.

Ribuffo, Leo. "Why Is There So Much Conservatism in the United States and Why Do So Few Historians Know Anything about It?" *American Historical Review* 99 (April 1994): 438–49.

Schiff, Lawrence F. "Dynamic Young Fogies—Rebels on the Right." *Trans-Action* 4 (November 1966): 31–36.

———. "The Obedient Rebels: A Study of College Conversions to Conservatism." *Journal of Social Issues* 20 (October 1964): 74–95.

Westby, David L., and Richard G. Braungart. "Class and Politics in the Family Backgrounds of Student Political Activists." *American Sociological Review* 31 (October 1966): 690–92.

BOOKS

Albert, Judith C., and Stewart E. Albert, eds. *The Sixties Papers: Documents of a Rebellious Decade*. New York: Praeger, 1984.

Allitt, Patrick. *Catholic Intellectuals and Conservative Politics in America, 1950–1985*. Ithaca, N.Y.: Cornell University Press, 1993.

Ambrose, Stephen E. *Eisenhower,* Vol. 2, *The President*. New York: Simon and Schuster, 1984.

Anderson, Terry. *The Movement and the Sixties: Protest in America from Greensboro to Wounded Knee*. New York: Oxford University Press, 1995.

Andrew, John A., III. *The Other Side of the Sixties: Young Americans for Freedom and the Rise of Conservative Politics*. New Brunswick, N.J.: Rutgers University Press, 1997.

Bachrack, Stanley D. *The Committee of One Million: "China Lobby" Politics, 1953–1971*. New York: Columbia University Press, 1976.

Ball, Howard. *Justice Downwind: America's Atomic Testing Program in the 1950's*. New York: Oxford University Press, 1986.

Bartley, Robert. *The Seven Fat Years: And How to Do It Again*. New York: Free Press, 1995.

Bates, Tom. *Rads: The 1970 Bombing of the Army Math Research Center at the University of Wisconsin and Its Aftermath*. New York: Harper Collins, 1992.

Bauman, Robert. *The Gentleman from Maryland: The Conscience of a Gay Conservative*. New York: Arbor House, 1986.

Bell, Daniel, ed. *The Radical Right*. New York: Doubleday, 1963.

Bell, Jack. *Mr. Conservative: Barry Goldwater*. New York: MacFadden Books, 1964.

Bennett, David H. *The Party of Fear: From Nativist Movements to the New Right in American History*. Chapel Hill: University of North Carolina Press, 1988.

Bennett, William J. *The De-Valuing of America: The Fight for Our Culture and Our Children*. New York: Summit Books, 1992.

Berman, William C. *America's Right Turn: From Nixon to Bush*. Baltimore: Johns Hopkins University Press, 1994.

Blum, John Morton. *Years of Discord: American Politics and Society, 1961–1974*. New York: Norton, 1992.

Blumenthal, Sidney. *The Rise of the Counter-Establishment: From Conservative Ideology to Political Power*. New York: Harper and Row, 1986.

Boskin, Joseph, ed. *Opposition Politics: The Anti–New Deal Tradition*. Beverly Hills, Calif.: Glencoe Press, 1968.

Brennan, Mary C. *Turning Right in the Sixties: The Conservative Capture of the GOP*. Chapel Hill: University of North Carolina Press, 1995.

Brock, David. *The Seduction of Hillary Rodham Clinton*. New York: Free Press, 1996.

Broder, David S. *Changing of the Guard: Power and Leadership in America.* New York: Simon and Schuster, 1980.

Brownstein, Ronald, and Nina Easton, eds. *Reagan's Ruling Class: Portraits of the President's Top One-Hundred Officials.* New York: Pantheon, 1983.

Brudnoy, David. *Life Is Not a Rehearsal: A Memoir.* New York: Doubleday, 1997.

Buchanan, Patrick J. *Right from the Beginning.* Boston: Little, Brown, 1988.

Buckley, William F., Jr. *God and Man at Yale.* Chicago: Henry Regnery, 1951.

———. *Up from Liberalism.* New York: Bantam Books, 1968.

———, ed. *Odyssey of a Friend: Whittaker Chambers's Letters to William F. Buckley, Jr., 1954–1961.* New York: Putnam's, 1961.

Buckley, William F., Jr., with L. Brent Bozell. *McCarthy and His Enemies.* Chicago: Henry Regnery, 1956.

Bundy, McGeorge. *Danger and Survival: Choices about the Bomb in the First Fifty Years.* New York: Random House, 1988.

Burnham, James. *The Coming Defeat of Communism.* New York: John Day, 1950.

———. *Containment or Liberation?* New York: John Day, 1953.

———. *The Managerial Revolution: What Is Happening in the World.* New York: John Day, 1941.

———. *The Struggle for the World.* New York: John Day, 1947.

Burnham, Walter Dean. *Critical Elections and the Mainsprings of American Politics.* New York: Norton, 1970.

Cain, Edward. *They'd Rather Be Right: Youth and the Conservative Movement.* New York: Macmillan, 1963.

Chafe, William H. *Never Stop Running: Allard Lowenstein and the Struggle to Save American Liberalism.* New York: Basic Books, 1993.

Chalmers, David. *And the Crooked Places Made Straight: The Struggle for Social Change in the 1960's.* Baltimore: Johns Hopkins University Press, 1991.

Chamberlain, John. *A Life with the Printed Word.* Chicago: Regnery, 1982.

Chambers, Whittaker. *Witness.* New York: Random House, 1952.

Chodorov, Frank. *One Is a Crowd.* New York: Devin-Adair, 1952.

Cole, Wayne S. *Roosevelt and the Isolationists, 1932–1945.* Lincoln: University of Nebraska Press, 1983.

Collier, Peter, and David Horowitz. *Destructive Generation: Second Thoughts about the Sixties.* New York: Free Press, 1996.

———, ed. *Second Thoughts: Former Radicals Look Back at the Sixties.* Lanham, Md.: Madison Books, 1989.

Cook, Fred J. *Barry Goldwater: Extremist of the Right.* New York: Grove Press, 1964.

Crawford, Alan. *Thunder on the Right: The "New Right" and the Politics of Resentment.* New York: Pantheon, 1980.

Davies, Gareth. *From Opportunity to Entitlement: The Transformation and Decline of Great Society Liberalism.* Lawrence: University Press of Kansas, 1996.

de Toledano, Ralph. *The Winning Side: The Case for Goldwater Republicanism*. New York: MacFadden Books, 1964.

Diggins, John P. *The Promise of Pragmatism: Modernism and the Crisis of Knowledge and Authority*. Chicago: University of Chicago Press, 1994.

———. *Up from Communism: Conservative Odysseys in American Intellectual History*. New York: Columbia University Press, 1994.

Dionne, E. J., Jr. *Why Americans Hate Politics*. New York: Simon and Schuster, 1991.

Divine, Robert A. *Blowing in the Wind: The Nuclear Test Ban Debate, 1954–1960*. New York: Oxford University Press, 1978.

Doenecke, Justus D. *Not to the Swift: The Old Isolationists in the Cold War Era*. Lewisburg, Pa.: Bucknell University Press, 1979.

Donovan, Robert J. *Eisenhower: The Inside Story*. New York: Doubleday, 1956.

Dorrien, Gary. *The Neoconservative Mind: Politics, Culture, and the War of Ideology*. Philadelphia: Temple University Press, 1993.

Dworkin, Andrea. *Right Wing Women*. New York: Putnam's, 1983.

Edwards, Lee. *Goldwater: The Man Who Made a Revolution*. Washington, D.C., Regnery, 1995.

———. *The Power of Ideas: The Heritage Foundation at Twenty-Five Years*. Ottawa, Ill.: Jameson Books, 1997.

Edwards, Lee, and Anne Edwards. *You Can Make the Difference*. New Rochelle, N.Y.: Arlington House, 1968.

Ehrman, John. *The Rise of Neoconservatism: Intellectuals and Foreign Affairs, 1945–1994*. New Haven, Conn.: Yale University Press, 1995.

Evans, M. Stanton. *The Liberal Establishment*. New York: Devin-Adair, 1965.

———. *The Politics of Surrender*. New York: Devin-Adair, 1966.

———. *Revolt on the Campus*. Chicago: Henry Regnery, 1961.

———. *The Theme Is Freedom: Religion, Politics, and American Tradition*. Washington, D.C.: Regnery, 1994.

Farber, David, ed. *The Sixties: From Memory to History*. Chapel Hill: University of North Carolina Press, 1994.

Francis, Samuel. *Beautiful Losers: Essays on the Failure of American Conservatism*. Columbia: University Press of Missouri, 1993.

———. *Power and History: The Political Thought of James Burnham*. Lanham, Md.: University Press of America, 1984.

Fraser, Steve, and Gary Gerstle, eds. *The Rise and Fall of the New Deal Order, 1930–1980*. Princeton, N.J.: Princeton University Press, 1989.

Freedman, Samuel G. *The Inheritance: How Three Familes and America Moved from Roosevelt to Reagan and Beyond*. New York: Simon and Schuster, 1996.

Fried, Richard M. *Nightmare in Red: The McCarthy Era in Perspective*. New York: Oxford University Press, 1990.

Frum, David. *Dead Right*. New York: Basic Books, 1994.

Gaddis, John Lewis. *Strategies of Containment: A Critical Reappraisal of Postwar American National Security Policy.* New York: Oxford University Press, 1982.

———. *The United States and the End of the Cold War: Implications, Reconsiderations, Provocations.* New York: Oxford University Press, 1992.

———. *We Now Know: Rethinking Cold War History.* Oxford: Clarendon Press, 1997.

Garfinkle, Adam. *Telltale Hearts: The Origins and Impact of the Vietnam Antiwar Movement.* New York: St. Martin's Griffin, 1997.

Garrow, David. *The FBI and Martin Luther King, Jr.: From "Solo" to Memphis.* New York: Norton, 1981.

Garthoff, Raymond L. *Detente and Confrontation: American-Soviet Relations from Nixon to Reagan.* Washington, D.C.: Brookings Institution Press, 1985.

Gillon, Steven M. *Politics and Vision: The ADA and American Liberalism, 1947–1985.* New York: Oxford University Press, 1987.

Gitlin, Todd. *The Sixties: Years of Hope, Days of Rage.* New York: Bantam Books, 1987.

Goines, David Lance. *The Free Speech Movement: Coming of Age in the 1960's.* Berkeley, Calif.: Ten Speed Press, 1993.

Goldberg, Robert Alan. *Goldwater.* New Haven: Yale University Press, 1995.

Goldwater, Barry. *The Conscience of a Conservative.* Shepardsville, Ky.: Victor Publishing, 1960.

———. *Where I Stand.* New York: McGraw-Hill, 1964.

———. *With No Apologies: The Personal and Political Memoirs of United States Senator Barry M. Goldwater.* New York: William Morrow, 1979.

Goldwater, Barry, with Jack Casserly. *Goldwater.* New York: Doubleday, 1988.

Goodman, Walter. *The Committee: The Extraordinary Career of the House Committee on Un-American Activities.* New York: Farrar, Strauss, and Giroux, 1968.

Goodwin, Richard N. *Remembering America: A Voice from the Sixties.* New York: Harper and Row, 1988.

Gottfried, Paul, and Thomas Fleming. *The Conservative Movement.* Boston: Twayne, 1988.

Halberstam, David. *The Fifties.* New York: Fawcett Columbine, 1993.

Haley, J. Evetts. *A Texan Looks at Lyndon: A Study in Illegitimate Power.* Canyon, Tex.: Palo Duro Press, 1964.

Hamby, Alonzo L. *Liberalism and Its Challengers: FDR to Bush.* New York: Oxford University Press, 1992.

———. *Man of the People: A Life of Harry S. Truman.* New York: Oxford University Press, 1995.

Hayden, Tom. *Reunion: A Memoir.* New York: Collier Books, 1988.

Hayek, Friedrich A. *The Road to Serfdom.* Chicago: University of Chicago Press, 1944.

Heale, M. J. *American Anticommunism: Combating the Enemy Within, 1830–1970*. Baltimore: Johns Hopkins University Press, 1990.

Heineman, Kenneth J. *Campus Wars: The Peace Movement at American State Universities in the Vietnam Era*. New York: New York University Press, 1993.

Hess, Karl. *In a Cause That Will Triumph: The Goldwater Campaign and the Future of Conservatism*. Garden City, N.Y.: Doubleday, 1967.

Himmelstein, Jerome L. *To the Right: The Transformation of American Conservatism*. Berkeley: University of California Press, 1990.

Hixson, William B., Jr. *Search for the American Right Wing: An Analysis of the Social Science Record, 1955–1987*. Princeton, N.J.: Princeton University Press, 1992.

Hodgson, Godfrey. *America in Our Time*. New York: Doubleday, 1976.

———. *The World Turned Right Side Up: A History of the Conservative Ascendancy in America*. Boston: Houghton Mifflin, 1996.

Hoeveler, J. David, Jr. *Watch on the Right: Conservative Intellectuals in the Reagan Era*. Madison: University of Wisconsin Press, 1991.

Hoff, Joan. *Nixon Reconsidered*. New York: Basic Books, 1994.

Holmes, Stephen. *The Anatomy of Antiliberalism*. Cambridge, Mass.: Harvard University Press, 1993.

Hoover, J. Edgar. *J. Edgar Hoover on Communism*. New York: Random House, 1969.

Horowitz, David. *Radical Son: A Generational Odyssey*. New York: The Free Press, 1997.

Iverson, Peter. *Barry Goldwater: Native Arizonan*. Norman: University of Oklahoma Press, 1997.

Jackson, Henry F. *From the Congo to Soweto: U.S. Foreign Policy Toward Africa since 1945*. New York: William Morrow, 1982.

Jacobs, Paul, and Saul Landau. *The New Radicals: A Report with Documents*. New York: Random House, 1966.

Jeansomme, Glen. *Women of the Far Right: The Mothers' Movement in World War II*. Chicago: University of Chicago Press, 1996.

Judis, John B. *William F. Buckley, Jr.: Patron Saint of the Conservatives*. New York: Touchstone, 1988.

Kazin, Michael. *The Populist Persuasion: An American History*. New York: Basic Books, 1994.

Kelman, Steven. *Push Comes to Shove: The Escalation of Student Protest*. Boston: Houghton Mifflin, 1970.

Kendall, Willmoore. *The Conservative Affirmation*. Chicago: Henry Regnery, 1963.

Kennan, George F. *Democracy and the Student Left*. New York: Atlantic–Little, Brown, 1968.

Kessel, John H. *The Goldwater Coalition: Republican Strategies in 1964.* Indianapolis: Bobbs-Merrill, 1968.

Kirk, Russell. *The Conservative Mind: From Burke to Eliot.* 3d rev. ed. Chicago: Henry Regnery, 1960.

———. *The Politics of Prudence.* Bryn Mawr, Pa.: Intercollegiate Studies Institute, 1993.

———. *The Sword of Imagination: Memoirs of a Half-Century of Literary Conflict.* Grand Rapids, Mich.: Eerdmans, 1995.

Klatch, Rebecca E. *Women of the New Right.* Philadelphia: Temple University Press, 1987.

Klehr, Harvey, John Earl Haynes, and Fridrikh Igorevich Firsov. *The Secret World of American Communism.* New Haven, Conn.: Yale University Press, 1996.

Kolkey, Jonathon Martin. *The New Right, 1960–1968 with Epilogue 1969–1980.* Lanham, Md.: University Press of America, 1983.

Lefever, Ernest W. *Crisis in the Congo: A United Nations Force in Action.* Washington, D.C.: Brookings Institution, 1965.

Leffler, Melvyn. *A Preponderance of Power: National Security, the Truman Administration, and the Cold War.* Stanford, Calif.: Stanford University Press, 1993.

Lewy, Guenter. *America in Vietnam.* New York: Oxford University Press, 1977.

Liebman, Marvin. *Coming Out Conservative: An Autobiography.* San Francisco: Chronicle Books, 1992.

Lipset, Seymour Martin, ed. *Student Politics.* New York: Basic Books, 1967.

Lipset, Seymour Martin, and Earl Raab. *The Politics of Unreason: Right-Wing Extremism in America, 1790–1977.* 2d ed. Chicago: University of Chicago Press, 1978.

Lyons, Eugene. *The Red Decade: The Stalinist Penetration of America.* Indianapolis: Bobbs-Merrill, 1941.

Martin, William. *With God on Our Side: The Rise of the Religious Right in America.* New York: Broadway Books, 1996.

Matusow, Allan. *The Unraveling of America: A History of Liberalism in the 1960's.* New York: Harper and Row, 1984.

Mayer, George H. *The Republican Party, 1954–1964.* New York: Oxford University Press, 1964.

McAllister, Ted V. *Revolt against Modernity: Leo Strauss, Eric Voegelin, and the Search for a Postliberal Order.* Lawrence: University Press of Kansas, 1996.

McDowell, Edwin. *Portrait of an Arizonan: Barry Goldwater.* Chicago: Henry Regnery, 1964.

McQuaid, Kim. *The Anxious Years: America in the Vietnam-Watergate Era.* New York: Basic Books, 1989.

Meyer, Frank S. *In Defense of Freedom and Related Essays.* Indianapolis: Liberty Fund, 1996.

Miles, Michael W. *The Odyssey of the American Right.* New York: Oxford University Press, 1980.

Miller, James. *Democracy Is in the Streets: From Port Huron to the Siege of Chicago.* New York: Touchstone, 1987.

Mills, C. Wright. *The Power Elite.* New York: Oxford University Press, 1956.

Nash, George H. *The Conservative Intellectual Movement in America: Since 1945.* Wilmington, Del.: Intercollegiate Studies Institute, 1997.

Nash, Phillip. *The Other Missiles of October: Eisenhower, Kennedy, and the Jupiters, 1957–1963.* Chapel Hill: University of North Carolina Press, 1997.

Nock, Alfred Jay. *Memoirs of a Superfluous Man.* New York: Harper and Brothers, 1943.

————. *Our Enemy, the State.* New York: William Morrow, 1935.

————. *The State of the Union: Essays in Social Criticism,* ed. Charles Hamilton. Indianapolis: Liberty Fund, 1991.

Noer, Thomas J. *Cold War and Black Liberation: The U.S. and White Rule in Africa, 1948–1968.* Columbia: University of Missouri Press, 1985.

Novak, Robert D. *The Agony of the G.O.P.: 1964.* New York: Macmillan, 1965.

O'Neill, William L. *Coming Apart: An Informal History of America in the 1960's.* New York: Times Books, 1971.

Pauken, Thomas W. *The Thirty Years' War: The Politics of the Sixties Generation.* Ottawa, Ill.: Jameson Books, 1995.

Pearson, Hugh. *The Shadow of the Panther: Huey Newton and the Price of Black Power in America.* Reading, Mass.: Addison Wesley, 1994.

Pells, Richard H. *The Liberal Mind in a Conservative Age: American Intellectuals in the 1940's and 1950's.* Middletown, Conn.: Wesleyan University Press, 1989.

Phillips, Howard, ed. *The New Right at Harvard.* Vienna, Va.: Conservative Caucus, 1983.

Phillips, Kevin P. *The Emerging Republican Majority.* New Rochelle, N.Y.: Arlington House, 1969.

————. *The Politics of Rich and Poor: Wealth and the Electorate in the Reagan Aftermath.* New York: Harper and Row, 1990.

————. *Post-Conservative America: People, Politics, and Ideology in a Time of Crisis.* New York: Vintage, 1983.

Podhoretz, Norman. *Why We Were in Vietnam.* New York: Simon and Schuster, 1982.

Powers, Richard Gid. *Not without Honor: The History of American Anticommunism.* New York: Free Press, 1996.

Radosh, Ronald. *Divided They Fell: The Demise of the Democratic Party, 1964–1996.* New York: Free Press, 1996.

————. *Prophets of the Right: Profiles of Conservative Critics of American Globalism.* New York: Simon and Schuster, 1975.

Reagan, Ronald. *An American Life: The Autobiography.* New York: Simon and Schuster, 1990.

Reeves, Richard. *President Kennedy: Profile of Power.* New York: Simon and Schuster, 1993.

Regnery, Henry. *A Few Reasonable Words: Selected Writings.* Wilmington, Del.: Intercollegiate Studies Institute, 1996.

———. *Memoirs of a Dissident Publisher.* Chicago: Regnery Books, 1985.

Reinhard, David W. *The Republican Right since 1945.* Lexington: The University Press of Kentucky, 1983.

Rhodes, Richard. *Dark Sun: The Making of the Hydrogen Bomb.* New York: Simon and Schuster, 1995.

Ribuffo, Leo. *The Old Christian Right: The Protestant Far Right from the Great Depression to the Cold War.* Philadelphia: Temple University Press, 1983.

Roberts, James C. *The Conservative Decade: Emerging Leaders of the 1980's.* Westport, Conn.: Arlington House, 1980.

Roberts, Paul Craig. *The Supply-Side Revolution: An Insider's Account of Policymaking in Washington.* Cambridge, Mass.: Harvard University Press, 1984.

Rogin, Michael Paul. *The Intellectuals and McCarthy: The Radical Specter.* Boston: MIT Press, 1967.

———. *Ronald Reagan, the Movie and Other Episodes in Political Demonology.* Berkeley: University of California Press, 1987.

Rossiter, Clinton. *Conservatism in America: The Thankless Persuasion.* Cambridge: Harvard University Press, 1982.

Roszak, Theodore. *The Making of a Counterculture: Reflections on the Technocratic Society and Its Youthful Opposition.* Garden City, N.Y.: Doubleday, 1968.

Rothbard, Murray. *For a New Liberty.* New York: Macmillan, 1973.

Rusher, William A. *The Making of a New Majority Party.* Ottawa, Ill.: Green Hill Publishers, 1975.

———. *The Rise of the Right.* New York: William Morrow, 1984.

Saloma, John S., III. *Ominous Politics: The New Conservative Labyrinth.* New York: Hill and Wang, 1984.

Schlafly, Phyllis. *A Choice, Not an Echo.* Alton, Ill.: Pere Marquette Press, 1964.

Schlesinger, Arthur M., Jr. *The Vital Center: The Politics of Freedom.* New York: Houghton Mifflin, 1949.

Schwarz, Fred. *Beating the Unbeatable Foe.* Washington, D.C.: Regnery, 1996.

Seaborg, Glenn T. *Kennedy, Khrushchev and the Test Ban.* Berkeley: University of California Press, 1981.

Shadegg, Stephen. *Barry Goldwater: Freedom Is His Flight Plan.* New York: MacFadden Books, 1963.

Shirey, Keith. *Barry Goldwater.* Glendale, Calif.: Harlequin Press, 1964.

Smant, Kevin J. *How Great the Triumph: James Burnham, Anticommunism, and the Conservative Movement.* Lanham, Md.: University Press of America, 1992.

Smith, Richard Norton. *The Colonel: The Life and Legend of Robert M. McCormick, 1880–1955.* New York: Houghton Mifflin, 1997.

Steigerwald, David. *The Sixties and the End of Modern America.* New York: St. Martin's Press, 1995.

Stockman, David. *The Triumph of Politics: The Inside Story of the Reagan Revolution.* New York: Avon Books, 1987.

Strauss, Lewis L. *Men and Decisions.* Garden City, N.Y.: Doubleday, 1962.

Sundquist, James. *Dynamics of the Party System: Alignment and Realignment of Political Parties in the United States.* Rev. ed. Washington, D.C.: Brookings Institution, 1983.

Talbott, Strobe. *The Master of the Game: Paul Nitze and the Nuclear Peace.* New York: Knopf, 1988.

Tanenhaus, Sam. *Whittaker Chambers: A Biography.* New York: Random House, 1997.

Thayer, George. *The Farthest Shores of Politics: The American Political Fringe Today.* New York: Clarion Books, 1968.

Thompson, Tommy. *Power to the People: An American State at Work.* New York: Harper Collins, 1996.

Tischler, Barbara L., ed. *Sights on the Sixties.* New Brunswick, N.J.: Rutgers University Press, 1992.

Tucille, Jerome. *It Usually Begins with Ayn Rand.* New York: Stein and Day, 1971.

———. *Radical Libertarianism: A Right-Wing Alternative.* Indianapolis: Bobbs–Merrill, 1970.

Tyrrell, R. Emmett, Jr. *The Conservative Crack-Up.* New York: Simon and Schuster, 1992.

———. *The Liberal Crack-Up.* New York: Simon and Schuster, 1984.

Unger, Irwin. *The Movement: A History of the American New Left, 1959–1972.* New York: Dodd, Mead, 1975.

Viguerie, Richard. *The New Right: We're Ready to Lead.* Falls Church, Va.: Richard Viguerie Co., 1981.

Voss, Earl H. *Nuclear Ambush: The Test-Ban Trap.* Chicago: Henry Regnery, 1963.

Wattenberg, Martin P. *The Decline of American Political Parties, 1952–1984.* Cambridge, Mass.: Harvard University Press, 1986.

Weart, Spencer R. *Nuclear Fear: A History of Images.* Cambridge, Mass.: Harvard University Press, 1988.

Weaver, Richard M. *Ideas Have Consequences.* Chicago: University of Chicago Press, 1948.

Weinstein, Allen. *Perjury: The Hiss-Chambers Case.* New York: Knopf, 1978.

Wells, Tom. *The War Within: America's Battle over Vietnam.* Berkeley: University of California Press, 1994.

Whitaker, Robert W., ed. *The New Right Papers.* New York: St. Martin's Press, 1982.

White, F. Clifton. *Suite 3505: The Story of the Draft Goldwater Movement.* Chicago: Henry Regnery, 1968.

White, F. Clifton, and William J. Gill. *Why Reagan Won: The Conservative Movement, 1964–1981*. Chicago: Regnery Gateway, 1981.

White, F. Clifton, with Jerome Tuccille. *Politics as a Noble Calling: The Memoirs of F. Clifton White*. Ottawa, Ill.: Jameson Books, 1995.

White, Theodore H. *The Making of the President, 1960*. New York: Atheneum, 1961.

————. *The Making of the President, 1964*. New York: Atheneum, 1965.

————. *The Making of the President, 1968*. New York: Atheneum, 1969.

————. *The Making of the President, 1972*. New York: Atheneum, 1973.

Whitfield, Stephen. *The Culture of the Cold War*. Baltimore: Johns Hopkins University Press, 1991.

Wills, Garry. *Confessions of a Conservative*. New York: Penguin Books, 1980.

————. *Nixon Agonistes: The Crisis of the Self-Made Man*. New York: Houghton Mifflin, 1969.

————. *Under God: Religion and American Politics*. New York: Simon and Schuster, 1990.

Wood, Rob, and Dean Smith. *Barry Goldwater*. New York: Avon Books, 1961.

Zubok, Vladislov, and Constantine Pleshakov. *Inside the Kremlin's Cold War: From Stalin to Khrushchev*. Cambridge, Mass.: Harvard University Press, 1996.

Index

About the Author

Gregory L. Schneider is assistant professor of history in the Division of Social Sciences at Emporia State University, Emporia, Kansas. He received his Ph.D. in history in 1996 from the University of Illinois at Chicago, his M.A. from Ohio University, and his B.A. from Drake University. He has been an instructor in history at Columbia College in Chicago, Roosevelt University, and the University of Illinois at Chicago.